Henry Wadsworth Longfellow

His Poetry and Prose

Literature and Life: American Writers

Selected list of titles:

SAUL BELLOW	*Brigitte Scheer-Schäzler*
TRUMAN CAPOTE	*Helen S. Garson*
RACHEL CARSON	*Carol B. Gartner*
THEODORE DREISER	*James Lundquist*
WILLIAM FAULKNER	*Alan Warren Friedman*
F. SCOTT FITZGERALD	*Rose Adrienne Gallo*
ROBERT FROST	*Elaine Barry*
LILLIAN HELLMAN	*Doris V. Falk*
ERNEST HEMINGWAY	*Samuel Shaw*
JOHN IRVING	*Gabriel Miller*
THE NOVELS OF HENRY JAMES	*Edward Wagenknecht*
THE TALES OF HENRY JAMES	*Edward Wagenknecht*
KEN KESEY	*Barry H. Leeds*
MARY MCCARTHY	*Willene Schaefer Hardy*
JAMES A. MICHENER	*George J. Becker*
ANAÏS NIN	*Bettina L. Knapp*
JOHN O'HARA	*Robert Emmet Long*
THE PLAYS OF EUGENE O'NEILL	*Virginia Floyd*
EDGAR ALLAN POE	*Bettina L. Knapp*
J.D. SALINGER	*James Lundquist*
JOHN STEINBECK	*Paul McCarthy*
LIONEL TRILLING	*Edward Joseph Shoben, Jr*
MARK TWAIN	*Robert Keith Miller*
NATHANAEL WEST	*Robert Emmet Long*
EDMUND WILSON	*David Castronovo*
RICHARD WRIGHT	*David Bakish*

Complete list of titles in the series available from publisher on request. Some titles are also in paperback.

Henry Wadsworth Longfellow

His Poetry and Prose

Edward Wagenknecht

UNGAR • NEW YORK

For
RUTH B. NUZUM
of Boulder, Colorado

gentle reader, indefatigable collector,
and loyal fan

1986
The Ungar Publishing Company
370 Lexington Avenue, New York, NY 10017

Printed in the United States of America

Library of Congress Cataloging in Publication Data
Wagenknecht, Edward, 1900-
  Henry Wadsworth Longfellow, his poetry and prose.

  (Literature and life series)
  Bibliography: p.
  Includes indexes.
  1. Longfellow, Henry Wadsworth, 1807–1882 — Criticism
and interpretation. I. Title. II. Series.
PS2288.W27 1985   811'.3   84-16317
ISBN 0-8044-2960-X

Contents

I

Biography

Henry Wadsworth Longfellow was born on February 27, 1807, in what is now known as Portland, Maine, but was then a part of the Commonwealth of Massachusetts. His father, Stephen Longfellow (1776–1849), a lawyer and a member of the Hartford Convention, who served in both the state legislature and the Congress of the United States, came of a Yorkshire family that had been established in Massachusetts since 1651, and his mother, Zilpah Wadsworth Longfellow (1778–1851), counted among her ancestors not only Elder William Brewster but the John Alden and Priscilla Mullins about whom posterity derives most of its knowledge from *The Courtship of Miles Standish*. Her father was General Peleg Wadsworth of Revolutionary War fame, who had a house in Hiram, Maine, where young Henry came as close to the American frontier as did James Fenimore Cooper at Cooperstown, New York, and her brother, Henry Wadsworth, a naval lieutenant, for whom the poet was named, died in Tripoli harbor in 1804 when the *Intrepid* was blown up to keep her from falling into enemy hands. Zilpah Longfellow was an intelligent woman who had humor, courage, sound common sense, a mind of her own, and a deeply religious spirit. Unlike her son, she loved to watch the lightning play across the sky during a storm, but she was like him in

1

her revolt against the military tradition of her family and her detestation of war. There were eight children—four boys and four girls—of whom Henry was the second child and boy.[1]

He was a happy, lively, well-behaved little boy, who seems never to have contributed to the discomfort of his parents except as he tended to wear them out with his enthusiastic temperament. His education apparently began at an old-fashioned "dame school" when he was only three, and in 1815 he went to the Portland Academy, where he studied under Jacob Abbot (later Abbott), the father of Lyman Abbott and himself the author of the "Rollo" books. We are told that he was halfway through the Latin grammar at seven, but he had no love for arithmetic and was not naturally a good speller, and science never interested him greatly except for its romantic and spiritual suggestiveness. Probably his home, where Puritan highmindedness survived, shorn of all its earlier hardness and fanaticism, and where religion was viewed very much in the spirit of William Ellery Channing, who had been a college classmate of Stephen Longfellow's, meant considerably more in his development than the schools.

Though Stephen Longfellow was a Harvard man, he sent his two eldest sons together, in 1822, to the new Bowdoin College at Brunswick, Maine, of which he was a trustee. Actually they passed their entrance examinations in 1821, when Henry was fourteen, but did not take up residence before the beginning of their sophomore year. Henry did as well in college (and in life) as Stephen did badly,[2] graduating in 1825, in the same class with Hawthorne.

By this time, Longfellow's literary interests were already well developed. He had published both prose and verse serially, and his future had been made the subject of anxious correspondence between his father and himself. Stephen Longfellow did not fail to sympathize with his son's literary ambitions, but he did take his stand upon the quite unassailable ground that it would not be safe for him to entrust his livelihood to the products of his pen. With his temperament and in his milieu, it was natural that the father should see the law as the solution of the son's problem; many lawyers have become distinguished writers. To Henry, however, Blackstone's only merit was that he seemed to hold out the hope of a somewhat less harrowing kind of uncongeniality than either the horrors of the dissecting room or the terrors of the pulpit.

The young man was not at all inclined to be rebellious or unreasonable about the matter. Having secured the generous promise of a year of postgraduate reading in literature at Harvard, he might well have accepted the law if he had not been delivered by an inspired Bowdoin trustee, Benajmin Orr, who had been so much impressed by his translation of one of Horace's odes that he proposed offering him the newly established professorship of modern languages (only the fourth to be set up in the United States) at Bowdoin College. This proposal was accepted by the board on condition that Longfellow should go to Europe at his own expense to fit himself for his duties.

He sailed from New York on May 15, 1826 and landed on June 14 at Havre. The basic purpose of the journey was to perfect his knowledge of French and Spanish. Before sailing, however, he talked with George Ticknor, who urged him on no account to neglect Germany, in his view the inevitable center of literary scholarship even in the Romance field. Longfellow's first visit to Europe stretched itself out accordingly to the at first quite uncontemplated length of three years, which he divided between France, Spain, Italy, and Germany. At one point the college reneged on the professorship, offering an instructorship instead, which Longfellow indignantly rejected. On August 11, 1829, the young scholar was back in America;

on September 6 the Bowdoin trustees voted him his professorship at an annual salary of eight hundred dollars (the original understanding had been a thousand), with an extra hundred for his services as college librarian. Since the library was open only one hour a day, this did not add greatly to his duties.[3]

Longfellow remained at Bowdoin from 1829 to 1835. Finding no textbooks available in a then largely uncultivated field, or at least none that suited him, he set to work to make and publish his own: *Elements of French Grammar* (1830); *French Exercises* (1830); *Manuel de Proverbes Dramatiques* (1830); *Novelas Españolas* (1830); *Syllabus de la Grammaire Italienne* (1832); *Saggi de' Novellieri Italiani d'Ogno Secolo* (1832). His first poetic publication between covers was his translation of the *Coplas de Don Jorge Manrique* (1833), and his first independent work in prose was the Irving-like *Outre-Mer: A Pilgrimage Beyond the Sea,* published in parts, in imitation of *The Sketch Book,* in 1833–34, and in book form in 1835. He also contributed a number of learned articles on linguistic and literary subjects to *The North American Review* and other periodicals.[4] This, in fact, was the only period in his life when Longfellow seemed more interested in scholarship than in creative writing.

On September 14, 1831, Longfellow was married to Mary Storer Potter, daughter of the Portland jurist, Barrett Potter. Since the Longfellows and the Potters were acquainted, Henry must have seen Mary during his youth, but she was five years younger than he, and he evidently had paid no attention to her until after his return from Europe, when he saw her one day at church and is said to have been so taken with her that he followed her home—though without venturing to speak to her. Compared to her successor Fanny Appleton, she is a rather shadowy figure in his biography, but this is probably because we know so much less about her. She was married to Longfellow only a little over four years, and he burned her journals after her death. A few letters have survived however, and they leave no doubt that she was both intelligent and highminded. Though as we have seen her husband's junior, she was no more in awe of him than Emerson's girl-wife was of her husband, nor did she apparently regard him as a practical man; "a good little dear," she calls him. When he was making almost frantic efforts to escape from Bowdoin and entertaining all kinds of impossible ideas toward achieving that end, she wisely acted as a restraining influence, evidently fearful that, in his impatience, he might get himself into a less congenial situation than that which galled him.

In 1834 Harvard College offered Longfellow the Smith Professorship of French and Spanish that George Ticknor was eager to relinquish, at an annual salary of $1,500, or, more accurately, assured him that it would be offered to him after he had, once more, taken himself to Europe for "a more perfect attainment of the German" and other studies. Acceptance would make him, as we should now say, the "head" or chairman of the department of modern languages, imposing responsibilities not only for teaching but for organization and supervision as well. Though there can never have been any question in Longfellow's mind of declining this call from the Athens on the Charles, he conducted the negotiations with cautious restraint, apparently taking pains not to appear too eager.

In April 1835 he sailed for Europe with his wife and two of her friends, Clara Crowninshield and Mary Goddard.[5] After a brief visit to London, the party journeyed by way of Hamburg to Denmark and Sweden and thence to Holland, where Longfellow experienced the first great sorrow of his life. On the night of October 5, at Amsterdam, Mary suffered a miscarriage, and though she rallied and was able to continue to Rotterdam, she relapsed there, and on November 29 she died. Longfellow, sorely stricken, spent the winter in Heidelberg, attempting to drown his grief in hard study and only succeeding in finding his dead wife in everything he tried to read; in an 1842 sonnet he would describe his ordeal as "sorrow and a grief that almost killed." His only comfort was that Mary had promised on her deathbed that she would not leave him, and he felt "assured of her presence" with him after her death; this seems to have been as close as he ever came to a mystical experience. In "Footsteps of Angels," written in 1839, he would speak of her as

> the Being Beauteous,
> Who unto my youth was given,
> More than all things else to love me,
> And is now a saint in heaven.
>
> With a slow and noiseless footstep
> Comes that messenger divine,
> Takes the vacant chair beside me,
> Lays her gentle hand in mine.
>
> And she sits and gazes at me
> With those deep and tender eyes,
> Like the stars, so still and saint-like,
> Looking downward from the skies.

In the spring the newly widowed Longfellow went to the Tyrol, whence he intended proceeding to Italy. Passport difficulties caused him to go to Switzerland instead, and this turned out to be one of those fortunate "accidents" than can transform a life, for it was there, during the summer, that he met Fanny Appleton and her family, whom, though they lived on Boston's Beacon Street, he does not seem to have encountered before. In December 1836 he arrived in Cambridge where, some eight months later, he rented quarters in the historic Craigie House at 105 Brattle Street, which was to be his home for the rest of his life and is now the Longfellow Historic Site.

Longfellow remained at Harvard until his resignation in 1854, when Lowell succeeded him, but for a man who was in general so little of a complainer, he finds enough fault with both his academic appointments to raise serious doubts in the reader's mind that he really enjoyed teaching or was made to be a teacher. This was not at all either because he did not believe in what he was doing or did not do it well. Nobody ever regarded the teacher's function as nobler, more necessary, or more important than he did. As we have already seen, he made his own textbooks at Bowdoin, and his historic position as one of the pioneer giants in establishing the modern languages as a basic part of American education has never been questioned.[6] He prepared his lectures in a responsible manner, sometimes investing "the labor of weeks" in a single discourse. The examination of his unpublished notes and manuscripts has left me with the feeling that while as a lecturer he may have achieved less in the way of a blanket coverage of his subject than would be expected today, he took more of his materials from first-hand sources in a number of languages than many modern professors do. He attempted little critical analysis and was much given to the reading of extracts which permitted the writer under consideration to speak for himself, but this might certainly be defended as sound pedagogic practice at a time when many of the texts with which he dealt were difficult or impossible for his students to come by at first hand. Among his books there is an 1831 edition of *Faust* bound up with blank leaves for memoranda, from which he taught. Some of his notes are explications of the text, but more are quotations from a wide range of authors whom Goethe's work in some way recalls or resembles.

Longfellow adhered to the principle then too little recognized that in order to be successful, education must enlist the vital interest of the pupil, and though his relations with his students do not seem to have been intimate, they were cordial and polite and, for the period at least, relaxed and comfortable. He "sat and read his lectures in a simple manner" (by all accounts he had an uncommonly pleasant and melodious voice, and nobody has ever denied his personal charm), and, especially in the more advanced courses, he created the effect of a gentleman addressing gentlemen. He was capable of discipline when it was required, but he relied more upon the dignity of his presence and the "atmosphere" he had created around himself than upon the harsher, more mechanical methods many others employed.

Yet he complains of the monotony, even the "anguish and exhaustion" of teaching and calls himself fool and madman to lead the life he does. He tired of adapting his mind to the minds of boys "instead of grappling with men's minds" (it must be remembered that college students in his time were considerably younger than they are today). Bowdoin was a freshwater college that did not afford him the resources to do his work as he wished to do it; his liberal religious views made him an object of suspicion to many, and he probably never quite ceased to resent the attempt the college had made to deprive him of professorial rank. Harvard of course was much better in these respects, but his responsibilities were much greater there than they had been at Bowdoin. He and the administration did not always see eye to eye; he knew that the modern languages were regarded by the conservatives as less respectable academically than the classics; he was sometimes compelled to teach more elementary courses than he liked; and keeping in order the "*four-in-hand* of outlandish animals, all pulling the wrong way, expect one" who taught under him took far more out of him than his students did.

Whether all this completely covered the case however is a question that probably nobody will ever be able to answer authoritatively. Longfellow himself speaks of "such an ardent temper as mine," and once he says frankly that he could be happy at Harvard if he were satisfied to be a professor and nothing else. As we shall see in Chapter II, there had been a time when he thought he had given up poetry for scholarship or at least put his muse "in the House of Correction," but it is also abundantly clear that during both his first two trips to Europe, he gave his attention to much that must have been of far more interest to the burgeoning poet than to the teacher of foreign languages. In 1839 he even contemplated resigning his professorship to go to Europe as tutor and guide to a young scion of the House of Astor, and he might indeed have committed this act of folly if the boy's father had not decided otherwise.

In 1839, to be sure, Longfellow had abundant reason for being upset and uncertain. As has already been noted, he had met Fanny (Frances Elizabeth) Appleton, the daughter of a wealthy New England industrialist, three years before in Switzerland, where he read and translated German poetry with her and her sister. Fanny was nineteen at the time, a little more than ten years and seven months younger than Longfellow. She was intelligent, socially cultivated, deeply religious and serious-minded, and she was also, it would seem, at this period in her development, somewhat inclined to pertness. She and Longfellow were clearly attracted to each other, and it is possible that their intimacy might have proceeded faster if he had not had to leave earlier than he had intended in order to escort Clara Crowninshield back to America. What is certain is that he got nowhere with Fanny for a long time after they had both returned home. Jacob served seven years for Rachel, and Fanny put Longfellow through a purgation of exactly the same length before, after he had just about given up hope, she put an end to his agony by telling him, upon a chance encounter, that her brother was going away and that he must come and comfort her.

Her reasons are still none too clear. After the long ordeal was over, she herself could not understand why it had lasted so long; her heart, she told her Aunt Matty, had "always been of tenderer stuff than anybody believed." She was very young when it all began, and she may just not have been ready for marriage. Longfellow may have frightened her also by too precipitate wooing. The one thing we can be sure of is that she was offended by *Hyperion* (1839), in which he portrayed her as Mary Ashburton and himself as Paul Flemming. Thus to parade their connection and his passion before all Boston and Cambridge was the very worst thing he could have done to further his suit, as it was the very best to show us how far his passion had carried him away. Surely Fanny Appleton never performed a more generous act than when, upon their marriage, she presented her husband with her European sketchbook inscribed "Mary Ashburton to Paul Flemming."

Before that happy time however, Longfellow had suffered everything that aspiring lovers suffered in the medieval romances, and since he knew these so well, he can hardly have been unaware that he was following in their footsteps. "And first of the 'Dark Ladie,' who holds my reason captive." "The lady says she *will not!* I say she *shall!* It is not pride but the madness of passion!" "But my passion is mighty; gigantic; or it would not have survived this." "I shall win this lady, or I shall die." And much more to the same effect. We do not have it all, for he inked out what he thought the most revealing passages in his records. Once, as with Dante and Beatrice, he met her in the street and *"looked* and *passed. . . .* It is ended." They were married at her home, 39 Beacon Street, on July 13, 1843, and Nathan Appleton's wedding present to them was the Craigie House, which in those days was a much more extensive property than it is today, with grounds on the other side of Brattle Street, clear down to the Charles.

Fanny made up to Longfellow for his seven years of serving with eighteen years of as perfect domestic happiness as we have the record of in the life of any man of letters. "My whole life is bound up now in my home and children," she once wrote. "I am spoiled by it for society, which now seems to me very barren and unsympathetic." There were six children.[7] Of course they brought cares and sorrows with them. The third child and first daughter, Fanny's namesake, lived little more than a year. The older son, Charles, presented his parents with disciplinary problems, and in 1856 he mutilated his left hand by the explosion of a gun that his firearms-hating father had rather surprisingly allowed him to have in spite of his mother's objection. But whatever love and understanding and common sense could do was done.

One event in the domestic life of the Longfellows was, in its context, more than a little sensational. When little Fanny was born, on April 7, 1847, her mother became the first woman in the Western world to bear a child under anesthesia. She undertook the experiment deliberately, despite the element of risk involved, with her husband's sanction, and felt proud "to be the pioneer to less suffering for poor weak womankind." We have all heard enough and to spare about the courage of Lady Mary Wortley Montagu in inoculating her child against smallpox in eighteenth-century England; here are the supposedly timid Longfellows performing an equally daring act of which only the Longfellow specialists seem ever to have heard.

Whatever roadblocks Longfellow's work at Harvard may have thrown up in the way of his writing, he published much during his tenure there, both before and after his marriage. We have already noted the appearance of *Hyperion,* but the same year, 1839, witnessed a more important publication, *Voices of the Night,* his first collection of original poems. Two years later he published *Ballads and Other Poems.* In 1842 he secured a leave of absence

from his college duties to spend six months at a water cure
in Germany, and on his way home, during a stormy
voyage, he wrote the *Poems on Slavery* which constituted
his contribution to the great moral-political conflict of his
time. In the year of his marriage came his first dramatic
composition, *The Spanish Student,* and in 1845 another
collection, *The Belfry of Bruges and Other Poems.* Then in
1847 he brought out the tremendously popular
Evangeline.

Longfellow had not yet, however, committed himself
exclusively to the composition of poetry or, for that matter, to the production of original work. In 1845 he had
published an immense anthology, *The Poets and Poetry of
Europe.* He also edited two small collections of fugitive
verses, suggestively called *The Waif* (1845) and *The Estray*
(1846). After that he let anthologizing alone until
1876–79, when he edited what is probably the most extensive anthology ever published in this country, the thirty-one volumed *Poems of Places.* He had already taken his
leave of prose with *Kavanagh* (1849), a tale of New
England village life.

The half-century mark brought the only volume
Longfellow devoted to short poems between 1846 and
1867, *The Seaside and the Fireside.* The most important
poem was in the "Seaside" section, "The Building of the
Ship," that eloquent expression of pre-Civil War hopes
that so moved Lincoln. In 1851 he permitted himself the
luxury of an elaborate and somewhat Faustian piece of
medievalism, *The Golden Legend,* which was destined to
form the middle third of his most ambitious, though not
most successful, undertaking, *Christus: A Mystery.* But
whatever ground he may have lost here with the general
reader was more than regained with *The Song of Hiawatha*
four years later, a considerably more elaborate work than
Evangeline and if possible even more fantastically successful. He had resigned his professorship the year before,

among other reasons to give him more time for writing, but it was not until 1858 that he published *The Courtship of Miles Standish and Other Poems,* another rousing success and his last publication during Fanny Appleton's lifetime.

The crowning sorrow of Longfellow's life came upon him just as the Civil War was getting under way. The ninth of July 1861 was a hot, windy day in Cambridge, and Mrs. Longfellow was sitting near an open window in the library, sealing up in small packets some locks of her two younger daughters' hair. By some fluke a lighted match or some hot sealing wax fell upon the light summer dress she was wearing and in a moment she was enveloped in flames. Frightened, she ran for help to her husband in his adjoining study. Longfellow wrapped a rug about her and held her close, trying to extinguish the flames and burning his own face and hands badly.

After a brief period of intense suffering, she was put to sleep with ether and slept into the night, when she awoke calm and free of pain. In the morning she was able to drink some coffee, but she soon fell into a coma from which she never awakened, and before the day had ended she was dead.

She was buried in Mount Auburn on July 13, the eighteenth anniversary of her marriage, her head, which was unmarred by the flames, crowned by a wreath of orange blossoms. Her husband, too badly burned to leave his bed, was unable to attend the funeral; half-delirious, he heard, through his open door, echoes of the services in the library, where neither men nor women were able to control their sobs.

One of the best things ever said about Longfellow was said by James Russell Lowell in a birthday tribute:

> Some suck up poison from a sorrow's core,
>   As nought but nightshade grew upon earth's ground;

Love turned all his to heart's-ease, and the more
Fate tried his bastions, she but forced a door
Leading to sweeter manhood and more sound.

Perhaps it was this, above all his other resources, that
helped him to survive. Nevertheless his sufferings were
terrible. "How can I live any longer?" "The terrible days
go by and bring no relief." "Perhaps some men could
bear up even under such sorrow as mine. But I cannot."
His only comfort was the memory of the life he and Fanny
had shared. As he wrote her sister, "I never looked at her
without a thrill of pleasure; she never came into a room
where I was without my heart beating quicker, nor went
out without my feeling that something of the light went
with her. I loved her so entirely, and I know she was very
happy."

Exteriorly the change in Longfellow after Fanny's death
was marked by the growth of a full beard, his burns having
made shaving impossible or inadvisable. Nobody ever
thinks of him now without this patriarchal adornment,
snowy white during his later years, and it is hard to realize
that neither of his wives ever saw him thus.

One other resource—and care—he had: the children, to
whom he must now be both father and mother.
Longfellow was in all things an unusual combination of
tenderness and reserve. He never romped with his
children, never apparently lost his dignity with them, but
no one could have given them better care. The endless
supplies of childish treasures he kept for them, all the way
from what Alice calls "small cakes of chocolate for cases of
extreme need" to "delightful books of German songs with
captivating pictures, and a tiny little book of negro
melodies, and the marvelous Jim Crow" have vanished
into the wallet of time, but we still have in manuscript
some of the stories and nonsense verses he wrote for them.
Neither Ernest nor the three girls ever seem to have caused
him any trouble beyond that inevitably involved in their

being children. His study was always open to all the members of his household, and Alice remarks that he carried on his writing almost "imperceptibly." We may be sure that he alone knew what it cost him to do this.

Charley continued to be the problem child. He did not behave like his Uncle Stephen nor like Stephen's son (that much at least his father was spared), nor did he lack either sensitiveness or devotion to his family, but he could be irresponsible, and when in 1874 he traveled in the Far East, buying all the Oriental furniture and objets d'art that took his fancy (some of which are still in the Longfellow House), he had spent half his inheritance from his mother before his father peremptorily ordered him home. The most hilarious of Charley's misadventures occurred at Nahant, where the Longfellows summered, when the redoubtable Jessie Frémont had him arrested for naked bathing, but this story has a happy ending, for the case was dismissed when it was shown that she could not have seen him without binoculars. But the worst trouble he caused his father came in 1863, when, despite his mutilated hand, he ran off and enlisted in the Union army. Though Longfellow disapproved and expressed his disapproval, he did not attempt to exert his authority and order his son to come home. Instead he made two trips to Washington to nurse him, the first when he came down with camp fever and the second when he was wounded and permanently put out of commission so far as military service was concerned.[8]

Though Longfellow's relations with women were always entirely proper, he was obviously fond of them, and since he was only fifty-four when Fanny Appleton died, it was not unnatural that he should have enjoyed friendships with a number of ladies during his later years. Most of them were writers or other artists, considerably younger than himself, and some were in a sense his protégées and partakers of his bounty. I do not know whether his

daughters disliked Blanche Roosevelt, who seems rather to
have wormed her way into the Longfellow circle, because
they thought she had designs on their father or whether
they merely thought she was using him to further her own
career, but though he seems to have thought much better
of her than they did, there is no reason to suppose that he
cherished amatory feelings toward her, and I would say the
same thing about his relations with the Mississippi local
color writer Sherwood Bonner, whom he befriended and
who at one period acted as his amanuensis. It is amusing,
however, that his letters to the aspiring young Wisconsin
singer, Frances Rowena Miller, who seems to have been a
very charming girl and who, judging by her letters, was in-
nocently fond of him, should begin "My Dear Protégée,"
"My Dear Child," "My Dear Fran," "Cara la mia Fran-
cesca," "Gentilissima Signora," and "Cara Signora
Roena" except when he was dictating to his daughter Annie Allegra and his correspondent became "Dear Miss
Miller"!

Two young ladies call for rather more careful consideration however. The first was Cornelia Fitch and the
second was Alice Frere.

Longfellow met Cornelia Fitch, of Auburn, New York,
who was thirty-one years his junior, at Nahant, where both
were summering, in June 1864. We have none of her letters to him; the eight we have from him to her are wholly
proper, but the Fitch family legend adds considerable
color, indicating both that Charley Longfellow shared his
father's interest in Miss Fitch and that her family rushed
her into her marriage in February 1865 because they
wished to end her relations with the Longfellows.

About Alice Frere we know a little more. She was a
lovely English girl whom he met briefly in Boston and
Cambridge, when she visited there in 1867 with her
father, William Frere of Bitton, Judge of the High Court
of Bombay, and though she was thirty-four years younger

than he, it is *possible* that he may have asked her to marry
him, for we have a letter in which she tells him of her
engagement of three years' standing to Major Godfrey
Clerk and of the difficulties that had so far prevented their
union, in reply to which Longfellow wrote that he was sure
the "secret" he had told her the other night, which was
the "cry" of his "soul," would be safe in her keeping, to
which he added, "And yet I would not have told it, had I
known yours." Alice Frere married Clerk, lived with him
in Egypt and India, and bore him at least one son. In 1873
she published a volume of tales translated from the Arabic
of which she sent Longfellow a copy. Whatever else may be
said about this matter, it seems clear that she inflamed his
imagination beyond any other woman he met after Fanny
Appleton's death and that both parties cherished the
memories of their meeting.[9]

Longfellow's first publication after the death of his wife
came along in 1863, in a volume which comprised "Part
First" of his *Tales of a Wayside Inn* and the "second
flight" of the lyric poems he called "Birds of Passage,"
whose "first flight" had already appeared in the same
volume with *The Courtship of Miles Standish.* Another
collection of lyrics, *Flower-de-Luce,* appeared in 1866
(dated 1867). *The New England Tragedies (John Endicott,*
which had been written some time before, and *Giles Corey
of the Salem Farms)* were published in 1868. In 1867 came
his translation of *The Divine Comedy of Dante Alighieri,*
and in 1871 *The Divine Tragedy,* Longfellow's dramatic
treatment of the life of Jesus. In 1868, the poet, accompanied by members of his family, made his last trip to
Europe, which took on almost the aspect of a royal
"progress." Both Oxford and Cambridge bestowed doc-
torates upon him, and he was received by Queen Victoria.
In 1872 *The Divine Tragedy, The Golden Legend,* and
The New England Tragedies were brought together in
Christus: A Mystery, and *Three Books of Song* (1872) was

made up of the "Part Second" of *Tales of a Wayside Inn;*
"Judas Maccabeus," a brief tragedy based on the Old
Testament Apocrypha; and "A Handful of Translations."

The *Tales of a Wayside Inn* were completed in 1874 in
Aftermath, which also carried the third flight of the
"Birds of Passage." The most distinguished work in *The
Masque of Pandora and Other Poems* (1875) was not in the
title piece but in the "Morituri Salutamus," Longfellow's
fiftieth-anniversary poem for a Bowdoin College reunion,
and a collection of sonnets which, taken with what he had
previously produced and what was still to come in the
Kéramos volume and later, would give him his high place
among English and American sonneteers. A fourth flight
of the "Birds of Passage" was also included in this
volume, along with his most elaborate celebration of the
domestic virtues, "The Hanging of the Crane," which had
already been published separately the year before in an
elaborately illustrated volume.

"Kéramos," the poem about potters and pottery in
which Longfellow became something of an imagist before
imagism, was handled in the same way, first appearing
alone in 1877, then giving its name to *Kéramos and Other
Poems* in 1878, in which the "Birds of Passage" undertook their fifth and last flight, and which also contained more sonnets and translations. Suggestions of en-
croaching mortality were widely recognized and deplored
when *Ultima Thule* appeared in 1880, and Longfellow's
instinct in the matter proved sound, for this was the last
book he ever saw in print. The poems he had left uncollected at his death were published posthumously in *In
the Harbor* (1882). In 1882–83 there also appeared the immense fragment, *Michael Angelo.*

Two of Longfellow's children, Ernest and Edith,
married before his death, and it was from Edith's children
that he derived the greatest pleasure of his last years. His
health began to fail in 1881, and his death, of peritonitis,

came after only a few days of illness, on March 24, 1882, less than a month after his seventy-fifth birthday had been celebrated all over America. He was taken sick during the night of March 18–19 but characteristically chose to suffer in silence, though in great pain, rather than disturb his family before morning.

Though Emerson would follow him only a month later, he was the first of the front-ranking American poets of his generation to go, and his death was widely recognized as marking the beginning of the end of an era.

II

Poetic Theory and Practice

Longfellow was never much given to the formulation of dogma in any area, and an age that is more interested in poetic theory than in poetry has made him pay for this. Yet here as elsewhere he knew what he believed, though he often expressed it with such disarming simplicity that sophisticated modern readers find it easy to fail to understand him. Take, for example, "The Day Is Done," in which the poet turns away, for the moment, from "the grand old masters" and

> the bards sublime
> Whose distant footsteps echo
> Through the corridors of Time.
>
> For, like strains of martial music,
> Their mighty thoughts suggest
> Life's endless toil and endeavor;
> And to-night I long for rest.
>
> Read from some humbler poet,
> Whose songs gushed from his heart,
> As showers from the clouds of summer,
> Or tears from the eyelids start.

The poem ends with some of Longfellow's best-known lines:

> Then read from the treasured volume
>   The poem of thy choice,
> And lend to the rhyme of the poet
>   The beauty of thy voice.
>
> And the night shall be filled with music,
>   And the cares, that infest the day,
> Shall fold their tents, like the Arabs,
>   And as silently steal away.

Strictly speaking, these verses do not formulate a creed but merely express a mood, for the same man who wrote them was capable of pondering for many years the "loftier strain" which finally eventuated in *Christus*. On the other hand, the whole Romantic doctrine of the character—or, if you prefer, of the "psychology"—of the poetic inspiration is implied in them, and to be unaware of its presence is to reveal a greater simplicity than some critics have found in Longfellow himself. If he generally composed in the Key of C, we might do well to remember that, in the view of Richard Strauss, the Key of C was also the Key of Heaven.[1]

This is not to say that Longfellow was completely incapable of indirectness and obscurity. Towards the end of his life, when he had become a literary monument, he blew both hot and cold on the "new poets" of the time, but in his youth he had himself been a "new poet," and "new poets" must, as Wordsworth had realized, create the taste by which they are understood. When he received his copy of *Voices of the Night,* Longfellow's brother Alexander wrote him: "To you must be accorded the merit of giving to these western shores a new species of poetry—the mental in contradistinction to the sentimental—the healthy, in opposition to the morbid." And if the modern reader rubs his eyes at this and sets it down to family partiality, what shall be made of the related fact, as pointed out by Clarence Gohdes, that *"Fraser's Magazine,* in 1853, initiated its discussion of . . .

[Longfellow] with a charge that might be levelled at the metaphysical poets of the twentieth century, namely, a tendency toward the farfetched and the extravagant''?

Generally speaking, however, one can certainly say truly that though Longfellow admitted the value of an implicational manner of presentation in some kinds of writing, he did set a high valuation upon clarity and simplicity, generally eschewing all the advantages that depend upon the suggestion of deep profundities beyond the reach of the everyday reader or comprehensible only to a clique, and that above all he disliked flashiness and gimcrack ornamentation. He wished to write not only for ''the few who think'' but also for ''the many who feel,'' assuming a certain community of nature, interest, and cultural inheritance between himself and his readers, and it was in this sense that he was a ''public'' poet, as distinguished from the obscure, often arcane, and extremely private ''confessional'' poets of today. Reviewing the *Poems and Prose of Writings* of Richard Henry Dana I in 1833, he complained that ''he sometimes follows out a brilliant train of thought farther than minds less metaphysical than his own are capable of accompanying him or willing to do.'' He condemned Browning's obscurity and disliked the ''very cumbrous phraseology'' that Coleridge often used ''to express an idea, where simple and direct language would have stood him in better stead.'' He comes very close to Milton's criteria—''simple, sensuous, and passionate''—when he compliments Frederick Locker-Lampson, telling him that his poems are ''very elastic and full of life and animal spirits which are the leaven of life.'' This is why he loved the popular ballads, ''the gypsy-children of song, born under green hedgerows, in the leafy lanes and by-paths of literature—in the genial summertime'' and valued the early English dramatists and other old writers for the ''directness and earnestness'' of ''broad daylight'' that he

found in them. To his way of thinking there was a difference between the simplicity of the backwoods ranter
and the kind of simplicity we find in the parables of Jesus,
which latter he suggested very well in his translation of
Tegnér's "The Children of the Lord's Supper":

> Friendly the Teacher stood, like an angel of light there
>   among them,
> And to the children explained the holy, the highest,
>   in few words,
> Thorough, yet simple and clear, for sublimity always is simple,
> Both in sermon and song, a child can seize on its meaning.

None of this means however that technical considerations were unimportant to him. His range as
prosodist was very wide, and Cecil B. Williams sums up
very well:

He could handle dexterously all the verse forms he attempted.
He was by no means limited to the iambic foot which prevails in
English poetry, but he handled trochees, anapests, and dactyls
frequently and with great skill. His lines range in length from
trimeter to octameter; his range of stanza patterns includes
couplets, triplets, simple quatrains and ballad meter, the varied
patterns of the ode and the elegy, sonnets, and blank verse.[2]

He was extraordinarily fertile in plans and ideas also,
though perhaps this can be fully realized only by those
who have examined his manuscript "Book of
Suggestions," in which he described so many projects that
life was not long enough to bring them to fruition.[3] Here
clearly is the man who while he was still only a boy, and
even before it was clear that he was to become a poet,
wrote his father that he was determined to "be eminent in
something."

But let us return for a moment to Alexander
Longfellow's distinction between the mental and the sentimental. *Was* Longfellow then, it may be asked, not a

romantic, a sentimentalist, a didactic poet, an idealist, a weaver of rhymed moralities? Certainly there can be no doubt that he saw art as inevitably both moral and religious. In "The Singers" he gives poetry a threefold function: "To charm, to strengthen, and to teach." And much later he wrote in *Michael Angelo:*

> Art is the gift of God, and must be used
> Unto His glory. That in art is highest
> Which aims at this.

But this is by no means all that he has to say upon this count.

He gave the imagination a very large and important share in literature, and he displeases many modern readers when he finds Jane Austen too detailed and matter-of-fact. In an early lecture on the "Lives of Literary Men" he distinguished between two "Schools of Poetry . . . : The Ideal and the Actual."

The first endeavors to invest ideal scenes and characters with truth and reality:—The second, on the contrary, clothes the real with the ideal, and makes actual and common things radiant with poetic beauty.

Of the former are Byron, Schiller, Percival:—of the latter, Goethe, Wordsworth, Bryant. The former are poets of passion:—the latter are poets of observation, and reflection. I would not willingly compare these schools and decide between them, but rather admire what is excellent in both. Our feelings tell us which we prefer; and our feelings vary, and with them our judgment. At times our spirits need the sunshine of a bold, brave impulse;—at times, the soothing quiet of reflection;—and the poets of each class commend themselves to us according to the mood we are in.

For his own part, however, he did not believe that the purpose of the imagination was "to devise what has no existence, but rather to perceive what really exists . . . not creation but insight.''

> By the mirage uplifted, the land floats vague in the ether,
>> Ships and the shadows of ships hang in the motionless air;
> So by the art of the poet our common life is uplifted,
>> So, transfigured, the world floats in a luminous haze.

How such beliefs affected Longfellow's own writing may be seen among other things in the use he made of the past. Unlike most poets, he was a professional scholar; consequently he knew better than most poets that the past was not really more romantic than the present but only looks so to us because it is farther away.

We see the tree-tops waving in the wind, and hear the merry birds singing under their green roofs; but we forget that at their roots there are swine feeding upon acorns. With the Present it is not so. We stand too near to see objects in a picturesque light.

Sometimes, however, Longfellow seems to prefer to ignore such considerations and frankly surrender himself to

> Dreams that the soul of youth engage
>> Ere Fancy has been quelled;
> Old legends of the monkish page,
> Traditions of the saint and sage,
> Tales that have the rime of age,
>> And chronicles of old.

So it was part of the charm of the Wayside Inn that it had become

> A kind of old Hobgoblin Hall,
> Now somewhat fallen to decay,
> With weather-stains upon the wall,
> And stairways worn, and crazy doors,
> And creaking and uneven floors,
> And chimneys huge, and tiled and tall.

The poet admits—and accepts—his own romanticism in the very last poem he wrote, "The Bells of San Blas," where he speaks of himself as

> a dreamer of dreams,
> To whom what is and what seems
> Are often one and the same.

No doubt we often think of Longfellow in this aspect. We think of him too, and justly, as the gentle poet of the domestic affections, but this does not mean that harsher themes and emotions lay altogether out of his range. If this had been true, the action-subjects to which he was predisposed through his sympathy for early and primitive peoples would have been impossible for him.

Longfellow was quite aware of the temptations of the romantic imagination and presented them in the dreamy Mr. Churchill of *Kavanagh*. Like Hawthorne in the custom house, Churchill knows that native sources of literary material and inspiration lie all around him, but in practice he overlooks them, for to him the near always suggests the far. His basic difficulty however is not that he is enthralled by the past but rather that he lacks the energy required to turn his dreams into literature. When a writer has such energy, when his imagination is sufficiently vital to be able to use the past so that it takes on fresh life in the present, then past and present have coalesced.

Longfellow did this on many occasions. He did it with "The Village Blacksmith." The actual smithy described stood on Brattle Street between the poet's house and Harvard Square, but in writing the poem Longfellow intended also to praise his own blacksmith ancestor in Newberry. Again, his very first poem, "The Battle of Lovell's Pond," took its inspiration from American history and from his teacher Thomas Upham's earlier treatment of the same subject. But the young writer could not bear to leave un-

controverted his predecessor's assertion that the heroes of
the battle were to be forgotten. Instead he asserts that

> They are dead, but they live in each Patriot's breast,
> And their names are engraven on honor's bright crest.

It is true then that the past inspired a feeling of piety in
Longfellow and a desire to preserve whatever it had held
that was lovely and of good report. He felt this even about
his beautiful house, and it was this feeling that saved from
materialism his devotion to it and its contents; he served as
a kind of priest at the sanctuary to hold the place inviolate
because Washington had been there. In this aspect, his
poetry is the utterance of a sensitive, cultivated man,
brooding over and assimilating the past and possessing
himself of his moral and aesthetic inheritance. But for him
this was not the basic consideration. He saw "the impulse
of the present as strengthened by [both] the memory of
the past and the anticipation of the future." Human
desire is "quickened by imagination, which casts its spell
upon us, till the deformed seems beautiful, and the sen-
sual is clothed upon with the ideal." For this reason,
"men do not love truth less, in seeming to love fiction
more. They love truth because it *is* truth, and they love fiction, not because it is fiction, but because it resembles
truth." Whether he deals with the past or the present or
both, it is the creative man who functions in the highest
possible human aspect.

Neither Longfellow's "sentimentalism" nor his didacticism is a very profitable subject for discussion now, for
the modern rebellion against both these tendencies in
literature is too recent to permit us to approach the subject
dispassionately. To be sure, Longfellow himself sometimes
rebelled against sentimentality—in Silvio Pellico, for
example, whose work would have been better, he thought,
"for a blast or two of the North." But there are times too
when he succumbs to it. He thinks it a high tribute that

Felton should have wept over ''Footsteps of Angels,'' and
he created some of his poems—''The Reaper and the
Flowers,'' for example—in a very tearful mood. One
might indeed make a pretty strong case for the view that
''The Reaper and the Flowers'' is *not* sentimental from the
point of view of one who shares the faith expressed in it,
but it is more important to remember that two of
Longfellow's most trusted advisers—Charles Sumner and
President Felton of Harvard—had grave doubts about the
wisdom of publishing ''The Skeleton in Armor,'' because
they considered it to represent too daring a departure from
the dominant didacticism of the time; that a Philadelphia
newspaper declined to review the *Poems on Slavery*
because the very word ''slavery'' was taboo in its columns;
and that one Boston newspaper roundly condemned
Hiawatha for having employed

the silly legends of the savage aborigines. His poem does not
awaken one sympathetic throb; it does not teach a single truth.
. . . In verse it contains nothing so precious as the golden time
which would be lost in the reading of it.

The poet's brother-biographer misrepresented him
when he wrote that he valued his art ''not for its own sake,
but as a vehicle for noble, gentle, beautiful thought and
sentiment''; the condescension implied in that ''not for its
own sake'' simply shows that the writer had no comprehension of how the creative imagination works. For
though Longfellow did not reject the poet's teaching function, neither did he, at his best, begin with it nor permit it
to swallow up everything else. In *The New England
Tragedies* to be sure he felt it worth while to resurrect the
errors of his ancestors

> ''For the lesson that they teach:
> The tolerance of opinion and of speech.''

But this ''moral'' is inherent in the subject, not superim-
posed upon it; this is what *The New England Tragedies*

mean, and Longfellow could not have understood his own materials if he had failed to perceive it. But this is a very different thing from conceiving of him as one who thought of moralizing as the sole end of the poet's striving.

> And the Poet, faithful and far-seeing,
>   Sees, alike in stars and flowers, a part
> Of the self-same, universal being,
>   Which is throbbing in his brain and heart.

That the poetic gift operated spontaneously Longfellow never ceased to believe.

> As the birds come to the Spring . . .
>
> As the rain comes from the cloud . . .
>
> As the grape comes to the vine . . .
>
> As come the white sails of ships
>   O'er the ocean's verge . . .
>
> So come to the Poet his songs,
>   All hitherward blown
> From the misty realm, that belongs
>   To the vast Unknown.

So he wrote at seventy-three. It was true all his life.

The most puzzling feature in Longfellow's poetic activity is the curious poetic hiatus in his career from 1826 to 1837. This cessation of poetic activity for eleven years has puzzled many students of his life and work, including his grandson, Henry Wadsworth Longfellow Dana, who once remarked to Robert Stafford Ward that these very years (age nineteen to thirty) are those during which many poets do much of their best work; would Longfellow have been a greater poet, he wondered, if he had not lost these years? In March 1826 he wrote Caroline Doane from Portland, ''I have not stopped writing, but I have stopped publishing, for certain reasons which I cannot go into at length in a letter." But in a letter to George Bancroft, from Auteuil, August 20, he went further: "I grow daily more certain of the fact,—that when I left my native land I left with it whatever poetical inspiration Heaven had blessed me with," and in 1829 he wrote his sister Elizabeth from Göttingen:

My poetic career is finished. Since I left America, I have hardly put two lines together. I may indeed say, that my muse has been sent to the House of Correction—and her last offspring were laid at the door of one of those Foundling Hospitals for poor poetry—a New Year's "Souvenir."

Even after he had settled down at Bowdoin Longfellow wrote George Washington Greene: "If I ever publish a volume it will be many years first. Indeed, I have such an engrossing interest in the studies of my profession that I write very seldom except in connection with those studies." It was not until after five more years had passed and he found himself in Europe again, that he noted in his Danish journal having

Sat up late at night writing poetry—the first I have written for many a long, long day. Pleasant feelings of the olden time came over me; of those years when as yet a boy, I gave so many hours to rhymery! I wonder whether I am destined to write anything in verse that will live?

But even this turned out to be a trial balloon.

Lawrance Thompson does not get much further in explaining this matter than to conjecture that Longfellow was discouraged about the quality of his early poetry (as well he might have been) in view of the criticisms that had been made of it by his own father and Theophilus Parsons. Horace E. Scudder and some of the other earlier interpreters of Longfellow threw out pentrating hints here and there. But the only scholar who has really grappled with the problem is the late Robert Stafford Ward in his unpublished 1951 doctoral dissertation, "Longfellow's *Lehrjahre.*"

It is noteworthy that even in the renunciatory utterances just quoted Longfellow does not seem at all out of sorts with poetry itself. There are simply obstacles in the way of his continuing his poetic career as of now. When, in 1832, in the midst of the hiatus, he was asked to give the Phi Beta Kappa poem at Harvard, he was even pleased that he had been thought of as a poet.

Ward suggested, accordingly, that Longfellow never really intended to give up poetry for good. He was merely postponing further composition in accordance with a well-laid and carefully prepared plan that he had worked out under the influence of the Swiss historian Jean Charles Sismondi and others. "With his increasing preoccupation with careful preparation and finished style, it is likely that he became concerned lest inferior work jeopardize his literary future. It seems clear that the cessation was due to his literary theories."

When Longfellow first encountered Sismondi is not known. He refers to him however in his first Inaugural Address at Bowdoin and also in his article on the French language in *The North American Review* for April 1831. But Sismondi was not the only influence in the direction indicated. Ward stressed that of Giovanni Vico also, with his cyclical theory of history, likewise reflected clearly, he thought, in the Inaugural Address.

Moreover, before he had read either Vico or Sismondi, Longfellow had come under the influence, at Bowdoin, of the teacher Thomas Cogswell Upham, whose ideas appear in many aspects of his poetic theory and practice. Like Longfellow, Upham was strongly antimaterialist. Like Longfellow's own, his temperamental bias was away from metaphysical speculation and in the direction of what would later be called pragmatism. The early Longfellow may well reflect him also in being more inclined than the later Longfellow would be to insist upon the use of American themes in poetry. But more important than any of this were Upham's views on the cultivation of the poet's talent. Upham saw genius as an inherited trait and believed the human heart the most important object of a poet's study. But he also believed that in the nineteenth century no poet could be what is commonly called "original." Innate talent must be assumed, but it could not be relied upon to take him the whole way. On the contrary, the poet must cultivate his gift by study and learning and practice of the most rigorous sort. Consequently,

> The first part of [Longfellow's] literary career was to be in prose, as it was for the ensuing decade. But his studies had been largely in the history of poetry, and he had been translating. Translation was to occupy him, too, during the decade of prose composition. These facts are consistent with, not an abandoned, but a deferred project for a poetic career. It was, indeed, deferred until after he had subsumed in his experience the literatures of Northern Europe as well as the Romance ones. In its "House of Correction" his muse was engaged in the "hard labor" of translation.

Such plans and convictions might a priori be thought likely to inhibit poetic spontaneity or facility, but this does not seem to have been the case with Longfellow.

> As the ink from our pen, so flow our thoughts and
>   our feelings
> When we begin to write, however sluggish before.

In *Hyperion,* the Baron tells Paul Flemming that "what we call miracles and wonders of Art are not so to him who created them, for they were created by the natural movement of his own great soul," which is a statement quite in harmony with Bernard Shaw's opinion that "fine art of any sort is either easy or impossible."

Of "The Wreck of the Hesperus," which was written in

its first form at a sitting, immediately after the idea had
entered his mind, Longfellow records that it came not by
lines but by stanzas. "The Arrow and the Song" was
jotted down under a similar sudden inspiration one Sunday morning before church. And of "Blind Bartimeus" he
sent this interesting account to Sam Ward:

> I was reading this morning, just after breakfast, the tenth
> chapter of Mark, in Greek, the last seven verses of which contain
> the story of blind Bartimeus, and always seemed to me
> remarkable for their beauty. At once the whole scene presented
> itself to my mind in lively colors,—the walls of Jericho, the cold
> winds through the gate-way, the ragged, blind beggar, his shrill
> cry, the tumultuous crowd, the serene Christ, the miracle; and
> these things took the form I have given them above.

Longer works too were often produced, once they had
got under way, with great rapidity: "The Saga of King
Olaf" in little more than fifteen days, "Judas Maccabeus"
in eleven, *The Divine Tragedy* in less than a month. "If I
had a hundred hands, I could keep them all busy with
'Hiawatha.' Nothing ever absorbed me more." For thirty-
four successive days he translated a canto of the "Inferno"
every day.

This of course was when the "estro" was upon him,
when he knew the truth of what he wrote in "The Poets,"
that the glory not of recognition but of achievement
eclipses, for the artist, all his pains:

> Yes; for the gift and ministry of Song
>   Have something in them so divinely sweet,
>   It can assuage the bitterness of wrong;
> Not in the clamor of the crowded street,
>   Not in the shouts and plaudits of the throng,
>   But in ourselves, are triumph and defeat.

"I have thought all the while," he once wrote Colin Grant
Mackenzie, thanking him for the gift of his poems, "what
a blessing it must be to you, as it is to any one, to possess

this gift of song, so as to set toil to music, and to turn the routine of daily life into verse."

But of course it was not always like that. If it could be, then, as Shelley observed, "man"—or at least the artist-man—"were immortal and omnipotent." There were times when it would not come at all—"Tried to work at Evangeline. Unsuccessful"—or when an interruption would break up the writing mood and make it impossible to recover it: "One bad effect the visit to East Greenwich had; it broke up entirely my poetic mood, and I cannot bring it back again. Any change produces this effect. The mind whirls off in a new direction; and there is no astronomy can calculate its return."

Moreover, even the rapid writing often required long years of rumination behind it. The *Christus,* conceived in 1841, was not completed until 1873. "The great theme of my poem haunts me ever," he wrote in 1851, "but I cannot bring it into act." "Judas Maccabeus" was not written until more than twenty years after the idea had been noted down. "His especial interest in the American Indian and Miles Standish," observes Carl Johnson, "dates from 1823, but *Hiawatha* was begun only in 1854 and *The Courtship of Miles Standish* in 1857." Even with short poems, the expression of the idea did not always follow conception. "I have had an idea of this kind on my mind for a long time," he observes of "The Reaper and the Flowers." "This morning it seemed to crystallize at once, without any effort of my own."

"Crystallize" is the key word here. Properly understood, it indicates the combination of spontaneity and careful craftsmanship which Longfellow achieved. "My poetry . . . is written seldom; the Muse being to me a chaste wife, not a Messalina to be debauched in the public street." Thus he put it to Sam Ward in 1839. And he added, "Your idea of mental *crystallization* is fine."

One would expect such a writer as Longfellow to revise

carefully. As a matter of fact, he revised with reasonable care, but he was not an extremist. Nor did he revise and recharacter already published work, like Henry James, James Branch Cabell, or Walter de la Mare. He himself says of *Evangeline* that the portions he wrote in the morning at his standing desk required no revision. Yet we know that he submitted the poem, unpublished, to three friends—Sumner, Folsom, and Felton—and went over their suggestions with great care. What revision he made was always neat and thorough.

By the same token, one would not expect such a writer to be much given to occasional poetry, and again Longfellow fulfills our expectations. Of one affair, in 1856, he records that "both Holmes and Lowell read poems; the first, serious; the second, humorous, and both good. I contributed nothing but my 'august presence.' " When George William Curtis begged him for a national song, he replied, "I am afraid the 'Go to, let us make a national song' will not succeed. It will be likely to spring up in some other way." In 1848 Samuel Longfellow wrote to Fanny, asking her whether she thought it would be possible for Henry to write a hymn for his ordination. "I should be more than glad to have it, but have not asked him, knowing his little inclination for that kind of composition." He wrote the hymn, and a good one too, but he was unable to produce another, ten years later, for the dedication of Sam's new church in Brooklyn, having "just written one for the new College Chapel" and being unable consequently to find anything "more to say on the topic."

The brilliant exception to all this is of course the "Morituri Salutamus," one of his most distinguished poems.

After telling my classmates that I could not write a poem for their Fiftieth Anniversary, I have gone to work and written one; some two or thee hundred lines in all, and quite long enough.

Whether I shall have the courage to read it in public, when the time comes, is another question.

What happened here, as in the case of his few other successful occasional poems—"A Ballad of the French Fleet," for example, which was written to help save the Old South Meeting House, or "The Three Silences of Molinos" for Whittier's seventieth birthday—was that a suggestion from outside had dropped into his inner consciousness and come to life there. His trouble had never been that he could not take *suggestions;* he was no self-centered, autobiographical poet; none was ever less so. The point is simply that his muse would not be fettered; he could not create to order.

There is no better illustration of the way inner and outer coalesced in his imagination than is afforded by his touching sonnet in memory of Fanny Appleton, "The Cross of Snow." This is one of his most personal utterances, and it is the most intensely, poignantly personal of all—so much so indeed that he never published it, but left it to be found among his papers and published by others after his death. Yet it took its point of departure—and its central image—from a picture of an actual cross of snow in "a book of Western scenery" which he chanced to examine, and he might never have written it at all had he not encountered that picture and found his imagination stimulated by it. Longfellow was always more comfortable with a suggestion when it came to him in such an unplanned way than he was when somebody came to him saying, "Look, here is something you ought to write a poem about."

All this is a part of the curious, unforcible independence of his character, which is all the more striking because of his extraordinary gentleness. In this sense, he illustrated the Blakian or Shavian ideal of the virtuous life, as Shaw expounded and illustrated it in *Caesar and Cleopatra;* he lived *out* from the center of his life, and all he said or thought or did was the expression of his own nature. We can see this in technical matters, as in his persistent use of English hexameters, in spite of the ridicule of his critics and the serious doubts of his friends. He made this experiment in an age much less sympathetic toward literary experimentation than our own and much more generally familiar with the classics, and coming, as it did, from a professional scholar, it was all the more striking on that account. Moreover, he never weakened nor shifted his ground. Sending *Evangeline* to Barry Cornwall, he wrote, "I hope you will not reject it on account of the metre. I could not write it *as it is* in any other; it would have changed its character entirely to have put it into a different measure. Pray agree with me, if you can, on this point." And he even told the Duke of Argyll that Homer would never be properly translated into English except in hexameters.[4]

But Longfellow's independence embraces more than technical matters. If he seems to us a "safe" person, the reason is less that he walked obediently in the paths his predecessors had marked out for him and never glanced over the fence into Bypath Meadow and more that he established his rebellions and departures with such complete success that it is difficult for us to realize that there was ever a time when they did not exist. We have already observed this in connection with his choice of a profession, but it appears in other aspects as well. Insofar as he was on the conventional side, it was because his own nature inclined him in that direction and not because he had forced himself into a mold to please somebody else. He achieved worldwide popularity without in any way deliberately seeking it or modifying his characteristic product for the sake of achieving it. The famous author of *Hiawatha* and *The Courtship of Miles Standish* still looked in his heart to write.

III

Longfellow's Prose Works

Longfellow's publications in prose comprise three books—*Outre-Mer: A Pilgrimage Beyond the Sea; Hyperion;* and *Kavanagh*—plus a sizeable number of contributions, both scholarly and belles-lettristic, to periodicals.

We first hear of what was to become *Outre-Mer* in a letter the author wrote his father from Göttingen on May 15, 1829: "I am also writing a book, a kind of Sketch-Book of scenes in France, Spain, and Italy." When, in 1831, Joseph T. Buckingham asked him to contribute to *The New-England Magazine,* he sent him, under the general title of "The Schoolmaster," some material which, he said, he had begun to write while abroad. The first installment, written in the first person and beginning with a sketch of the author, appeared in July 1831, the sixth and last, with which both magazine publication and the fiction of the schoolmaster-author were abandoned, in February 1833. The material is desultory and lacking in unity, and, as he proceeded, Longfellow evidently lost interest in its original form. Some of it was taken up into *Outre-Mer,* however, the publication of which was begun in parts, the first published by Hilliard, Gray & Company of Boston in 1833 and the second by Lilly, Wait & Company of the same city in 1834. Neither of these nor the two-volume

edition of the complete work which Harpers brought out
in 1835 carried the author's name, and in Bentley's
English edition of the same year he was merely "An
American." [1]

Though Longfellow says he had begun his writing
abroad, the bulk of the work must have been done after he
had "come home to rest," and, as he says in his
"Colophon," "for the most part, when the duties of the
day were over, . . . and the world . . . hushed in sleep,"
with his pen "a feather stolen from the sable wing of
night." There is an "Epistle Dedicatory" addressed to the
"Worthy and Gentle Reader," and the title is carefully explained at the outset:

The Pays d'Outre-Mer, or the Land beyond the Sea, is a name
by which the pilgrims and crusaders of old usually designated the
Holy Land. I, too, in a certain sense, have been a pilgrim of
Outre-Mer; for to my youthful imagination the Old World was a
kind of Holy Land, lying afar off beyond the blue horizon of the
ocean; and when its shores first rose upon my sight, looming
through the hazy atmosphere of the sea, my heart swelled with
the deep emotions of the pilgrim, when he sees afar the spire
which rises above the shrine of his devotion.

In both its content and its initial manner of publication
in parts, *Outre-Mer* was an imitation of Washington Irving's *Sketch-Book*. [2] The general pattern was derived from
the author's travels and reflections through France, Spain,
and Italy; the journey northward from Italy is merely
suggested in the last few pages as if he had wearied of his
subject or run out of space. The travel sketches are
frequently broken in upon however by character studies
and occasionally by stories, which may be narrated by a
member of the company. The character sketches may be
integrated into the record of the journey or, as with "The
Sexagenarian," presented by themselves. The style is
always carefully wrought, generally highly rhetorical,

sometimes exclamatory. There is considerable moralizing, never more than in the section "Père la Chaise," about the cemetery which is "the Westminster Abbey of Paris." Epigraphs, quotations, and literary allusions abound. Longfellow made considerable use of the letters he had written home from Europe, and there is one passage in "The Pilgrim's Breviary" in which he actually speaks of turning over "the leaves of this journal." He also included materials he had previously published elsewhere. Such critical articles as "The Trouvères," "Ancient Spanish Ballads," and "The Devotional Poetry of Spain," unpretentious as they are, break new ground on pioneering themes, then completely unfamiliar to American readers.

Of the tales included, "Martin Franc and the Monk of St. Anthony" is much the best, which is a bit surprising since, though Longfellow disparages the fabliaux in "The Trouvères," this tale is clearly fabliau material, but the wife who tricks the libidinous monk into believing that she desires an assignation with him in order that her husband may have a chance to chastise him is as chaste as the merry wives of Windsor. The tale is not pornographic, but it is macabre, for the husband accidentally kills the monk, and the rest of the story is so ingeniously and elaborately involved with the attempts made by a number of persons to dispose of the corpse and the peregrinations the latter undergoes in the process that Cecil B. Williams has not unreasonably been reminded of Faulkner. When a contemporary writer accused Longfellow of having stolen his fable from George Colman's "The Knight and the Friar," the author replied that he had found it in a collection of fabliaux and in several other places, including *The Arabian Nights*. "Thus the story has passed through as many hands as did the body of Friar Gui. Mr. Colman evidently drew the incidents of 'The Knight and the Friar' from the same source whence I drew those of Martin Franc. . . . Unfortunately I was not aware . . . that any modern writer had availed himself of the old fiction."

"The Notary of Périgueux" is a considerably less effective comic tale about a man who imagines himself to
have contracted scarlet fever when he has only burned
himself by thrusting a lighted pipe into his pocket. On the
other hand, nothing could be in more deadly earnest than
"The Baptism of Fire," which describes the martyrdom of
a Huguenot under Henry II. Coming from Longfellow, it
is as surprising an item as "Martin Franc," for the
execution is almost sadistically described. "Jacqueline,"
however, is as sentimental as "The Wife" and "The
Broken Heart" in *The Sketch-Book*. The detailed account
of confession and extreme unction contained in it, reflect-
ing the interest in Catholic beliefs and practices that
Longfellow developed during his European visits, is
perhaps its most interesting feature for modern readers. In
"The Village of El Pardillo," however, where a catechism
lesson is rehearsed, he objects to perplexing "the spirit of a
child with these metaphysical subtleties, these dark,
mysterious speculations, which man in all his pride of in-
tellect cannot fathom or explain."

Longfellow's most ambitious prose work, *Hyperion*, is
often called a novel, but it can be so denominated only by
a fairly generous extension of the term. Actually it is as
variegated as *Outre-Mer*, a kind of extension of *Outre-Mer*
through Germany and Switzerland. It has, to be sure, a
fictional hero, Paul Flemming, who had "a good heart,
and a poetic imagination," but "acted more from impulse
than from fixed principles," and who falls vainly in love
with Mary Ashburton, but though his disappointment in
love brings the book to a conclusion, the love story embraces only a portion of its contents. Nor is Paul himself a
much more disguised Longfellow than the "I" of *Outre-
Mer;* he comes to us still grieving because "the friend of
his youth was dead," and though the friend's sex is not
immediately indicated, before we reach the end of the
paragraph, we read that "he could no longer live alone
where he had lived with her."

The Baron of Hohenfels and the Englishman Berkley are introduced as Flemming's principal interlocutors, and even some of the literary and critical material is presented in dialogue form. But the dialogue is often stiff and formal; the characters do not so much converse as deliver lectures to each other. There is much romantic vocabulary, and there are many apostrophes to the Gentle Reader, epigraphs, quotations, translations, and literary allusions; in everything except the actual form, many passages are more poetry than prose. The method of narration is loose and chatty throughout: "But I will not attempt to describe the Rhine; it would make this chapter much too long"; "And this reminds me that I have not yet described my hero." And of Mary Ashburton: "I will not disguise the truth. She is my heroine, and I mean to describe her with great truth and beauty, so that all shall be in love with her, and I most of all."

There are whole chapters on Jean Paul Richter, Goethe, and E. T. A. Hoffmann, as well as on "Lives of Scholars" and "Literary Fame," all carefully discriminative, even in their enthusiasm. Longfellow had himself had his difficulties with Goethe and at one time considered calling the Goethe chapter "Old Humbug." Interpolated tales appear as in *Outre-Mer,* and the character sketch intrudes everywhere, most elaborately in the chapter devoted to Brother Bernardus, a renegade Catholic on his way to America to establish the true universal church, who plans to excommunicate the pope next Christmas. But Longfellow himself, who enjoyed Jean Paul's apparent confusion, finds a dignified term to describe all this. "This book," he writes, "does somewhat resemble a minster, in the Romanesque style, with pinnacles and flying buttresses, and roofs,

> "Gargoyled with greyhounds, and with many lions
> Made of fine gold, with divers sundry dragons."

On September 13, 1838, Longfellow looked over his notes and papers for *Hyperion* and longed "for leisure to begin once more." This longing must shortly have been satisfied, for he completed the work the first week of the following April, and in August Samuel Colman published it in New York in two volumes bound in boards and covered with pale olive-colored paper sides as "by the Author of *Outre-Mer.*" Friends and reviewers praised and blamed, and the initial sale was respectable, but the publisher failed almost at once, and twelve hundred copies, about half the first printing, were temporarily sequestered from the market.

At one time Longfellow considered making Hyperion the name of his hero, but this plan was abandoned. After the name "St. Clair" had also been weighed and rejected, the hero became Paul Flemming, but "Hyperion" was retained as a title to indicate that the subject was "the life of one who in his feelings and purposes is 'a son of Heaven and Earth,' and who, though obscured by clouds, yet 'moves on high.' Further than this," wrote the author, "the name has nothing to do with the book, and in fact, is mentioned only once in the course of it." Again he says, "I called it 'Hyperion,' because it . . . expresses the various aspirations of the soul of man." He fully expected to be "mightily abused" for this. "People will say I am the hero of my own romance, and compare myself to the sun, to Hyperion Apollo. This is not so. I wish only to magnify certain feelings which are mine, not to magnify myself." Miss Fanny Appleton granted that the title was "cousin *German* to the book" but beyond that could discern "no natural relationship" between the two. She thought the hero obviously Longfellow himself, but though she did not deny that there were "some exquisite things" in the work, nor that the style was "infinitely polished and sparkling with many beautiful poetical concetti," she dismissed the whole as "desultory, objectless, a thing of shreds and patches like the author's mind.''

I have said that *Hyperion* describes the German and
Swiss journeyings that Longfellow had treated only sum-
marily in *Outre-Mer,* but it must be remembered that this
material has been derived mainly from his second
European journey, not the first. James Taft Hatfield made
a determined effort to trace the details and identify the
originals of the Baron, Berkley, and others. Longfellow
himself met the sculptor Dannecker, and even the seduction of Emma of Ilmenau had a real-life original.[3] In a
sense all the German literature that Longfellow had ever
read might be called sources of *Hyperion,* but the most
important sources were obviously Goethe and Jean Paul.

Lawrance Thompson believed that ''Longfellow borrowed his motivation and general outline and prose style
. . . from Jean Paul,'' especially from his ''introductory
remarks in *Quintus Fixlein,* about finding how to enjoy
pleasure by soaring above the clouds of life'' and that ''he
borrowed only the action-philosophy and conclusion based
upon it, from Goethe,'' blending this with or superim-
posing it upon Jean Paul. Though this is not unreasonable
in itself, it may allow insufficiently for the importance of
Goethe's *Wilhelm Meister's Apprenticeship,* which, like
Hyperion, is a *Reisenovelle* or *Wanderroman,* with an obvious affinity to the ''educational'' novels whose vogue in
England antedated but was greatly stimulated by Henry
Brooke, Thomas Day, and others in the late eighteenth
century, for *Wilhelm Meister* too stresses the idea of
development through suffering. ''The Everlasting Yea''
philosophy of Carlyle, whom Longfellow met in 1835, may
have contributed something also, as may both Heine and
Novalis.[4]

Mary Ashburton is obviously Fanny Appleton and Paul
Flemming's hopeless wooing of her quite as obviously
Longfellow's (as it then appeared) vain wooing of Fanny.
Though it is hard to believe that he, of all writers, could at

this point have been so "confessional" and so gauche, the fact is that he actually considered calling his heroine "Frances" or "Francisca," and even as the book stands, "Mary" was the name of Fanny's only sister, and "Ashburton" was not far from "Appleton." How he could have expected Fanny not to resent this, especially in a book that should end with Paul's resolutely turning his back upon his passion, which, in life, Longfellow at times thought he had done but never really succeeded in doing, baffles the imagination, but he seems to have thought that since he had violated no confidences, avoided giving an "exact portrait" of the lady (he made her English, not American), and glorified both her character and her appearance out of all mortal semblance, he must be safe.

The words of power that Paul finds on a funeral urn at St. Gilgen to strengthen his high resolves, and which Longfellow himself actually found in that place and made the epigraph for his book, have worn much better than anything in the closely-related "Psalm of Life": "Look not mournfully into the Past. It comes not back again. Wisely improve the Present. It is thine. Go forth to meet the shadowy Future, without Fear, and with a manly heart." It sounds even better in the original German: *"Blicke nicht traurend in die Vergangenheit. Sie kommt nicht wieder. Nütze weisse die Gegenwart. Sie ist dein. Der düstern Zukunft geh ohne Furcht mit männlichen Sinne entgegen."*

Longfellow wrote George Washington Greeme that *Hyperion* was "a *sincere* book; showing the passage of a morbid mind into a purer and healthier state." Like "A Psalm of Life," it has much greater historical significance than contemporary readers might suppose. When he had finished his work, the author said it would "take a great deal of persuasion" to convince him that it was not good. What is more surprising is that as late as 1849 he should have considered writing a sequel in which he would bring

Paul Flemming to America. Hawthorne called *Hyperion*
"a most precious and rare book, as fragrant as a bunch of
flowers and as simple as one flower. . . . It is entirely
original, a book by itself, a true work of genius, if ever
there was one," and in 1852 Washington Irving chose it as
his favorite among all Longfellow's works. European
travelers used it as a guidebook for decades; at the time of
Longfellow's last trip to Europe, the English novelist and
Egyptologist Amelia B. Edwards wrote him that for seventeen years it had been her "constant friend and companion. It has accompanied me in all my wanderings—I
know every word in it by heart—and my first novel . . . was
saturated through and through with Hyperionisms."
James Taft Hatfield called it "the most important single
document having to do with Longfellow's transmission of
German culture to the American people." It cites as many
as twenty-five German writers, and even the hero was
given the name of a German poet. It included many translations of German ballads and folk songs, and it introduced Wilhelm Müller, now best remembered as the
poet of the two great Schubert song cycles, *Winterreise*
and *Die schöne Müllerin,* to English readers.

Longfellow's third and last independent publication in
prose postdated *Hyperion* by ten years, a late date for so
successful a poet to return to prose. It was on the day he
finished *Evangeline* (February 27, 1847, his fortieth
birthday) that he wrote in his journal, "Now for a little
prose: a romance which I have in my brain, 'Kavanagh' by
name." It seems to have been begun promptly, but the
bulk of the work was not done until the autumn of 1848,
when, writing *"con amore,"* he finished it on November
4. In February he took the first sheets to the printer "with
some doubts and misgivings," never having "hesitated so
much about any of my books, except the first hexameters,
'The Children of the Lord's Supper.' " In March he made
up his mind he must add Chapter XVIII, the account of

Kavanagh's spiritual background and experience, and fit it into the book "as the keystone into the arch."

The story was published on May 12, 1849, and Emerson called it "the best sketch we have seen in the direction of the American Novel. For here is our speech and manners, treated with sympathy, taste, and judgment." At a later date Howells was equally enthusiastic, finding the story "quite unapproached by the multitude of New England romances that had followed it in a certain delicate truthfulness, as it is likely to remain unsurpassed in its light humor and pensive grace." Mrs. Longfellow, however, though finding in it "many very beautiful thoughts . . . and a background of Yankee life humorously depicted without the vulgar element," still believed that it needed "more filling out," as it did, and doubted that it would be "as popular as *Hyperion,* for Germany is Henry's native country."

Brief as *Kavanagh* is (less than half the length of *Hyperion*), there can be no question that this time Longfellow had produced a novel and one that antedates the whole local color movement at that. Yet though superficially *Kavanagh* is much better unified than *Hyperion,* he had introduced far more material than anybody could have fully developed in a book of this length. His local color is altogether right as far as it goes, even to the traveling shows, the Temperance Jubilee, the visiting fanatics announcing the end of the world, the advertisements drawn from contemporary newspapers, and the deterioration Fairmeadow suffers through the coming of the Grand Junction Railroad during the three years Kavanagh and his bride are away, yet compared to the documentation that was coming from Mrs. Stowe, Sarah Orne Jewett, and their successors, all this seems a little thin, and much the same must be said of the characterization. The people are quite all right as far as they go, but we do not get to know any of them well enough to care very deeply about them.

Allusions to literature, art, and music abound. Classical and Northern mythology and European legendry are drawn upon, as well as the writings of the great mystics. German critics have found Jean Paul again in the style. The reference to "the 'Lilawati' of Bhascara Acharya, translated from the Sanscrit," with the poetical treatment of the "divine . . . science of numbers," is the more interesting because Longfellow, unlike Emerson and Thoreau, was not, generally speaking, much interested in Oriental writings, nor, for that matter, in mathematics either.

Certainly there can be no excuse for any English or American reader failing to discern the influence of Dickens. Take "Moses Merryweather, Dealer in Singing-Birds, foreign and domestic." Take Sally Manchester, the Archers's maid, "a treasure, if you can get her," whose disposition, like the flavor of some apples, is "a pleasant sour." Jilted by Martin Cherryfield, who, when turning to another woman, exhorts Sally, as a professing Christian, to be resigned to her lot in this world, so that, in time to come, they may both be "prepared to join the great company in heaven," she is so thoroughly disillusioned about men and marriage that she lives out her life in single blessedness, unmoved even by the pleas of Mr. Vaughan's hired man Silas, who sends her letters "written with his own blood,—going barefooted into the brook to be bitten by leeches, and then using his feet as inkstands." The butcher Mr. Wilmerdings weighs the village babies in his scales like meat and takes his wife on their bridal tour "to a neighboring town to see a man hanged for murdering his wife." But the most Dickensian character of all is Hiram A. (later H. Adolphus) Hawkins, whose "shiny hair went off to the left in a superb sweep, like the handrail of a banister," and who displays himself, "with strange gyrations," and all decorated with rings and strange waist-coats, to Cecilia Vaughan, of whom he is enamored, before his shop door, on the street, and on the church steps on Sunday, all in a vain attempt to attract her attention.

Though the story is named for the Reverend Arthur Kavanagh, who becomes the pastor of the village church after the aging sour Calvinist Pendexter has gone on his way, the schoolmaster Mr. Churchill (he is never given a first name), who dreams about writing a romance but never gets to work at it, is brought in earlier and gets more space. In introducing us to Olive Chancellor and Verena Tarrant in *The Bostonians* Henry James was to write that they represented "one of those friendships between women that are so common in New England"; of Cecilia Vaughan and Alice Archer in *Kavanagh,* who communicate by carrier pigeon, Longfellow says that "they were in love with each other." Since there is no question of a physical relationship between either pair, both writers might well have expressed themselves differently had they been writing in our own time.[5] Longfellow indeed adds, "It was, so to speak, a rehearsal in girlhood of the great drama of woman's life," and, as his story develops, the performance follows quickly, for both girls fall in love with Kavanagh, who loves Cecilia, after which Alice accommodatingly pines away. There is one other girl in the story, the teen-aged orphan Lucy, who has been virtually adopted by the Churchills and employed as their domestic, and whose history becomes a rerun with variations of the Emma of Ilmenau tragedy in *Hyperion.* Lucy runs off with a queer creature who deserts her, after which she returns to Fairmeadow and drowns herself in the brook, but all this is told so briefly and parenthetically that, except perhaps for a moment at her death, which has obviously been modeled upon Ophelia's, the reader has no chance to be moved by it.

In 1964, in his study of Longfellow in Twayne's United States Authors Series, Cecil B. Williams argued not only that Mr. Churchill, not Arthur Kavanagh, was the principal character in the novel but also that through him Longfellow was rationalizing "his own failure to achieve the literary distinction he had envisioned for himself." Six years later, Steven Allaback,[6] taking his cue from this suggestion, worked out a much more elaborate interpretation, according to which Longfellow is not only Churchill but also Kavanagh, the two characters representing different sides of his personality. Moreover, Mrs. Churchill is Fanny Appleton Longfellow, and "the slightly sour elements in the Churchill marriage are reflections of the Longfellows' own marriage." From here it was only a step to finding resemblances between Longfellow's wooing of Fanny and the egregious Hawkins's attempt to ingratiate himself with Cecilia or even to seeing Longfellow's anxiety about his own eyesight reflected in Mrs. Archer's blindness and in Alice's fear of blindness.

It is quite true that there are likenesses between Churchill's resentment at being chained to the schoolroom when he would much rather be writing (or thinks he would) and Longfellow's own chafing under the restrictions of his Harvard professorship, and it is also true that some of those who break in upon Churchill's time and attention without having any reasonable claim upon either have obviously been derived from those who intruded upon Longfellow.[7] But it is hard to see how the latter could have been rationalizing "his own failure to achieve . . . literary distinction" in 1849, two years after *Evangeline,* when he had already won it, and he must have been a self-castigator indeed if he either consciously or unconsciously presented himself in the semblance of a man who, save for a few articles, never wrote but only dreamed of writing. There is not the slightest indication that Churchill even has an idea of what the romance he is forever talking about is to deal with; as he tells his wife, he has "so many things to do, so many books to write" that he really does not know where to start, to which she very sensibly replies that "it will not make much difference, if you will only begin!" But in her heart she knows he never will, and Arthur Kavanagh knows this too. "If you had looked nearer for the materials of your Romance," he tells Churchill at the end, "and had set about it in earnest, it would now have been finished." No, Mr. Churchill is not Longfellow; rather, as Newton Arvin observed, he is "a sort of Spoon River character long before Masters."

Neither am I convinced by Professor Allaback's argument that Kavanagh's relations with his father are autobiographical ("obviously the shadows cast by fathers over one is a theme in *Kavanagh*"), nor yet that the treatment of sex in this novel indicates that Longfellow "wants to explore forbidden territory but never quite makes it." On the other hand, I do agree with Allaback that Alexander H. Smith is a more likely original for Mr. Hathaway than the much better known literary nationalist Cornelius Mathews, who was nominated by Perry Miller[8] and accepted by Arvin. Finally, though Williams's guess that Hathaway's projected magazine, "The Niagara," was suggested by Lowell's *The Pioneer* seems to me pretty wild, his idea that Cecilia's reply to Kavanagh's proposal—"Come to me"—was based upon "the still unpublished note of Fanny to Longfellow which brought him to her in such urgency of joy" may well be right.

The two things in *Kavanagh* that are likely to interest modern readers most have very little to do with the plot, such as it is. The first of these concerns Arthur Kavanagh's religious views and background, and the second is Mr. Churchill's discussion with Mr. Hathaway of nationalism versus universalism in literature.

Kavanagh is the actual name of "an ancient Catholic family" of Maine, and Arthur has been subjected to a sound Jesuit training. Long before we encounter him as pastor of the Fairmeadow church, he had of course liberated himself from "the dogmas of that august faith, whose turrets gleam with such crystalline light, and whose dungeons are so deep, and dark, and terrible." When he became a Protestant, it seemed to him however that "he had but passed from one chapel to another in the same vast cathedral. . . . Out of his old faith he brought with him all he had found in it that was holy and pure and of good report. Not its bigotry, and fanaticism, and intolerance; but its zeal, its self-devotion, its heavenly aspirations, its human sympathies, its endless deeds of charity." Though he is far from being a fanatic like Brother Bernardus in *Hyperion,* the "great design and purpose of his life" is now "the removal of all prejudice, and uncharitableness, and persecution, and the union of all sects into one church universal."

More space is given to the discussion of nationalism and universalism in literature in connection with Hathaway's attempt to enlist Churchill as a contributor to his projected magazine, and here there can be no question that Churchill *is* Longfellow's spokesman. Hathaway wants "a national literature commensurate with our mountains and rivers, . . . a national epic . . . that shall be to all other epics what Banvard's Panorama of the Mississippi is to all other paintings, . . . a national drama in which scope enough shall be given to our gigantic ideas, . . . a national literature altogether shaggy and unshorn, that shall shake the earth, like a herd of buffaloes thundering over the prairies!" (If only the dates were right, critics would surely see Longfellow striking out at Whitman here!) But Churchill replies that "great has a very different meaning when applied to a river, and when applied to a literature" and that while "nationality is a good thing to a certain extent, . . . universality is better." If we are natural, "we shall be national enough. Besides our literature can be strictly national only so far as our character and modes of thought differ from those of other nations," and this cannot be "the growth of a day." "As the blood of all nations is mingling with our own, so will their thoughts and feelings finally mingle in our literature. We shall draw from the Germans, tenderness; from the Spaniards, passion; from the French, vivacity . . . and this will give us universality, so much to be desired."

I shall try to be selective in commenting upon Longfellow's uncollected prose, dividing my examples between the belles-lettristic and the scholarly items, though some may overlap. Perhaps the best of the stories is "The Wondrous Tale of a Little Man in Gosling Green," which appeared in *The New Yorker* on November 1, 1834, and was completely forgotten until it was reprinted in 1931.[9] Longfellow submitted this tale under the pseudonym of George F. Brown in a prize contest, and the prize of one hundred dollars was divided between him and a "Miss Leslie of Philadelphia."

The Little Man comes to Bungonuck and finally settles there, arouses intense curiosity, gives rise to many baseless conjectures, and finally dies. There is some Maine local color as well as some satire: "To be sure, no light had been thrown upon his past history, but it had been ascertained from his own confession, that he believed in the existence of a devil, and he was immediately taken under the wing of the Dorcas Society," thus showing that "there are some places in the world where it is easier to die than to live." Like "The Bald Eagle," which had appeared in *The Token* the year before, "The Wondrous Tale" exemplifies the kind of story best represented by Irving's "The Stout Gentleman" in which an elaborate buildup means nothing and leads nowhere. Irving's influence is clear, and there may be some Sterne also, very likely filtered, as Hatfield suggested, through Jean Paul. Some of the chapter headings are rather clever in a knowing, self-conscious way; see, for example, Chapter II: "In which things are said concerning Bungonuck, and nothing at all concerning the Little Man in Gosling Green; whereby the reader's curiosity is wonderfully sharpened." In "The Bald Eagle," which is the name of an inn "in one of those villages sprinkled through the delicious valley of the Connecticut," the variation presents a "knot of village politicians" assembled on "a calm autumn evening," awaiting Lafayette's visit, which is expected sometime within the next two days. Elaborate preparations are made for his reception, but he travels by another route, and all his aspiring hosts get is a storm.

"The Indian Summer" (*The Token,* 1832) is, like "Jacqueline," a painfully sentimental tale. It opens with a good display piece of Irvingesque prose, but it is less interesting than either of the other tales.

In the melancholy month of October, when the variegated tints of the autumnal landscape begin to fade away into the pale and sickly hue of death, a few soft, delicious days, called the Indian Summer, steal in upon the close of the year, and, like a second spring, breathe a balm round the departing season, and light up with a smile the pallid features of the dying year. They resemble those calm and lucid intervals, which sometimes precede the last hour of slow decline; mantling the cheek with the glow of health; breathing tranquillity around the drooping heart; and, though seeming to indicate that the fountains of life are springing out afresh, are but the sad and sure precursors of dissolution; the last earthly sabbath

> Of a spirit who longs for a purer day,
> And is ready to wing her flight away.

The narrator stumbles upon a house of mourning, views the corpse, attends the funeral of the dead girl, where he hears a sermon of the sob-sister variety, and explores the pathos of her grief over her wayward brother and her lingering illness. The sentimental pietism of the account of her passing matches anything in nineteenth-century Sunday School literature, but the most shocking thing in the story is the morbid curiosity of the narrator and the way he intrudes himself into the death chamber. "The coffin was placed upon a table in the middle of the room. Several of the villagers were gazing upon the corpse, and as they turned away, speaking to each other in whispers of the ravages of death, I drew near and looked for a moment upon those sad remains of humanity." At least he has the grace to feel that "there was something cold and heartless in thus gazing idly upon the relics of one whom I had not known in life; and I turned away with an emotion of more than sorrow."

Two tales with a Spanish military background have been attributed to Longfellow. "Torquemadea: A Tale of the Peninsular War" appeared in *The New-England Magazine* in 1832 and "The Convent of the Paular, Translated from a Spanish Manuscript" in *The Token and Atlantic-Souvenir* for 1834. I can see nothing in either that seems characteristic of Longfellow. In the first story Torquemada is a town, so named because it has been burned four times. "The Convent of the Paular" has an atmosphere of death and desolation and creates an eerie frisson unmatched, so far as I am aware, anywhere in Longfellow. I have already spoken of "The Schoolmaster" in connection with *Outre-Mer.* "The Lady Monastery" papers, which ran in the *United States Literary Gazette* in 1824–25, are earlier and similarly rambling, and here again the persona of the rambler and minor littérateur tends to disappear as the work unfolds. The installment for April 1, 1825, includes a discussion of "The Literary Spirit of Our Country," in which the author advances the thesis that America is now an excellent field for the development and exhibition of literary talent and explores the forces working for and against this. In "Poets and Common-sense Man" (June 1,

1825), he acknowledges that the poetical temperament "unfits men in some degree for life's ordinary scenes and duties" and divides poets in two classes, "those who have within them the light of original genius, and those who borrow their lustre and draw their inspiration from the full urns of others."

Most of the more technical, scholarly, and academic pieces appeared in *The North American Review*. Such are "Origin and Progress of the French Language" (April 1831); "Spanish Devotional and Moral Poetry" (April 1832); "History of the Italian Language and Dialects" (October 1832); "Spanish Language and Literature" (April 1833); "Old English Romances" (October 1833); "Anglo-Saxon Literature" (July 1838); and "The French Language in England" (October 1840). In the same class with these pieces was his ambitious Inaugural Address at Bowdoin in 1830, "Origin and Growth of the Languages of Southern Europe and of Their Literature," which remained unpublished until the Bowdoin College Library made a small book of it to celebrate the Longfellow centennial in 1907, and "Ancient French Romances" in the *Select Journal of Foreign Periodical Literature* (January 1833). Like "Anglo-Saxon Literature," this last piece was reprinted in part in the Craigie Edition, where will also be found a number of other *North American* pieces of less restricted interest: "The Great Metropolis" (April 1837); "Frithiof's Saga" and "Twice-Told Tales" (both July 1837); and "Paris in the Seventeenth Century," a charming essay on the age of Louis XIV, drawn from several sources. "The Youth of Mary Stuart" in *The Token and Atlantic-Souvenir* of 1835 is hack work, interesting only because it shows Longfellow's sympathy with the Queen, but there is more substance to the controversial piece on "Heinrich Heine" in *Graham's Lady's and Gentleman's Magazine* in 1842.

It must be obvious that a really definitive judgment of

the value of Longfellow's more academic papers could be entered only by a committee of experts in the various fields he surveyed, and in order to be fair these would of course be obliged to make due allowance for his doing pioneering work. What stands out first of all is the extraordinary range of his linguistic interests; who, in these days of specialization, would try to match it? The paper on "Anglo-Saxon Literature," to take only one example, seems to me to show a surprising knowledge of the period for 1838, especially on the part of a man whose main interest was in the modern languages.

Some of Longfellow's pieces are book reviews. In the essay on Heine much of the space is taken up with two long quotations from the *Reisebilder,* and in "Old English Romances" there is much material from William J. Thoms's three-volume collection of 1829, which occasioned the discussion. In the paper on Tegnér's *Frithiof's Saga,* Longfellow goes over the story canto by canto, but this is much less interesting than his account of rural life in Sweden, which was derived not from Tegnér but from the reviewer's own experience. And considering that it is a review of such an early book, the article on *Twice-Told Tales* certainly reveals an extraordinary awareness of Hawthorne's special quality. [10]

The lover of Longfellow may well find himself most interested, however, in the revelations of the writer's own interests and personality that appear in even his scholarly writings. These reflect both his professional interests and his personal convictions. "We hold the study of languages, philosophically pursued, to be one of the most important which can occupy the human mind"—thus he writes in "History of the Italian Languages and Dialects." The morality of the old English romances "is not of a very austere nature; nay, it is very lewdness itself," and Heine, who adds "the sentimentality of Sterne" to "the recklessness of Byron" and seeks "to establish a religion of

sensuality on the ruins of the church," is "not sufficiently
in earnest to be a great poet" in spite of all his lyric
beauties. But religious faith and practices do not get a
clean bill of health either. In the Bowdoin Inaugural, for
example, we may read of "the mummeries of the church
festivals and the spiritual farces by which the temples of
Religion were profaned," of the medieval mind as having
wasted itself "on such speculations as the manner of the
miraculous conception of the Virgin, and the digestion of
the eucharist," and of the Crusades as exhibiting "a lively
portrait of the ill-directed zeal and the hoodwinked superstition of those centuries."

I have purposely left for the last what is by all means the
most significant of Longfellow's critical papers, "The
Defence of Poetry" in *The North American Review* for
January 1832. As the title indicates, this was occasioned by
the publication of a new edition of Sir Philip Sidney's
famous essay, but this provides only the jumping-off place
for a vindication of literature and a discussion of its
relationship to national character which in some respects
anticipates Emerson's address on "The American
Scholar." Longfellow sees true greatness as "the greatness
of the mind" and the real glory of the nation as "moral
and intellectual preeminence." By citing the examples of
Homer, Dante, and Milton, he combats the notion that
literary study is morally debilitating; on the contrary, "the
legitimate tendency of poetry is to exalt, rather than to
debase—to purify rather then to corrupt"; fiction,
moreover, may be "true in the impression it conveys"
without being "true to fact." When, as with Byron, the
impressions a writer conveys to the mind present nature
garbled and falsified, it is the individual artist, not art itself, that must be blamed. A literature is "national" when
"it bears upon it the stamp of national character," and in
order to "give a national character to their writings," our
poets must write "from their own feelings and impressions

and not from any preconceived notions of what poetry ought to be, caught from reading many books, and imitating many models," for a national literature "embraces every mental effort made by inhabitants of a country through the medium of the press." A nightingale, therefore, is as much out of place in an American poem as an elephant or a rhinoceros in an American landscape.

IV

Early Poems

On December 29, 1839, Fanny Appleton, still at odds
with Longfellow, wrote, "The Prof has collected all his
vagrant poems into a neat little volume christened mournfully *Voices of the Night.* He does not look like a night bird
and is more of a mocking-bird than a nightingale, though
he has some sweetly plaintive notes. All the Psalms are
fine, but the rest *peu de chose."* Published the same year
as *Hyperion,* this was Longfellow's first collection of his
own verses—nine of recent composition and seven more
selected from his earlier writings, dating clear back to
college days—with a new introductory "Prelude" and a
closing "L'Envoi." There was also a group of translations.[1]

Fanny was quite right in observing that Longfellow did
not look like a night bird, and night did not have the same
connotations in his title that it would have had for Poe[2] or
even Hawthorne. In "Hymn to the Night," the "calm,
majestic presence" addressed—

> I heard the trailing garments of the Night
> Sweep through her marble halls!—

is "welcome, . . . thrice prayed for, . . . most fair," and
the poet drinks repose from "the fountain of perpetual
peace" that flows "from the cool cisterns of the midnight

air.'' There is no fool's paradise here; from ''holy Night''
one may ''learn to bear / What man has borne before!''
But the net result is comfort:

> Thou layest thy finger on the lips of Care,
>   And they complain no more.

Longfellow knew whereof he spake; in an earlier version,
the last two verses of the fourth stanza, referring more
directly to his disappointed wooing, read ''That saved me
from the frenzy of despair, / The apathy of grief.'' There
is more autobiography in ''Footsteps of Angels,'' which
was quoted in Chapter I, and there is autobiography too in
the ''Prelude,'' which begins like a nature poem, recalling
how

> Pleasant it was, when woods were green
>   And winds were soft and low
> To lie amid some sylvan scene.

But the seductive invitation implied in such
things—''Come, be a child once more!''—cannot be accepted, for the poet is no longer a child. For a man the
''land of Song'' lies ''within'' and in the world around
him, in ''a forest where the din / of iron branches sounds!''
even though ''the heavens there'' may be ''all black with
sin.''

> ''Look, then, into thine heart, and write!
>   Yes, into Life's deep stream!
> All forms of sorrow and delight,
> All solemn Voices of the Night,
> That can soothe thee, or affright,—
>   Be these henceforth thy theme.''

''Look, then, into thine heart and write!'' is of course
from Sidney. The credo expounded here may seem too

close to that of the realist or even naturalist adequately to
cover Longfellow's own practice, but he was quite con-
sistent in always being true to his own experience and in
maintaining that not nature but human life was the poet's
true preoccupation.

All this is quite in harmony with the best-known poem
in the collection, perhaps the best-known short poem
Longfellow ever wrote, "A Psalm of Life." Unfortunately
it is also one of his poorest poems, and nothing has
harmed his reputation more than its inclusion in every
selection from his work. Commonplace in expression
throughout, it is more a rhymed morality than a poem.
The last verse of the first stanza, "And things are not what
they seem," is plain prose, from which the writer proceeds
to such obviously mixed and ill-chosen figures that point-
ing them out is like breaking a butterfly on the wheel.

> In the world's broad field of battle,
>   In the bivouac of Life,
> Be not like dumb, driven cattle!
>   Be a hero in the strife!

Cattle do not participate in battles, nor are battles fought
in bivouacs.

> Lives of great men all remind us
>   We can make our lives sublime,
> And, departing, leave behind us
>   Footprints on the sands of time;
>
> Footprints, that perhaps another,
>   Sailing o'er life's solemn main,
> A forlorn and shipwrecked brother,
>   Seeing, shall take heart again.

"The sands of time," if anything definite is indicated,

would presumably indicate the sand in an hourglass, but since footprints could not possibly appear here, Longfellow must be thinking of the sand on the seabeach. If a man wishes to be remembered, however, to leave his footprints there must be about the last thing he could desire, for the first tide that comes in will wash them away. It is hard to see also how the "forlorn . . . brother" could, at the same time, find himself "shipwrecked" and "sailing o'er life's solemn main," how, if he were thus sailing, he could see the footprints in the sand, or why, if he did see them, he should be heartened by them.

Nevertheless, to dismiss "A Psalm of Life" thus would be insensitive. Though it may be hard to realize now, even Baudelaire was influenced by it, and there can be no question that, in its own time, for uncounted multitudes of men and women, it ranked with the literature of power. Ruskin said that it was "known by heart by nearly all the modern reformers, good and bad, but *does good* to all of them" and doubted whether all Byron's poems put together had exerted comparable influence, and Whittier rashly declared that it was "worth more than all the dreams of Shelley, and Keats, and Wordsworth." Like Tennyson's "Ulysses," though without that poem's literary distinction, it expressed the aspiring, exploratory spirit of the age, while for Longfellow himself it signified a turning away from the softer and dreamier aspects of German romanticism in the direction of Goethean reality and heroic striving. He himself said that, having written the poem, he kept it by him for some time, "unwilling to show it to any one, it being a voice from my inmost heart at a time when I was rallying from depression." [3]

Since Fanny Appleton singled out the psalms as the best poems in *Voices of the Night,* she may be presumed to have admired not only "A Psalm of Life" but also "The Reaper and the Flowers" (originally subtitled "A Psalm of Death"), "The Light of Stars" ("A Second Psalm of Life" in *Knickerbocker's Magazine),* "Footsteps of Angels" (first called "Evening Shadows," then "Voices of the Night: A Third Psalm of Life"), and "Midnight Mass for the Dying Year" ("The Fifth Psalm" in *Knickerbocker's).*

"The Reaper and the Flowers," which borrows its opening verse ("There is a Reaper, whose name is Death") from an old German hymn *("Es ist ein Schnitter und er heisst Tod"),* inculcates resignation rather than striving, seeking to comfort those who have lost children by assuring the grieving mother that "the Lord of Paradise" had need of these "flowers," that the saints will wear the "sacred blossoms," on "their garments white," and that she who has lost them will surely "find them all again / In the fields of light above." But the bracing tone of "A Psalm of Life" recurs in "The Light of Stars," where "The first watch of the night is given / To the red planet Mars" which radiates not "love and dreams" but the gleam of "a hero's armor."

> O star of strength! I see thee stand
>   And smile upon my pain;
> Thou beckonest with they mailed hand,
>   And I am strong again.

Just how "the star of the unconquered will" imparts its strength to the disappointed poet is not made very clear, for he seems left at the end with no reliance except upon himself:

> Oh, fear not in a world like this,
>   And thou shalt know ere long,
> Know how sublime a thing it is
>   To suffer and be strong.

As for the other psalms, in "Footsteps of Angels," quoted elsewhere in this volume, comfort comes from the writer's sense of continued union with Mary Storer

Longfellow and with his brother-in-law George W. Pierce, who died in the prime of life less than a month after Mary. "Midnight Mass for the Dying Year," the most literary of the psalms, is full of echoes of *King Lear,* and the death of the old year is compared to that of the aged monarch.[4] The pious exhortatory conclusion, which might seem forced in another poem, seems justified here by the resemblances intended to a mass:

> Kyrie, eleyson!
> Christe, eleyson!

Except for the "L'Envoi," which again stresses the healing power of night, I have now commented upon all the new poems in *Voices of the Night* except "Flowers" (originally "Floral Anthology") and "The Beleaguered City." In "Flowers," which was written to be sent to Fanny with a floral offering, flowers are to the earth what the stars are to the sky, and Longfellow, seeing nature as revelation more clearly than usual, develops a fairly elaborate analogy between flowers and human beings ("How akin they are to human things"). But the line "Stand like Ruth amid the golden corn" seems an echo of Keats's far superior "alien corn" in the "Ode to a Nightingale," and this time the pious reference at the end to our seeing in flowers

> Emblems of our own great resurrection,
> Emblems of the bright and better land,

seems unprepared for in spite of the poet's concession that we "behold" this "with childlike, credulous affection." Longfellow's imagination burns more brightly, however, in "The Beleaguered City," whose basic idea of the "midnight host of spectres pale" that "beleaguered the walls of Prague" was derived from a note in Scott's *Minstrelsy of the Scottish Border,* though Poe preferred to believe it had been taken from his own poem, "The Haunted Palace." For once, night is sinister in Longfellow, for when "the glorious morning star" rises upon the scene, "the troubled army fled." So, too, it is with man's own night fears, and Longfellow develops the analogy, as he loved to do, with considerable skill.

Among the "Earlier Poems" in *Voices of the Night,* the blank verse "Autumn" is interesting for the passage toward the end, which virtually paraphrases Bryant's "Thanatopsis," and "Burial of the Minnisink" has usually been regarded as Longfellow's first Indian poem, though Scudder objected that "the red chief is only a mere transliteration of a mediaeval knight." It has three companions, however, among the pieces printed in the Craigie appendix: "Jeckoyva," "Lover's Rock," and "The Indian Hunter," all 1825 and all melancholy in tone, though the tragedies recorded are personal rather than racial. "Dirge over a Nameless Grave" and "The Lunatic Girl" are authentic nineteenth-century morbid sentimentalism, and "The Battle of Lovell's Pond," an imitation of Byron's anapests in "The Destruction of Sennacherib," is interesting as Longfellow's very first published poem, in the Portland *Gazette,* November 17, 1820, when the poet was only thirteen.

Voices of the Night was followed (on December 18, 1841) by the slim *Ballads and Other Poems,* whose prime significance as indicating advance in Longfellow's poetic career is its having marked his discovery that he could tell a story in verse, always one of the things he did best. Among the original poems in this volume were five which, if not all true ballads, were in some sense narrative: "The Skeleton in Armor," "The Wreck of the Hesperus," "The Village Blacksmith," "Blind Bartimeus," and "Excelsior." The other seven were lyrical or meditative poems.

Though "The Skeleton in Armor" was by all means the most impressive piece in this collection, only "The Wreck

of the Hesperus'' was in the real old English and Scottish
common measure ballad meter: four-line iambic stanzas
(four, three; four, three: rhymed a b a b), with dialogue
and reference to folk beliefs, as in the unforgettable
warning of the ''old sailor'' who ''had sailed the Spanish
Main,''

> ''Last night, the moon had a golden ring,
>   And to-night no moon we see!''

to the hubris-driven skipper, who''blew a whiff from his
pipe, / And a scornful laugh laughed he,'' disregarded the
warning, and drove on to the destruction of his ship, himself, and the ''little daughter'' he had taken ''to bear him
company.'' The moon reference was probably drawn from
the traditional ballad ''Sir Patrick Spens'':

> ''Late, late yestreen I saw the new moone
>   Wi the auld moone in hir arme,
> And I feir, I feir, my deir master,
>   That we will cum to harme.''

But the immediate inspiration for the poem came from the
report of an actual wreck, though not ''on the reef of Norman's Woe,''[5] and Longfellow wrote it between midnight
and three o'clock (''It hardly cost me an effort. It did not
come into my mind by lines but by stanzas'') in the night
of December 29–30, 1839. Though the ''little daughter''
is idealized, the ending is stark:

> At daybreak, on the bleak sea-beach,
>   A fisherman stood aghast,
> To see the form of a maiden fair,
>   Lashed close to a drifting mast.

''The Village Blacksmith'' is concerned wholly with the
presentation of an ideal character; one wonders how many

young Americans have been introduced to Longfellow, and sometimes to poetry itself, through this simple but lovely poem. After the "spreading chestnut tree" on Brattle Street had been cut down, the children of Cambridge had a chair made out of its wood, which is still in the Longfellow House. The stanza form runs to six lines instead of four, and there are irregularities in the rhyme scheme and some imperfect rhymes, all of which is managed well, with a rather daring variation in the iambic meter at the beginning of the penultimate stanza:

> Toiling,—rejoicing,—sorrowing,
> Onward through life he goes.

Only the directly didactic and exhortatory final stanza,

> Thanks, thanks, to thee, my worthy friend,
> For the lesson thou hast taught!

is a serious blemish.[6]

Newton Arvin has praised "Blind Bartimeus" for "its association of literal and spiritual blindness, and its bold use of actual Greek phrases from St. Mark," but the retention of the Greek ("perforce," the poet says) for "the expressions of entreaty, comfort, and healing" at the end of each of the four stanzas makes it caviar to the general and veils its full effectiveness from those ignorant of that language.

Mrs. Longfellow recorded that the day the German translation of "Excelsior" appeared in an Innsbruck newspaper, students, meeting the translator on the street, "rushed towards him, [and] embraced and kissed him with . . . joy and transport." One can hardly imagine such a scene being reenacted today, for "Excelsior" has become as definitely a period piece as "A Psalm of Life." The youth who passes through "an Alpine village" while "the shades of night" are "falling fast," bearing "a banner with the strange device, / Excelsior!" rejects love, along with all warnings of physical danger, and even the consecrated life represented by "the pious monks of St. Bernard," to continue his climbing until at last his lifeless body "half-buried in the snow was found." In his letters Longfellow described the poem as "simply a fancy of my own," denying that it had a source, and said that his idea was "to display in a series of pictures the Life of a man of genius, resisting all temptations, laying aside all fears, heedless of all warnings and pressing right on to accomplish his purpose,"[7] but since in the poem nothing whatever is accomplished by the youth's climb, the modern reader is more likely to be reminded of the critic who called the boy who stood on the burning deck an inspired idiot. Incidentally it all comes rather oddly from Longfellow, who, in reading of Western exploration, only sighed over the hardships and when his son Charley was abroad, requested to be informed why he felt that he must climb every mountain he encountered.

"The Skeleton in Armor" was no inevitable expression of Longfellow's own personality either, except as it testified to his ability to grasp and project the spirit of the sagas and as the first notable expession of what the nineteenth century at least must have considered his understanding of primitive ways. It employs an eight-line stanza in which both iambics and trochees appear, and the line length varies. It was suggested by the discovery of an ancient skeleton at Fall River, Massachusetts, and the so-called Round Tower at Newport. Though it was never proved that the skeleton was that of a Norseman nor yet that the Vikings had built the Round Tower, Longfellow thought all this "sufficiently well established for the purpose of a ballad," as indeed it was. Everything except the first two of the twenty stanzas and the very last line of the twentieth is put into the mouth of the poet's "fearful guest,'' who with ''hollow breast / Still in rude armor drest,'' demands of his host that he his ''tale rehearse'' or ''dread a dead man's curse.'' He describes his youthful exploits in ''the Northern Land,'' where he ''tamed the gerfalcon,'' tracked the ''grisly bear,'' followed ''the werewolf's bark,'' and much besides. He became a pirate and a wassailer and was apparently quite contented with this life until he fell in love with a ''blue-eyed maid,'' old Hildebrand's daughter. The maiden returned his love, but her father merely laughed at the thought of giving ''a prince's child'' to ''a Viking wild.'' They eloped, but Hildebrand and his followers pursued them at sea.

> ''And as to catch the gale
> Round veered the flapping sail,
> 'Death!' was the helmsman's hail,
>   'Death without quarter!'
> Mid-ships with iron keel
> Struck we her ribs of steel;
> Down the black hulk did reel
>   Through the black water!
>
> ''As with his wings aslant,
> Sails the fierce cormorant,
> Seeking some rocky haunt,
>   With his prey laden,—
> So toward the open main,
> Beating to sea again,
> Through the wild hurricane,
>   Bore I the maiden.''

Three weeks of sailing brought them to America, where the lover built as ''my lady's bower'' the ''lofty tower'' that still stands. There they lived for many years, there she became a mother, and there at last she died.

> "Still grew my bosom then,
> Still as a stagnant fen!
> Hateful to me were men,
>   The sunlight hateful!
> In the vast forest here,
> Clad in my warlike gear,
> Fell I upon my spear,
>   Oh, death was grateful!"

Except for his love for his wife, the warrior's savagery is nowhere modified, nor is there any touch of moralizing in Longfellow's presentation of him. But it may be that human sympathy, understanding of a human being wholly different from the writer, and comprehension of a completely alien way of life are themselves moral. [8]

Four of the lyrics—"God's-Acre," "To the River Charles," "The Goblet of Life," and "Maidenhood"—are meditative, rather loosely organized pieces. The last named has two lines that have passed into common speech, describing the girl as

> Standing, with reluctant feet,
> Where the brook and river meet.

The first, a religious interpretation of death and burial, is mainly interesting for its high percentage of run-on lines.

> God's-Acre! Yes, that blessed name imparts
>   Comfort to those who in the grave have sown
> The seed that they had garnered in their hearts,
>   Their bread of life, alas! no more their own.

"To the River Charles" offers the river a song in return for the pleasure it has given the poet to watch its winding, but interest is somewhat divided between the river itself and the "three friends, all true and tried," who have dwelt beside it. "The Goblet of Life," a comparatively long and complicated poem, is also the most astringent, the closest in tone to "A Psalm of Life" and the inscription Paul Flemming found at St. Gilden. Fennel gives bitterness to the drink in the goblet of life, but it also imparts "new light and strength." Arvin well remarks that Longfellow "rarely comes so close to . . . an almost Hardyesque harshness as here."

"Endymion," "It Is Not Always May," and "The Rainy Day," however, are all perfectly balanced. In "The Rainy. Day" indeed the balance achieved is almost mathematical, for stanza 1 describes the rainy day, stanza 2 draws the analogy to the poet's "cold, and dark, and weary life," and stanza 3 interprets the meaning of the juxtaposition. "It Is Not Always May," which takes its text from a Spanish proverb *("No hay pajáros en los nidos de antaño")* has only two divisions, the first of which is predominantly nature poetry, while the second develops a carpe diem philosophy, urging the "maiden, that read'st this simple rhyme" to "enjoy the Spring of Love and Youth" while it lasts.

"Endymion" is more elaborately structured. Stanza 1 is a nocturne, presenting a moonlight landscape, while stanza 2, developing this theme, brings in the first reference to the moon goddess Diana, which, in stanza 3, reminds the poet how

> On such a tranquil night as this,
> She woke Endymion with a kiss,
>   When, sleeping in the grove,
>   He dreamed not of her love.

From this we shift, in stanzas 4–6, to exploring the nature of love, which, like "Diana's kiss, unasked, unsought," must always be as free as was Diana's. The closing stanzas (7–8) are poetry of comfort and direct exhortation to "weary hearts, . . . slumbering eyes, . . . and drooping souls," whom the poet promises, "Ye shall be loved again!"

"Endymion" is beautifully done up to the last three stanzas, which are quite the weakest in thought, sentiment, and expression. It may be true that no one is so utterly desolate

> But some heart, though unknown,
> Responds unto his own,

but surely not all are "loved again," nor even once, for that matter, and so long as the heart capable of responding remains unknown, it can never be of much use to the lonely one. In "The Rainy Day," on the other hand, the last stanza, though often criticized, seems to me a necessary addition, without which the poem would have little meaning. Nothing could be much more trite than that

> Into each life some rain must fall,
> Some days must be dark and dreary,

but it is also true that we continually forget it and rebel against it, and we can only do this at our peril.

Longfellow's next little book (or pamphlet), *Poems on Slavery* (1842), contained only eight pieces, several of which are in a modified common measure ballad stanza form, and all save one, "The Warning," were written in the poet's berth during a stormy voyage home from Europe. He had always been opposed to slavery and in Brunswick days had contemplated a play about Toussaint L'Ouverture, "that I may do something in my humble way for the great cause of negro emancipation," but he had read Dickens's *American Notes,* with its "grand chapter" on slavery, during a fortnight spent with the novelist in London, and it seems reasonable to posit some influence here. [10] Perhaps the poem that comes closest to distinction is the last, in which he warns that the "poor, blind Samson" Americans keep in bondage may finally bring the temple down around their ears. But "The Slave's Dream" is not ineffective in the contrast it develops between the captive's life of agony under "the driver's whip" and the world of memory into which he escapes when in sleep he is a king again where "the lordly Niger flowed," and "The Quadroon Girl" dares to touch upon the most horrifying aspect of slavery when it introduces us to the planter who sells his own flesh and blood. Whitman found even Longfellow's anger gentle, and the *Poems on Slavery are* gentle compared to what people like Garrison were saying; Longfellow wrote John Forster that he had tried to reach the hearts of people who were accustomed to seeing blacks presented only in comic aspects. Nevertheless Hawthorne was "never more surprised than at your writing poems about slavery," and Whittier, committed abolitionist and professional agitator that he was, was sufficiently impressed to urge Longfellow to run for Congress! He had taken a stand at a time when there was some risk involved in doing so, and he did pay a price for it, especially in the South. When Carey and Hart brought out a Longfellow collection, they omitted the *Poems on Slavery,* and even the New England Tract Association, reprinting the slavery pieces for propaganda purposes in 1843, found it politic not to include "The Good Part," describing a rich woman who

> gave up all
> To break the iron bands
> Of those who waited in her hall,
> And labored in her lands,

after which she earned her own "daily bread" and had only the prayers of those she had served to "clothe her with such grace'' as to produce ''the light of peace / That shines upon her face.''

Longfellow's next collection, *The Belfry of Bruges and Other Poems,* came out at the end of 1845, though it was dated 1846. Of the twenty-two original poems it contained Longfellow called seven ''Songs,'' and there were three ''Sonnets'' (''Mezzo Cammin,'' which was added to these in the collected editions, though written at this time, was not published until much later). I quote ''Mezzo Cammin'' to illustrate his adherence to the Italian form (he never used the looser English or Shakespearian form), but the ''Dante'' is equally distinguished. Both ''Mezzo Cammin'' and ''Autumn'' end with an alexandrine, and ''The Evening Star'' is one of the only two sonnets he ever ended with a rhymed couplet. [11]

> Half of my life is gone, and I have let
>   The years slip from me and have not fulfilled
>   The aspiration of my youth, to build
>   Some tower of song with lofty parapet.
> Not indolence, nor pleasure, nor the fret
>   Of restless passions that would not be stilled,
>   But sorrow, and a care that almost killed,
>   Kept me from what I may accomplish yet;
> Though half-way up the hill, I see the Past
>   Lying beneath me with its sounds and sights—
>   A city in the twilight dim and vast,
> With smoking roofs, soft bells, and gleaming lights,—
>   And hear above me on the autumnal blast
>   The cataract of Death far thundering from the heights.

''The Belfry of Bruges'' (to which the briefer, more personal ''Carillon'' is a pendent) and ''Nuremberg,'' both comparatively long poems, are drawn directly from Longfellow's own European sight-seeing, giving the impression that he was setting out to produce a travel journal in verse. Both follow essentially the same plan: the poet begins by describing what he sees; then, drawing upon his imagination, he revives the past, achieving a virtual review of the history of the place and a roll call of the famous persons involved. The principal difference between the two is that the artists in "Nuremberg" meant much more to Longfellow personally than did anybody he calls up in "The Belfry of Bruges." The outstanding "Nuremberg" figures include Hans Sachs, of *Meistersinger* fame (Walther von der Vogelweide gets a separate tribute among the "Songs"), and, best of all, Dürer:

> Here, when Art was still religion, with a simple, reverent
> heart,
> Lived and labored Albrecht Dürer, the Evangelist of Art.

This shifting between past and present is very characteristic of Longfellow in general but especially in this collection. He does it in "To an Old Danish Song Book," in "The Old Clock on the Stairs," and even in so personal a poem as "To a Child," where he roams over the earth to account for the child's rattle, reviews the history of the house in which he plays with it, and, this time, even attempts to forecast the future. But he is faithful in all his work to the ingrained conviction upon which he overtly insists at the end of "Rain in Summer," that only the poet-prophet ever really understands what lies before his eyes. For him imagination never meant taking refuge in the unreal but in penetrating to the significance of what was.

Personal experience, the here and now, remains nevertheless the indispensable taking-off place, and Longfellow makes freer use of his own experience in this book than was his wont. I have already mentioned "To a Child." "A Gleam of Sunshine" preserves the memory of a happy day in Brookline. The sonnet "The Evening Star" has been called Longfellow's only love poem, and "The Bridge"—

> I stood on the bridge at midnight,
>   As the clocks were striking the hour—

once more shifting between past and present, revives his agony during his wooing of Fanny Appleton and contrasts it with his present happiness. "The Old Clock on the Stairs" was inspired by a visit to the homestead of Mrs. Longfellow's maternal grandfather at Pittsfield, Massachusetts, and even "The Arsenal at Springfield" was suggested by an incident on their wedding trip. This admirably constructed poem is perhaps Longfellow's most effective plea for peace. "The burnished arms" piled up "from floor to ceiling" at the arsenal reminded the poet of organ pipes, which led to his contrasting organ music with the anti-music of exploding shells. Again he roams back through history for his illustrations, from which he turns finally to lament and promise. The explicit statement of the moral—

> Were half the power, that fills the world with terror,
>   Were half the wealth bestowed on camps and courts,
> Given to redeem the human mind from error,
>   There were no need of arsenals or forts—

led Newton Arvin to prefer the "more dramatic and less oratorical" peace propaganda in "The Occultation of Orion": "How fine . . . is the sense of radiance and harmony that, with his language and his imagery, Longfellow creates in this poem!" These things are certainly there, and so is the propaganda. But "The Occultation of Orion" is one of Longfellow's few really difficult poems, and it depends for its full impact upon the reader's knowledge of astronomy. [12]

Prosodically *The Belfry of Bruges* volume is full of interest and variety. Both the "Belfry" and "Nuremberg" use a basically trochaic, fifteen-syllabled line which may contain as many as eight stresses. "To the Driving Cloud" is a much more important Indian poem than the earlier "Burial of the Minnisink" (much as he regrets the Indian's passing, Longfellow seems to accept it as inevitable), and he himself thought its hexameters superior to those he had achieved in his translation of "The Children of the Lord's Supper." "The Norman Baron" is a brief narrative, suggested by Augustin Thierry, of an incident in Anglo-Norman times, in a four-line trochaic stanza whose first two lines rhyme with each other while lines three and four rhyme with the corresponding lines in the following stanza. Again, in "Afternoon in February," which Harry Hayden Clark compared to the work of the imagists,[13] the first two lines of each four-line stanza rhyme, but the last line rhymes with the last line of the following stanza while the third line does not rhyme with anything. "Rain in Summer" and "To an Old Danish Song Book" might be called free verse, though the first has abundant, irregular rhyme, but Arvin takes it and "Curfew" along with the later "Birds of Passage," as exemplifying what Gerard Manley Hopkins was to call "sprung rhythm." "Curfew" too is very successful in virtually reproducing the sound it indicates. Among the "Songs," several of which have already been mentioned, "The Arrow and the Song," which was set to music by Balfe,[14] and "The Old Clock on the Stairs" are probably the best known, and "The Day Is Done" closes with the simple yet musical passage quoted at the beginning of Chapter II.

The Seaside and the Fireside was published at mid-century, three years after *Evangeline.* Longfellow would not collect any more of his short poems until 1858, when *The Courtship of Miles Standish and Other Poems* appeared, nor bring out a volume devoted entirely to short pieces until *Flower-de-Luce* in 1866. Consideration of *The Seaside and the Fireside* may then fittingly conclude this chapter.

The volume was divided into two sections, "By the Seaside" and "By the Fireside." The "Dedication" leaves its closing emphasis upon the latter:

> Therefore I hope, as no unwelcome guest,
>   At your warm fireside, when the lamps are lighted,
> To have my place reserved among the rest,
>   Nor stand as one unsought and uninvited!

Nevertheless the "Seaside" section predominates, not only because it contains by all means the longest, most ambitious, and most famous piece, "The Building of the Ship," but also because its contents are so much less miscellaneous.

"The Building of the Ship" is Longfellow's most important utterance upon public affairs. "Standing out upon the platform, book in hand, trembling, palpitating, and weeping, and giving every word its true weight and emphasis," the great actress Fanny Kemble may have been the first and most gifted of its "readers," but her successors were innumerable. Lincoln too wept over the poem ("it is a wonderful gift to be able to stir men like that"), and it was widely imitated by poets and poetasters alike. Though it tells a story, its structure, probably suggested by Schiller's *"Das Lied von der Glocke,"* is basically that of an ode,[15] and it employs with freedom a variety of metrical forms. The "text" is enunciated by the personified vessel at the outset and repeated in the middle of the poem:

> "Build me straight, O worthy Master!
>   Stanch and strong, a goodly vessel,
> That shall laugh at all disaster,
>   And with wave and whirlwind wrestle!"

Unity is served by having the launching of the vessel and the marriage of the master's daughter to his apprentice take place simultaneously as if one were dependent upon the other, though one is not quite sure why this should be.

> She starts,—she moves,—she seems to feel
> The thrill of life along her keel,
> And, spurning with her foot the ground,
> With one exulting, joyous bound,
> She leaps into the ocean's arms!

And at the same time the master's daughter is exhorted:

> Sail forth into the sea of life,
> O gentle, loving, trusting wife,
> And safe from all adversity
> Upon the bosom of that sea
> Thy comings and thy goings be!

"Like a beauteous barge" does not however seem the happiest possible figure to apply to a young woman, and though it is true that the terror of the sea is not felt very strongly in this poem save in the passage describing the master's sea tales, one wonders how the bride could have been thought the best possible model for the ship's figurehead.

> On many a dreary and misty night,
> 'T will be seen by the rays of the signal light,
> Speeding along through the rain and the dark,
> Like a ghost in its snow-white sark,
> The pilot of some phantom bark,
> Guiding the vessel in its flight,
> By a path none other knows aright!

Effective as this passage is, one might expect it to produce at least a slight shudder on the part of those who loved the model.

The political bias of the poem is never overtly stressed before the end save in one passage:

> "Cedar of Maine and Georgia pine
> Here together shall combine,
> A goodly frame, and a goodly fame,
> And the UNION be her name"

But after the vessel has been launched, the last division begins

> Thou, too, sail on, O Ship of State!
> Sail on, O UNION, strong and great!
>
> Humanity with all its fears,
> With all the hopes of future years,
> Is hanging breathless on that fate!

and it ends, more like a hymn than a lyric, with

> Our hearts, our hopes, are all with thee,
> Our hearts, our hopes, our prayers, our tears,
> Our faith triumphant o'er our fears,
> Are all with thee,—are all with thee!

There are seven other poems in the "Seaside" section. "Sir Humphrey Gilbert" is a ballad, inspired by the subject's reputed statement that heaven was as close to those who died by sea as on land. "Chrysaor," which Saintsbury called "the most Browningesque thing in Longfellow," was first called "The Evening Star." It shines into the sea, but the emphasis of the poem falls upon the star itself. The scene of "The Fire of Drift-Wood" is indoors, at Devereux Farm, near Marblehead, where Longfellow had visited, but the proximity of its inhibitants to the ocean is much upon their minds, and in "Twilight" the family in the fisherman's cottage can think of nothing but the peril of the absent husband and father; simple as this poem is, it is effective in its concentration upon fear, anxiety, and foreboding. "Seaweed" brings in Longfellow's fondness for analogy again; as the seaweed drifts in from everywhere and nowhere, so the poet draws his inspiration from he knows not where, but since the seaweed is not "at length in books recorded" or "hoarded" like "household words," the comparison seems a bit strained. There is no such use of analogy in "The Lighthouse," but there is personification; the lighthouse is called "a new Prometheus, chained upon the rock," and at the end it even speaks. The least concentrated of these poems is "The Secret of the Sea," in which fragments of sea lore, followed by an anecdote, mingle in the poet's meditation. As always, Longfellow can vary his musical patterns as masterfully as Richard Strauss could shift keys, without disturbing basic harmonies or interfering with the creation of a unified impression. Thus the first stanza of "The Lighthouse" is regularly iambic, almost without the minutest variation, while stanzas 2 and 3 are very different.

The sonnet "On Mrs. Kemble's Readings from Shakespeare," which was presented to the actress at a dinner Longfellow gave for her after one of her performances, is in the "Fireside" section, where four other poems also, in a way, relate to poetry. "The Singers" presents three different types of poet, refuses to choose between them, and defines the threefold function of poetry—"to charm, to strengthen, and to teach." "Gaspar Becerra," which was based on a story told in William Stirling-Maxwell's *Annals of the Artists of Spain,* is didactic also; the "anxious master" who has been unable to carve his Virgin out of "the precious wood" that had been imported "from a distant Eastern island" succeeds unexpectedly with a slab seized from "the smoking embers" of his own hearth.

> That is best which lieth nearest;
> Shape from that thy work of art.

Longfellow himself did not always follow this counsel however, and "Pegasus in Pound" and "Tegnér's Drapa" (i.e., dirge) are more impressive poems. The winged horse who represents poetry uses his wings to fly out of the pound in which the stupid villagers have placed him upon finding him as an estray (the poem was written for the collection of fugitive verses to which Longfellow gave that name), but a fountain flows from the place where his hoof marks broke the soil, and this

> Gladdens the whole region round,
> Strengthening all who drink its waters,
> While it soothes them with its sound.

"Tegnér's Drapa" honors the great Swedish poet whom Longfellow so much admired in a measure intended to suggest the old sagas, but the point stressed is that the ancient violence has now been replaced by the spirit which informs Tegnér's own work.

> The law of force is dead!
> The law of love prevails![17]

There are three distinctly religious poems. "Hymn for My Brother's Ordination," which takes its text from Christ's advice to the young man who wished to be made perfect, is probably the most conventionally religious piece Longfellow ever wrote, but there is no cant in it. Both "Suspiria" and "Resignation" deal with death; it is surprising as well as heartening that the latter, which was directly occasioned by the poet's grief over the death of his little daughter Fanny, should have inspired perhaps his most triumphant expression of faith in immortality.

> There is no Death! What seems so is transition;
>   This life of mortal breath
> Is but a suburb of the life Elysian,
>   Whose portal we call Death.

In "The Open Window," however, the shadow of muta-
bility falls across the poet's soul as he passes a deserted
house,

> And the boy that walked beside me,
>   He could not understand
> Why closer in mine, ah! closer,
>   I pressed his warm, soft hand!

The imagery in "The Builders" seems a bit confused; it
is not quite clear whether we are building the wall or being
built into it, and "King Witlaf's Drinking Horn," derived
from Samuel R. Maitland's *The Dark Ages,* in which the
abbot apparently drinks himself to death while "the jovial
monks" in his charge simply go on drinking, seems an
unlikely subject for Longfellow. Much more effective is
"Sand of the Desert in an Hour-Glass"; this time it is a
concrete object which becomes "the spy of Time, / The
Minister of Thought" and sets the poet's imagination
roaming with those whose feet may have pressed this sand
in Bible times.

V

Evangeline

This is the forest primeval.The murmuring pines and the
hemlocks,
Bearded with moss, and in garments green, indistinct in
the twilight,
Stand like Druids of eld, with voices sad and prophetic,
Stand like harpers hoar, with beards that rest on their
bosoms.
Loud from its rocky caverns, the deep-voiced neighboring
ocean
Speaks, and in accents disconsolate answers the wail of the
forest.

Not so long ago, every school child in America could recite
these opening lines of *Evangeline: A Tale of Acadie,* and
many could add other selected passages, among them one
now universally condemned as "sentimental":

Silently one by one, in the infinite meadows of heaven,
Blossomed the lovely stars, the forget-me-nots of the angels.

It was the first long poem in American literature to live
beyond its own time, and it would be impossible to
exaggerate its vogue, either at home or abroad. Its
popularity cut through all class distinctions. It was read
and loved and pondered over in humble cottages, and

both the Honorable Mrs. Norton and King Leopold I of Belgium admired it so much that each, independently, had the name "Atchafalaya" cut upon a seal. In 1947 Hawthorne and Dana[1] counted over 270 editions and at least 130 translations. There have been plays, films, and musicals, and as late as 1934 the Longfellow-Evangeline State Park was established in Louisiana.

The historical basis of the story was supplied in 1755 by the expulsion of the French settlers from the vicinity of the Bay of Minas in Acadie (now known as Nova Scotia) as an incident of the conflict between France and England for possession of the North American continent. Their homes and possessions were destroyed, and some three thousand people were dispersed over the Atlantic Coast and as far away as Louisiana, where their descendants are still known as Cajuns. The rationale behind the atrocity was that the English colonies in America needed protection. A New England man, Governor William Shirley, had been active in urging the removal, the Boston firm of Apthorpe and Hancock furnished the ships, and the troops were commanded by Lieutenant-Colonel John Winslow, a great-grandson of Governor Edward Winslow.[2]

Longfellow heard the story of an Acadian maiden separated from her lover on what was to have been their wedding day, who "wandered about New England all her life-time" in search of him, "and at last, when she was old, . . . found [him] on his death-bed," from Hawthorne, who had received it from his friend, the Reverend Horace L. Conolly. Conolly wanted Hawthorne to make a story of it, but for some reason it did not strike the tale-teller as suitable literary material for himself. Longfellow, responding to it instantly, said, "If you really do not want this incident for a tale, let me have it for a poem."[3]

He set about "Gabrielle," as he then thought of it, on November 28, 1845, but it was far from smooth sailing; as he said afterwards, the poem was easy to read because it had been so hard to write. By January 12 he had completed two cantos, but soon he began to encounter roadblocks, and in May we find him complaining that "the Castalian fount is still." On December 17 he finished the first canto of the second half, and on January 16, 1847, he finished the last canto, but there were still three intervening cantos in "Part the Second" to be filled in. On February 27, his birthday, the poem was finished at last, and now he was tempted to see nothing in it but defects. On March 6 he began correcting and revising it, and by the time he saw the first proofs on April 3, he was "pretty well satisfied." It was published on October 30.

Sources for the historical material involved in the poem were much less abundant in Longfellow's time than they are now; indeed his own work may well have stimulated the publication of some of them. His principal source for the expulsion itself was certainly Thomas C. Haliburton's *An Historical and Statistical Account of Nova Scotia,* which makes use of the Abbé Raynal's account of the early French settlers. For the second part he himself mentions having consulted "Watson's 'Annals of Philadelphia' and the 'Historical Collections of Philadelphia.' Also Darby's 'Geographical Description of Louisiana.' " It was from Watson that he learned about the epidemic of yellow fever in Philadelphia. He also knew Frémont's account of his explorations in the West, from which he seems to have taken the name of his hero, Gabriel Lajeunesse, and W. I. Kip's *Early Jesuit Missions in North America* and Timothy Flint's *Recollections of the Last Ten Years, Passed in Occasional Residences and Journeyings in the Valley of the Mississippi,* and he may have drawn upon Chateaubriand's *Voyage en Amérique* and his own sister Mary Greenleaf's letters, describing her journey down the Ohio and Mississippi to New Orleans in 1840. Seasoned traveler though he was, Longfellow was not in the habit of traveling for his writing (he did not even bother to visit

Plymouth for *The Courtship of Miles Standish),* and fate
certainly humored him by sending John Banvard's
"moving diorama" of the Mississippi to be exhibited in
Boston just when he needed it. "The river comes to me,"
he wrote, "instead of my going to the river; and as it is to
flow through the pages of the poem, I look upon this as a
special benediction." So it surely was, and though "three
miles of canvas" must have been both less vivid and less
accurate than a film would have been, for the imagination
of a poet it served well enough.

He had, to be sure, seen both the Friends' almshouse in
Philadelphia, one day when he was "passing down Spruce
Street," and, on another walk, the Catholic cemetery
where both Gabriel and Evangeline were buried, but this
was pure chance, not zeal for research, and there is merit in
the suggestion of a number of writers that the pastoral setting of Acadie (there were no "forest primeval" nor
"murmuring hemlocks" there) may have been drawn
from what he remembered of the Maine of his boyhood or
his visit to Sweden during his second European sojourn.[4]
The bird song comes from Audubon. The French folklore
retailed by the notary René Leblanc is in Frédéric Plaquet's
Contes Populaires, and the Indian stories told by the
Shawnee woman are indebted to Schoolcraft. Indians,
however, are much less sympathetically treated in
Evangeline than they would be, only a few years later, in
Hiawatha.

There were more literary sources, however, than have yet
been indicated. If Longfellow used his own memories of
Sweden for the Acadian locale, this must at least have been
powerfully reinforced by what he read in Tegnér's
Frithiof's Saga, which probably contributed not only to his
background but to his conception of the early lives and the
courtship and betrothal of the hero and heroine, originally
intended to be treated more fully than now appears.
Newton Arvin may have been right also in suggesting that

"the Vergil of the *Eclogues* and the *Georgics*" exercised some influence, and even if we do not go all the way with Oliver Wendell Holmes, who declared that "Dorothea was the mother of Evangeline," Goethe's *Hermann und Dorothea* must have been in the picture, for this poem, which, like *Evangeline,* employs hexameters, also deals with displaced persons in much the same spirit as Longfellow's, and he of course had had occasion to lecture about it at Harvard.

The only sour note in the chorus of praise that greeted *Evangeline* was struck by those who could not stomach the hexameters and indeed insisted that they were not hexameters at all. In the strictly classical sense, of course they were not; probably the best description of what Longfellow produced is that of Edward Hirsh:

Encouraged by Goethe's example and by the experiments of Southey and Coleridge, he solved the immediate problems by using a basically dactylic line with a trochaic close and free trochaic substitution; the minimally necessary spondees he obtained by juxtaposing monosyllabic words and by coaxing the second syllable of trochees into an approximation of spondees.[5]

Longfellow himself had had his doubts about hexameters. In 1841, in his introduction to the translation of "The Children of the Lord's Supper" in *Ballads and Other Poems.* he wrote:

I have preserved even the measure, that inexorable hexameter, in which, it must be confessed, the motions of the English muse are not unlike those of a prisoner dancing to the music of his chains; and perhaps, as Dr. Johnson said of the dancing bear, the wonder is not that she should do it well, but that she should do it at all.

By the time he came to *Evangeline,* however, he had evidently been thoroughly converted. Not only did he now believe he had chosen the only measure suitable to the particular tale he had to tell, but he declared that "the English world is not yet alive to the beauties of that measure."

He won considerable support from his peers. Oliver Wendell Holmes did not "believe any other measure could have told that lovely story with such effect, as we feel when carried along the tranquil current of these brimming, slow-moving, soul-satisfying lines." Hawthorne conceded that

> The first impressions of many of his readers will be adverse; but, when it is perceived how beautifully plastic this cumbrous measure becomes in [Longfellow's] hands—how thought and emotion incorporate and identify themselves with it—how it can compass great ideas, or pick up familiar ones—how it swells and subsides with the nature and necessities of the theme—and, finally, how musical it is, whether it imitate a forest-wind or the violin of an Acadian fiddler—we fully believe that the final judgment will be in its favor.

Whittier, however, blew hot and cold. Though he found the hexameter measure "exceedingly well adapted to a descriptive and narrative poem," he was yet "constrained to think that the story of *Evangeline* would have been quite as acceptable to the public taste had it been told in the poetic prose of the author's *Hyperion*." When Longfellow thanked Hawthorne for his review of *Evangeline,* he acknowledged his debt to him "for being willing to forego the pleasure of writing a prose tale, which many people would have taken for poetry, that I might write a poem which many people take for prose"![6]

If I have so far said nothing about the story of *Evangeline,* I might plead in extenuation that there is little or no story to tell. Grand-Pré is destroyed and its inhabitants deported; Evangeline's father dies of shock; Gabriel's father survives to become a wealthy planter in

Louisiana; Evangeline spends her life searching for her lover, but only finds him at last, in an almshouse in Philadelphia, just before he dies. She "wandered about New England" in the account that reached Longfellow from Conolly through Hawthorne, but he widened the scope of her odyssey indefinitely, for she knows the Ohio and the Mississippi and the Ozarks and Louisiana and Michigan and the Western plains and at last Philadelphia, where, finally, having relinquished her search, she has become a Sister of Mercy, but New England she apparently touches not at all. Originally Part the Second was to begin with Evangeline already old and gray: "more than thirty years had lapsed since the burning of Grand-Pré." Apparently when he wrote these words, Longfellow had not yet planned to include all the material we now have about her wanderings. Time, as well as space, seems to manifest expansive powers in these pages. The actual expulsion of the Acadians from their homes took place, as has been observed, in 1755. But Part the Second, Canto IV, line 165—"Now in the noisy camps and the battle-fields of the army"—seems to indicate the period of the American Revolution, and the actual date of the yellow fever epidemic at the close was 1793.

Saintsbury criticized Evangeline's failure to find Gabriel until the very end of the story as one of those "possible improbabilities" that are worse than "probable impossibilities." Gabriel had left his father's plantation to trade for mules with the "Spaniards," "follow the Indian trails to the Ozark mountains," hunt "for furs in the forest," and trap the beaver on the rivers, just before Evangeline and Father Felician arrived there. But why does he never seem to come back? Even in those days of slow and difficult communication, is it conceivable that Evangeline could not have left a message for him that would have enabled him to find her? Probably the only sensible answer to such questions, if we must ask them, is

that there is no more point in applying a realistic test to
Evangeline than to *The Winter's Tale* or *The Merchant of
Venice*. Once Longfellow even teases the reader by having
Gabriel's boat and Evangeline's pass each other on the
river without recognition. Always mindful of what is now
called extra sensory perception, he made Evangeline, at
this point, mildly aware of what had happened.

> "O Father Felician!
> Something says in my heart that near me Gabriel wanders.
> Is it a foolish dream, an idle and vague superstition?
> Or has an angel passed, and revealed the truth to my spirit?"

Nor is this the only such touch in the poem. While
Evangeline tarries in the Ozarks, a "subtile sense . . . of
pain and indefinite terror" creeps into her heart "as the
cold, poisonous snake creeps into the nest of the swallow."
This is less like "earthly fear," than "a breath from the
region of spirits," so that, like the Shawnee Indian girl
whose story she has been hearing, she feels that "she, too,
was pursuing a phantom." And at the very end, before she
finds Gabriel, "something within her said, 'At length thy
trials are ended!' "

But *Evangeline* is an idyll, and the lovers are as idealized
as the picture of Grand-Pré itself. They are not elaborately
shaded characters, nor is there any reason in the poem itself why they should be; like Romeo and Juliet they were
created only to love, to suffer, and be faithful unto death.
To this one may easily reply that Romeo and Juliet are im-
mensely more vivid and more minutely shaded characters,
but this is the lagniappe that Shakespeare could not avoid
giving us; the gods endowed him with all gifts except one.
He could not create a character without having the creature
come alive on his hands, as witness the quite casual and in-
consequential Barnadine in *Measure for Measure*, who
simply declines, upon his own initiative, to perform the
one   function   in   the   play   for   which   he   was

designed and decides instead to behave more to his own liking.

Gabriel's position in the story is odd and in a way ungraceful. It is true that Evangeline herself speaks very little; it is her lot to suffer, not to contend. She is a pilgrim who passes across the scene, and she can hardly expect to reach the ultimate goal of her pilgrimage in this world. But at least the poet keeps her before our eyes, and of the two characters she has the active role. She is the pursuer and Gabriel is the pursued; she chases her man over a considerable portion of the North American continent. But if, as Longfellow makes clear at the very beginning, the poem was to focus on her, not on him, this was unavoidable.

> Ye who believe in affection that hopes, and endures, and
>   is patient,
> Ye who believe in the beauty and strength of woman's
>   devotion,
> List to the mournful tradition, still sung by the pines of
>   the forest;
> List to a Tale of Love in Acadie, home of the happy.

There is no suggestion at any point that Gabriel is less faithful than Evangeline (according to his father, he was highly restless in Louisiana); the plan of the poem simply requires that he must be kept out of sight and loved in absentia.

It is beside the point also to wonder how Evangeline could have moved unmenaced and unharmed among the rough men of the frontier through so many years. No matter whether this is true to life; it is true to art and to the spirit of the poem. Whittier was correct when he observed that he himself would not have been able to tell this story without expressing his indignation against the British, and he was right too in realizing that this would have spoiled the poem, at least the poem that Longfellow had conceived. There is one moment and only one, in the church at Grand-Pré, at the time of the evacuation, when violence threatens to break out, and this is quickly quelled. All this, of course, supports Longfellow's own view that the dreamy, langourous hexameter was right for this poem.[7] Newton Arvin perceived all this when he praised the "passages of melancholy and pathetic inaction" in *Evangeline* and the "moonlight mysteriousness" of the scene in which the heroine "wanders out into Basil's Louisiana garden in the 'magical moonlight,' " and at the end the colors of the Philadelphia scene, even in time of plague, are as muted as those of the frontier. But it is even more important to realize that the tone is as right for the "Enoch Arden"-like characters as it is for the setting against which they move. They are gentle people thrust into an ungentle situation not of their own making, and we and they alike must find what satisfaction we can in the reflection that if they cannot master it, neither can it corrupt them. There is dignity in endurance as well as contention.

VI

The Song of Hiawatha

Longfellow described *The Song of Hiawatha* in the following terms:[1]

This Indian Edda—if so I may call it—is founded on a tradition prevalent among the North American Indians, of a personage of miraculous birth, who was sent among them to clear their rivers, forests, and fishing-grounds, and to teach them the arts of peace. He was known among different tribes by the several names of Michabou, Chiabo, Manabozho, Tarenyawagon, and Hiawatha. Mr. Schoolcraft gives an account of his life in his *Algic Researches,* Vol. I, p. 134; and in his *History, Condition, and Prospects of the Indian Tribes of the United States,* Part III, p. 134, may be found the Iroquois form of the tradition, derived from the verbal narrations of the Onondaga chief.

Into this old tradition I have woven other curious Indian legends, drawn chiefly from the various and valuable writings of Mr. Schoolcraft, to whom the literary world is greatly indebted for his indefatigable zeal in rescuing from oblivion so much of the legendary lore of the Indians.

The scene of the poem is among the Ojibways on the southern shore of Lake Superior, in the region between the Pictured Rocks and the Grand Sable.

Longfellow recorded having hit upon both his plan and his meter on June 22, 1854, and a few days later be began work on "Manabozho." By the end of July he was calling it "Hiawatha," but in November both he and Fanny feared it might lack human interest. In January 1855 he was writing again. He finished the work in March and in April was copying and rewriting. When the proofs came in July he found himself "growing idiotic" about it, not knowing whether it was good or not. Ticknor and Fields published it early in November, and it sold thirty thousand copies within a few months.

The writings of Henry Rowe Schoolcraft (1793–1864), ethnologist, explorer, and Indian agent, who had married a half-Ojibway woman, and who would credit Longfellow with having, for the first time, portrayed the Indian correctly in literature, furnished the poet with his principal source, bequeathing to him, among other more valuable gifts, the confusion between the mythical Manabozho and the historical Hiawatha for which Longfellow himself has often been blamed. [2]

But there were other sources, both in literature and in life, and the poet's interest in Indians had already expressed itself in such poems as "Burial of the Minnisink" and "To a Driving Cloud." He had seen Algonquins in Maine and Black Hawk with his Sacs and Foxes in an exhibition on Boston Common and had entertained an Ojibway chief at his house after a lecture in Boston. A Harvard student who had traveled in the West had repeated some Indian legends to him. He was familiar with the writings of the Moravian missionary John G. E. Heckewelder (1743–1823), who also influenced Cooper and who, through Conrad Richter, was still affecting American literature in our own time, and Heckewelder had convinced him that the Indians possessed "magnanimity, generosity, benevolence, and pure religion without hypocrisy" and that they had been barbarously treated by the whites. The poet had read *A Narrative of the Captivity and Adventures of John Tanner* (1836), and if he had no Banvard this time, as with *Evangeline,* he may well have found a partial equivalent in George Catlin's 350 pictures illustrating *Manners and Customs of the North American Indians* (1841) and in Schoolcraft's own illustrator, Seth Eastman. He found the names Wenonah and Minnehaha in *Dahcotah; or Life and Legends of the Sioux around Fort Snelling* (1848) by Eastman's wife Mary.[3] Certainly there can be no question as to the influence he himself exerted upon Frederic Remington and other painters through his own poem.[4]

But he called *Hiawatha* an "Indian Edda," and this may well remind us that one important European influence was brought to bear upon it. Longfellow's rhymed trochaic tetrameter meter was that of the Finnish folk epic *Kalevala,* which had been put together from native folk singers by Elias Lönrott and which we know Longfellow to have been reading in the very month he began his own poem. He was angered by the allegation that he had also taken some of his stories from the *Kalevala,* though it is a little hard to see why this should have been different than taking them from Schoolcraft. In 1854 he wrote T. C. Callicott:

I have tried to do for our Indian legends what the unknown Finnish poets had done for theirs, and in doing this I have employed the same metre, but of course have not adopted any of their legends. Whatever resemblances therefore may be found between the poems of "Kalevala" and mine, in this respect, is not of my creating, but lies in the legends themselves. . . . All these strange stories are in Schoolcraft and the other writers on Indian matters, and this ought to shield me from any accusation of taking them from Finnish sources.[5]

Of course it is the meter itself, easily imitated and more easily read in a singsong manner, that has made *Hiawatha* the most parodied poem in the English language; more than a thousand such parodies were counted years ago, of which seven were almost as long as the poem itself.[6] The

keen-eyed Mrs. Longfellow had come pretty close to
foreseeing this. "It is very fresh and fragrant of the woods
and genuine Indian life," she wrote of her husband's
poem, "but its rhymeless rhythm will puzzle the critics,
and I suppose it will be abundantly abused." Longfellow
himself was always sure he had chosen rightly for a poem
which dealt with a primitive people. He would have been
pleased, I am sure, by C. Hugh Holman's demonstration
that, two decades before *Hiawatha,* "a metre approximate" to its own had commended itself to William
Gilmore Simms as a means of indicating the rhythm of Indian speech and song, and by the fact that though he was
no special admirer of *Hiawatha,* Newton Arvin showed
conclusively by both quotation and scanning that "the fall
of the accents" in the poem is sometimes more "shifting
and variable" than the parodists would suggest.[7]

Though *Hiawatha* has sometimes been called an epic,
Longfellow's own "Indian Edda" seems a more accurate
description, and it is generally regarded as a collection of
traditional tales about the culture hero of a primitive
people. It does however have some epic characteristics. Its
hero or his forebears are of supernatural origin, and epic
repetition and enumeration are employed. But wonderful
as Hiawatha's deeds are, he is not the founder of a nation,
and at the close he takes his leave of a people who are
about to be superseded as inhabitants of their land. When
in the last canto, the emissaries of the white men and the
white man's God arrive, Hiawatha commends them to his
people and himself departs

> To the Islands of the Blessed,
> To the Kingdom of Ponemah,
> To the land of the Hereafter!

The suggestion that

> "Many moons and many winters
> Will have come, and will have vanished,
> Ere I come again to see you,"

hardly seems more than an Arthurian echo. Neither he nor his people seem to expect him to come again, and Longfellow's readers knew that he had not come and was not coming. The poet himself recognized this as the weakest thing in his poem. "The contrast of Saga and History," he said, "is too sudden."[8]

Hiawatha is a long and many-sided poem, in which readers may be trusted to find their favorite passages in accord with their own tastes and interests, but one can hardly believe that many would fail to respond to the famous passage from "Hiawatha's Childhood" in Canto 3:

> Then the little Hiawatha
> Learned of every bird its language,
> Learned their names and all their secrets,
> How they built their nests in Summer,
> Where they hid themselves in Winter,
> Talked with them whene'er he met them,
> Called them "Hiawatha's Chickens."

Whatever else may or may not have lain comfortably within Longfellow's range, nobody has ever doubted that he was at home with domestic themes and emotions, and whatever answer we make to Rose M. Davis's question, "How Indian Is Hiawatha?"[9] there can be no question that Longfellow's hero is a less primitive and less discordant being than his sources might have been expected to inspire. The poet omits the wars between the Indian tribes, though he was obviously aware of them. Gitchie Manito, the "Maker of Life," strikes the keynote at the very beginning when he calls for an end to strife:

> "I am weary of your quarrels,
> Weary of your wars and bloodshed,
> Weary of your prayers for vengeance,
> Of your wranglings and dissensions;
> All your strength is in your union,
> All your danger is in discord;
> Therefore be at peace henceforward,
> And as brothers live together."

Hiawatha fasts like Christ in the wilderness. He teaches his people the arts of peace, wins maize for them to eat, builds a birch canoe, and invents picture writing that their records may be preserved. The trickster side of Manabozho is filtered out of him entirely and assigned instead to Pau-Puk-Keewis, and the violence largely disappears also, though not quite altogether. For all his love of his "chickens" and "brothers," Hiawatha remains a mighty hunter. He slays animals and monsters and at last brings about the death of Pau-Puk-Keewis, thus, a Freudian might say, destroying the element of violence in himself. Early in the poem he even attempts to slay his father, the West Wind Mudjekeewis, to punish him for seducing and deserting Wenonah, though, after he has failed to do so, the two become surprisingly good friends and Mudjekeewis even becomes a sponsor of Hiawatha's mission.

Stith Thompson, whose credentials as a folklorist were unimpeachable, wrote of the Hiawatha-Minnehaha love story, which is original with Longfellow, that it "does violence both to the myth and to the spirit of the life depicted."[10] Some readers have objected that Minnehaha is not a true Indian woman; perhaps it would be more to the point to say that she is not characterized at all. She hardly ever speaks, and she has nothing to do in the poem save to follow Hiawatha when he comes for her,[11] walk naked around the cornfields in an ancient fertility rite, and die in the famine. There are no children, and no love passages between the two are indicated. Their wedding feast, to be sure, is the most elaborately described incident in the poem, but the foreground is occupied not by the lovers but by Chibiabos, the sweet singer; Kwasind, the strong man; Iagoo, the boaster; and Pau-Puk-Keewis, the dancer. One whole canto is given over to the story of the Evening Star, as told by Iagoo. Later, Cantos 16–17, in which Pau-Puk-Keewis, now become an evil force of destruction, devoted to violence for violence' sake, must

be hunted down and destroyed, are so crammed full of action, magic transformations, and fairy lore that they become the most exciting in the poem.

At the beginning of their connection, Minnehaha seems rather more romantic than Hiawatha. Against the advice of his grandmother, he chooses to wed a Dacotah girl rather than one of his own people because he hopes the alliance may help to cement peace between the tribes, but her instantaneous capitulation to him seems largely independent of such considerations. Yet whatever Indian braves may or may not have felt for their wives, as the poem stands, nobody doubts Hiawatha's love for Minnehaha, whose very name has an atmosphere about it. Perhaps we are more moved by it and by her husband's grief when she dies[12] than we have any right to be over so undeveloped a love story. Perhaps too we may have been conditioned by the undeniable power of the two cantos ("The Ghosts" and "The Famine") which precede the account of her death. Yet it may be that neither of these considerations quite covers the case. After all, Hiawatha was "miles away among the mountains" when Minnehaha died, yet he

> Heard that sudden cry of anguish,
> Heard the voice of Minnehaha
> Calling to him in the darkness,
> "Hiawatha! Hiawatha!"

Schoolcraft may have been right in feeling that Longfellow had come closer to presenting the real Indian in literature than anybody had before him. Yet his poem antedates many modern studies in folklore and anthropology from which we have learned much that neither he nor his contemporaries had any way of knowing; consequently what we are tempted to call his concessions to contemporary taste were not concessions for him, for contemporary taste was his taste as well. That he understood

just what he was doing and why he was doing it is proved
by the way he defined his purpose and located his audi-
ence at the very beginning:

> Ye whose hearts are fresh and simple,
> Who have faith in God and Nature,
> Who believe that in all ages
> Every human heart is human,
> That in even savage bosoms
> There are longings, yearnings, strivings
> For the good they comprehend not.

In 1920, Christabel F. Fiske published an article that,
one might reasonably argue, still remains the finest single
study of *Hiawatha*.[13] In it she differentiates, brilliantly, ex-
citingly, and well-nigh unerringly, between those elements and incidents that are true to primitive life and
those that have been subjected to modification and
modernization. This article is, I believe, superior even to
the much later important study by Celia Millward and
Cecelia Tiche, "Whatever Happened to Hiawatha?"[14] in
which we are told that though Longfellow "cannot be
faulted with respect to the usual metrics and poetic devices
of heroic poetry," his moral values are inconsistent with its
general structure. He mingled the mythical with the
historical and undercut the heroic stature of his characters
by presenting them as "child-like and immature," not
universally human. Sometimes he presented nature as in-
different to human wants and sometimes as sympathetic.
Finally he infused the Protestant work ethic into his poem,
imposing an "American religio-progressive ethos" upon a
kind of poetry to which it is "generally alien." He "filled
Hiawatha with numerous events typical of epic poetry, yet
kept out of it the values usually manifested through those
events."

I have no quarrel with most of these specific findings as
such. What troubles me is that if, having accepted them,

we see *Hiawatha* as having been ruined by them, we shall also have to reject *Hamlet* and virtually every other work that deals with the past. In *Hamlet* Shakespeare took from the sagas a barbarous, pagan story that assumes the sacred duty of blood revenge, imposed a Catholic coloring upon it, and gave his hero all the complexities of a super-subtle Renaissance gentleman. Shall we therefore dethrone it from its eminence and put James Branch Cabell's *Hamlet Had an Uncle,* which *does* go back to the sagas, in its place? If Longfellow had produced a poem wholly faithful to traditional Indian values could he have interested anybody besides the anthropologists? Does anybody read *Beowulf,* great as it is, besides scholars and the college students to whom they assign it? Has the admitted confusion of values in *Hamlet* ever seriously interfered with either its theatrical effectiveness or its greatness as a work of art? Must Chaucer's *Troilus and Criseyde* be thrown into the discard because its characters behave more like fourteenth-century English ladies and gentlemen than ancient Trojans? Surely there can be only one answer to all these questions. The plain truth of the matter is that no matter what his intentions may be, no creator of literature *can* escape from his own time, though Longfellow came much closer to doing it in "The Saga of King Olaf" than in *Hiawatha.* Surely the fact that Cabell went back to the sagas no more prevented *Hamlet Had an Uncle* from being an extremely "modern" book than *The Song of Hiawatha* escaped being a nineteenth-century work by a New England poet. But if we are to accept it, we shall have to accept it for what it is. We cannot accept only the aboriginal portion and reject Longfellow's treatment of it. Once begin dissecting the baby and you will soon find you have no baby left.

VII

The Courtship of Miles Standish

The Courtship of Miles Standish may not be the most important, as certainly it was not the most ambitious, of Longfellow's "long" poems, but one might easily argue that it comes closest to perfection. The narrative is faultlessly managed, the atmosphere of "the old Colony days, in Plymouth the land of the Pilgrims," is skillfully invoked, and when action is called for, it is handled without faltering.[1] The characterization is more detailed than in either *Evangeline* or *Hiawatha,* and the characters are presented more realistically and with greater sophistication. Humor appears notably for the first time, and the balance is held nicely even between comedy and drama. The hexameters of *Evangeline* reappear, but they have been shorn of their languorousness. As Bliss Perry observed,[2] "frequent iambic substitutions" make them "more supple and racy than those of the earlier poem," and though the poet still uses repetition for calculated effect, he is now never in danger of wearying the reader with it, as he was at times in *Hiawatha.*

Shortly after he had finished *Hiawatha,* the conflict between the Puritans and the Quakers was suggested to Longfellow as a promising subject. To this he turned finally in "The New England Tragedies," and it is interesting that *The Courtship of Miles Standish* also began, late in 1856, as a play. This was aborted, and about a year later he began "a new poem, 'Priscilla,' to be a kind of Puritan pastoral; the subject, the courtship of Miles Standish. This, I think, will be a better treatment of the subject than the one I wrote some time ago." Again he calls it "an idyll of the Old Colony times." The writing did not all go smoothly, and once at least he was very discouraged about it, but the narrative was completed on March 22, 1858, and published, along with other poems, on October 16. Boston alone gobbled up five thousand copies by noon on publication day; two months later there were twenty-five thousand copies of the American edition in print.

William Bradford's *History of Plymouth Plantation* (1856) was a comparatively newly published book when Longfellow wrote, but his principal sources seem to have been Alexander Young's *Chronicles of the Pilgrim Fathers,* which includes Winslow's account of the expedition of Miles Standish against the Indians, and Charles Wyllys Elliott's *New England History.* Longfellow was himself descended through his mother from one of the eleven children of John Alden and Priscilla Mullins, whose famous reply to Alden, when he came to woo her on behalf of Miles Standish—"Why don't you speak for yourself, John?"—had been preserved in family tradition. Iris Lilian Whitman's suggestion that the plot was derived from a Spanish play is not convincing.

Though the poem was finally called *The Courtship of Miles Standish,* Priscilla remains the principal figure. She understands both her absurd suitors perfectly and is never at a loss how to eliminate the one and hold the other. The contrast between the two men is broad enough so that it might easily have run into caricature, but Longfellow never permits this to happen. Thomas Morton had called Standish, the commander of a twelve-man army, "Captain Shrimpe," and Longfellow tells us that

Short of stature he was, but strongly built and athletic,
Broad in the shoulders, deep-chested, with muscles
    and sinews of iron;
Brown as a nut was his face, but his russet beard was already
Flaked with patches of snow, as hedges sometimes in
    November.

He lives surrounded by

            "the warlike weapons that hang here
Burnished and bright and clean, as if for parade or
    inspection!"

He takes pains to keep them thus

                "as if in an arsenal hanging;
That is because I have done it myself, and not left it to others.
Serve yourself, would you be well served, is an
    excellent adage."

His three favorite books are

Bariffe's Artillery Guide, and the Commentaries of Caesar
Out of the Latin translated by Arthur Goldinge of London,
And, as if guarded by these, between them was standing the
    Bible.

He hesitates before deciding

Which of the three he should choose for his consolation and
    comfort,
Whether the wars of the Hebrews, the famous campaigns of
    the Romans,
Or the Artillery practice, designed for belligerent Christians.

But he finally chooses the Caesar, perhaps as most in harmony with his own maxim,

> "if you wish a thing to be well done,
> You must do it yourself, you must not leave it to others."

Even such a maxim must be used "discreetly," however, and not so as to "waste powder for nothing." So, since Standish realizes that he is "a maker of war, and not a maker of phrases," when it comes to offering himself to Priscilla, he must send John Alden, a scholar and a master of "elegant language," to woo her in his behalf.

> "I can march up to a fortress and summon the place to
>   surrender,
> But march up to a woman with such a proposal, I dare not.
> I'm not afraid of bullets, nor shot from the mouth of a
>   cannon,
> But of a thundering 'No'! point blank from the mouth of a
>   woman,
> That I confess I'm afraid of, nor am I ashamed to confess it!"

Alden, of course, "his friend and household companion," is a totally different kind of man.

> Fair-haired, azure-eyed, with delicate Saxon complexion,
> Having the dew of his youth, and the beauty thereof, as
>   the captives
> Whom Saint Gregory saw, and exclaimed, "Not Angles,
>   but Angels."

His problem is that he himself loves Priscilla, though he has never told her. His absurdity is altogether different from his friend's. Though he recognizes that the impossible has been asked of him, he knows too that "the name of friendship is sacred," and he has no power to deny what is asked of him in that name. For what came to be called "the New England conscience" is already well developed in him, and he tries not only to face up to his ordeal but to regard it as God's command and a sorrow that he has brought upon himself through his own wickedness—a conviction as artificial and unreal under the circumstances as the borrowed language he uses to try to convince himself of it.

> "This is the hand of the Lord; it is laid upon me in anger,
> For I have followed too much the heart's desires and devices,
> Worshipping Astaroth blindly, and impious idols of Baal.
> This is the cross I must bear; the sin and the swift
>   retribution."

Nothing could have prepared him worse for what he had to do. To Priscilla, who knows what she wants and whose sound common sense never deserts her, such posturing could only make Alden seem as ridiculous in his own way as Standish himself, but because she loves him and cares not a whit for his principal, she regards his shortcomings much more indulgently than those of the other, and she needs only seven words—seven of the most famous words in American literature—to blow all Alden's fine pleadings for his friend sky-high: "Why don't you speak for yourself, John?"

No other words in the language could have served her better, and few could have served her so well, but there may be more question about the buildup Longfellow gives them:

> Archly the maiden smiled, and with eyes overrunning
>   with laughter,
> Said in a tremulous voice, "Why don't you speak for
>   yourself, John?"

One reader at least believes that she might have said them, as the historical Priscilla probably did, but would she have said them "archly," that is, coquettishly? And would she have spoken "in a tremulous voice" at the same time that her eyes were "overrunning with laughter"? These things seem much more doubtful. For Priscilla is, in her love relations, a true Shakespearean heroine, a descendant of Juliet and the rest, who know what they want, admit it frankly, and if necessary guide the stupid male into giving it to them. As Juliet puts it,

> If that thy bent of love be honorable,
> Thy purpose marriage, send me word tomorrow,
> By one that I'll procure to come to thee,
> Where and what time thou wilt perform the rite;
> And all my fortunes at thy foot I'll lay
> And follow thee my lord throughout the world.

And Priscilla, her lover having rushed out of her house "like a man insane," is quick-witted enough to suspect that the Caesar-obsessed Miles Standish might, in his disappointment, now see him as his Brutus and that he himself might be silly enough to go back to England with the *Mayflower*. So she takes herself down to the shore to see that this does not happen and there confronts John Alden frankly and talks out their situation.

> "Are you so much offended, you will not speak to me?" said she.
> "Am I so much to blame, that yesterday, when you were pleading
> Warmly the cause of another, my heart, impulsive and wayward,
> Pleaded your own, and spake out, forgetful perhaps of decorum?"

She cannot indeed offer, like Juliet, to follow her lord throughout the world, for her lord has not yet declared himself, but she does everything any girl could do at this stage to make sure he will not get away. Never mind that contemporary feminists might find her too apologetic, and remember that she qualified her apology for violating decorum with a "perhaps."

> "It was wrong, I acknowledge; for it is the fate of a woman
> Long to be patient and silent, to wait like a ghost that is
>   speechless,
> Till some questioning voice dissolves the spell of its silence.
> Hence is the inner life of so many suffering women
> Sunless and silent and deep, like subterranean rivers
> Running through caverns of darkness, unheard, unseen,
>   and unfruitful,
> Chafing their channels of stone, with endless and profitless
>   murmurs."

When her lover meets this with nonsense about "the beautiful rivers that watered the garden of Eden" and "the river Euphrates, through deserts of Havilah flowing," all about as relevant to the situation in hand as his vision of himself worshipping Baal and Astaroth or his comparison of himself to David lusting after Bathsheba—"It hath displeased the Lord! It is the temptation of Satan!"—she loses her patience and interrupts him, for such silly talk only convinces her

> "How very little you prize me, or care for what I am saying.
> When from the depths of my heart, in pain and with secret
>   misgiving,
> Frankly I speak to you, asking for sympathy only and
>   kindness,
> Staightway you take up my words, that are plain and
>   direct and in earnest,
> Turn them away from their meaning and answer with
>   flattering phrases."

Nor will it do to argue that she has thought this out since John Alden's ambassadorial visit to her, for she had been equally clear-sighted and direct upon that occasion.

> "If the great Captain of Plymouth is so very eager to wed me,
> Why does he not come himself, and take the trouble to woo
>   me?
> If I am not worth the wooing, I surely am not worth the
>   winning!"

The resemblance to Juliet when her parents would thrust the County Paris upon her is very close here:

> I wonder at this haste that I must wed
> Ere he that should be husband comes to woo.

And her realism never shows more frankly than when Alden makes everything as bad as he possibly could by urging that Standish has no time for courtlhip, and she replies,

> "Has he no time for such things, as you call it, before he is married,
> Would he be likely to find it, or make it, after the wedding?"

But I must not leave the impression that only Priscilla is characterized realistically or psychologically and that John Alden is a lay figure. His romanticizing is as true to his character as her realism is to hers, and there is one startling moment of truth in Longfellow's portrayal of him that has not, I think, received its due meed of praise. The tale was skillfully plotted so that Miles Standish was obliged to go off to fight the Indians immediately upon John Alden's return from Priscilla, and though the lovers reach their understanding quickly, they do not venture to make plans for their marriage until after they have received the false news that he has been killed. Then,

> John Alden, upstarting, as if the barb of the arrow
> Piercing the heart of his friend had struck his own, and had sundered
> Once and forever the bonds that held him bound as a captive,
> Wild with excess of sensation, the awful delight of his freedom,
> Mingled with pain and regret, unconscious of what he was doing,
> Clasped, almost with a groan, the motionless form of Priscilla,

> Pressing her close to his heart, as forever his own, and
>   exclaiming:
> "Those whom the Lord hath united, let no man put
>   asunder!"

Even now he must express himself in terms of a pious quotation, yet what does the passage mean but that he is ecstatic because his friend's death has at last made it possible for him to claim his love, and what is human nature here if not quite naked and unashamed? This passage comes just after we have been told that when disentangling her yarn from her lover's clumsy hands, Priscilla sometimes inadvertently touched them, she sent "electrical thrills through every nerve in his body." Human passion is touched very lightly and delicately in both passages. But it is enough. [3]

The final canto, "The Wedding-Day," is effective both in itself and in its contrast to the more restrained, more Puritan tone of the rest of the poem. This has been noticed by a number of critics, but Edward Hirsh has described it so well that one can only quote:

The marriage of John and Priscilla, however humorous its preliminaries, is, nevertheless, in the barely surviving Plymouth colony that is the setting, an affirmation of faith in America's future and a promise of its fruitfulness. Thus the almost lush description of the climactic bridal day is without serious incongruity set forth in images of religious ritual and of fertility, as the sun issues forth like a high priest, with the sea a laver at his feet, and Priscilla rides on a snow-white bull to her wedding while golden sunlight gleams on bunches of purple grapes. Longfellow again introduces the imagery of Eden and expulsion as he describes the land of privation and hardship lying before John and Priscilla and adds,

> But, to their eyes transfigured, it seemed as the
>   Garden of Eden,
> Filled with the presence of God, whose voice was the
>   sound of the ocean.

The final balance of sometimes broad humor, romantic sentiment, and gravity is a tonal achievement of no small order.[4]

Nearly all the literary allusions in *The Courtship of Miles Standish* are Biblical, as befits a tale that deals with so Bible-centered a people as the Pilgrims. Possibly the military aspects of the poem gave the author a little trouble however. Except for Hobomok, who takes the part of the white men against his own people (one is never quite sure why), the Indians are more like those in *Evangeline* than in *Hiawatha,* and Standish and his men slaughter Pecksuot and Wattawamat without compunction. For that matter, at the very beginning of the poem, Standish had compared the brass howitzer on the church roof to "a preacher who speaks to the purpose." Later we are told that it was placed there to shoot down red devils, not red squirrels, and that this is the "only tongue that is understood by a savage." It is true that "the excellent Elder of Plymouth" tries to be conciliatory when the Indian challenge is received, but he seems to stand alone, and Standish is quite in the spirit of modern "gunboat diplomacy" when he takes the rattlesnake skin that the Indians had sent stuffed with arrows and sends it back stuffed with powder and bullets. Like "the mighty men of David," the Pilgrims are "giants in heart,"

> who believed in God and the Bible, —
> Ay, who believed in the smiting of Midianites ad Philistines.

Longfellow handles it all without much "tendency," but it is hard not to believe that he sympathized with Priscilla when the head of Wattawamat was mounted above the Pilgrims' fortress-church.

> All who beheld it rejoiced, and praised the Lord, and took
>   courage.
> Only Priscilla averted her face from this spectre of terror,
> Thanking God in her heart that she had not married
>   Miles Standish.

VIII

Tales of a Wayside Inn

Longfellow's gift for narrative being what it was, it became inevitable that sooner or later he should produce something like the *Tales of a Wayside Inn,* which Newton Arvin regarded as his major poetic achievement.[1] It was published in three parts, the first in 1863 in the same volume with "Flight the Second" of the "Birds of Passage" (who had flown first in 1858 with *The Courtship of Miles Standish*), the second in 1872 in *Three Books of Song,* along with "Judas Maccabeus" and "A Handful of Translations," and the last in *Aftermath* (1874), together with the third flight of the birds.[2] "The Saga of King Olaf," which is as much the most elaborate piece in the series as "The Knight's Tale" is in *The Canterbury Tales,* had been written as early as 1860 and what is now its first division, "The Challenge of Thor," about a decade before that and originally intended for inclusion in the *Christus.* It is amusing that Longfellow, who seldom troubled to visit the scenes of his poems, should have gone to the Red-Horse Tavern in Sudbury, Massachusetts, as the very end of October 1862, *after* he had begun writing the "Prelude" in which it is described. He had intended to go earlier, but the "damp weather" had made it "hardly worth while." Shortly after his visit, he wrote his publisher, James T. Fields, that "The Sudbury Tales," as he then planned to call his work, went on "famously" and that he had finished five stories.

The Red-Horse Tavern in Sudbury, Massachusetts is now, thanks to Longfellow, the Wayside Inn. Henry Ford bought it in 1923 and after it burned had it accurately rebuilt in every detail. The original building was erected in 1686 by an English family named Howe, and after they lost their fortune, they turned their house into an inn, or, as Longfellow says, "a house of call for travellers from Boston westward," which it remained until Lyman Howe, who belonged to the fifth generation of innkeepers, died in 1861. After his death the building was not again used as an inn until 1896.[3]

All the tale-tellers gathered at the inn in Longfellow's work were real people.[4] The Landlord was of course Lyman Howe. The Student was Henry Ware Wells, who died young and left his books to Harvard College. The Spanish Jew was Isaac Edrehi. The Italian was Luigi Monti, a post-1848 refugee, whom Longfellow had succored by making him a teacher of Italian in his department of modern languages. The Musician was the famous Norwegian violinist Ole Bull. The (amateur) Theologian was Daniel Treadwell, a professor of physics at Harvard, who appears in the "Prelude" as "still perplext / With thoughts of this world and the next" and as holding religious views much like those of Arthur Kavanagh in Longfellow's novel, believing that "the deed, and not the creed, / Would help us in our utmost need" and dreaming of a universal church

> Lofty as the love of God,
> And ample as the wants of man.

Finally, the Poet was Thomas William Parsons, best remembred today for his excellent translation of Dante's "Inferno."

The Landlord tells the first tale and the last—"Paul Revere's Ride" and "The Rhyme of Sir Christopher." The Student and the Spanish Jew each have four, the former "The Falcon of Ser Federigo," "The Cobbler of Hagenau," "The Baron of Saint Castine," and "Emma and Eginhard," and the latter "The Legend of Rabbi Ben Levi," "Kambalu," "Azrael," and "Scanderberg." All the rest get three apiece—the Sicilian "King Robert of Sicily," "The Bell of Atri," and "The Monk of Casal-Maggiore"; the Musician "The Saga of King Olaf," "The Ballad of Carmilhan," and "The Mother's Ghost"; the Theologian "Torquemada," "The Legend Beautiful," and "Elizabeth"; and the poet "The Birds of Killing-worth," "Lady Wentworth," and "Charlemagne."

Since Longfellow himself mentions *The Canterbury Tales,* it is impossible to avoid comparing his work with Chaucer's masterpiece. His smaller, stationary group of narrators is of course much less varied in type and background than Chaucer's.[5] In spite of the picturesqueness of the old inn with its romantic properties, Longfellow's reader fastens his attention on the tales themselves, tending to disregard their tellers, while with Chaucer, the prologue and the links hold their own in interest with the best of the stories. None of Longfellow's tales are awkwardly or inappropriately assigned, but none is a dramatic utterance in the sense that this term can be applied to "The Pardoner's Tale" or "The Tale of the Wife of Bath." About the most exciting thing that happens at the inn is the snapping of two strings on the Musician's Stradivarius.

The differences of opinion that develop between the tale-tellers (they are never really quarrels, as in Chaucer) concern aesthetic matters only. Innocent as "The Falcon of Ser Federigo" is, the Theologian seizes upon the Student's telling of it to compare Italian tales in general to "a stagnant fen," and the Student pays him back when he

finds the Theologian's own first tale, the horrible
"Torquemada," unsuited to the company at the inn. But
when the Poet, introducing "Lady Wentworth," disparages the European tales that have been told by describing them as

> "Flowers gathered from a crumbling wall,
> Dead leaves that rustle as they fall,"

and proposes instead

> "Something of our New England earth,
> A tale, which, though of no great worth,
> Has still this merit, that it yields
> A certain freshness of the fields,
> A sweetness as of home-made bread,"

he sets off a controversy which runs through several in-
terludes. The Student immediately objects that

> "if the flour be fresh and sound,
> And if the bread be light and sweet,
> Who careth in what mill 't was ground,
> Or of what oven felt the heat,
> Unless, as old Cervantes said,
> You are looking after better bread
> Than any that is made of wheat?"

After the Poet has told his tale, the Theologian reopens
the controversy concerning foreign versus native materials,
granting "Lady Wentworth" "a certain freshness as of
home-made bread," but insisting that it is "not less sweet
and not less fresh" than "many legends that I know, /
Writ by the monks of long ago," and later, even in Part
Three after the Theologian has told the story of
"Elizabeth," the Student will not let go. "Elizabeth," he
declares, is "a pleasant and a winsome tale," in spite of its
paleness and quietness,

> "As if it caught its tone and air
> From the gray suits that Quakers wear,"

but he is impish in finding it

> "worthy of some German bard,
> Hebel, or Voss, or Eberhard,
> Who love of humble themes to sing,"

and he adheres stubbornly to his own opinion in maintaining that it is "no more true / Than was the tale I told to you." At the end, all the tale-tellers take their departure, and Longfellow goes out of his way to assure us that "nevermore / Their feet would pass that threshold o'er."

> Two are beyond the salt sea waves,
> And three already in their graves.

Of the twenty-two tales told, only six have American settings. Italy predominates among the European countries represented.[6] Spain contributes only "Torquemada." "The Saga of King Olaf" and "The Mother's Ghost" represent Scandinavia. There are echoes from eastern Europe, the near East, and the Orient in four stories.[7] Religion is important in at least seven,[8] and at least six[9] involve the supernatural. There are two excellent ballads—"Paul Revere's Ride" and "The Ballad of Carmilhan"—and two—"The Cobbler of Hagenau" and "The Monk of Casal-Maggiore"—use fabliau material. In scope the tales vary from such brief, anecdotal, and comparatively insignificant pieces as "Rabbi Ben Levi," "Kambalu," "Azrael," and "Charlemagne" to "The Saga of King Olaf," with its twenty-one sections. The meters employed are as varied as the subject matter of the tales, including pentameter couplets, octosyllables, ottava rima, blank verse, dactylic hexameters, ballad stanzas, and others.[10]

The tenderness so characteristic of Longfellow predominates in "The Birds of Killingworth" and "The Bell of Atri," but "King Olaf" and "Scanderberg" are violent in the extreme, and "Torquemada" and "Kambalu" might well be called horror stories. In contrast to the piety of pieces like "King Robert of Sicily," both "The Falcon of Ser Federigo" and "Emma and Eginhard" are kindly and wordly-wise; the latter, in which Charlemagne discovers that his daughter has spent the night with his secretary and instead of punishing the lovers, as his advisers recommend, arranges for their marriage, is much the most erotic piece in the collection.[11] Sex is of some importance too in "The Baron of Saint Castine" and in "Lady Wentworth," where a May and December marriage between the governor and

> A thin slip of a girl, like a new moon,
> Sure to be rounded into beauty soon,
> A creature men would worship and adore,

who had been rebuked by one of the staid matrons of the town—

> "O Martha Hilton! Fie! how dare you go
> About the town half dressed, and looking so!"—

is presented with complete sympathy.

As to the derivation of the tales,[12] "Paul Revere's Ride" may have been based upon the rider's own narrative,[13] and "The Birds of Killingworth" appears to have been suggested by an actual war on birds in the Connecticut town named.[14] "The Ballad of Carmilhan," obviously Germanic or Scandinavian, bears a general resemblance to the legends of the Flying Dutchman, but no specific source seems to have been identified. The story told in "The Falcon of Ser Federigo" is as old as or older than the *Panchatantra*, but Longfellow follows Boccaccio's version

(*Decameron,* Fifth Day, ninth story) very closely, though
he fleshes out the characters considerably and comes up
with something far superior to Tennyson's one-act play,
The Falcon. This tale has what is now called an "O. Henry
ending." Monna Giovanna comes to her former, rejected,
and now impoverished suitor, to beg him to save the life of
her son by giving up his beloved falcon, which the dying
child craves, but he, unaware in his poverty of the object of
her visit, sacrifices his most cherished possession to provide
her with a delectable dinner dish. The boy dies, but the
mother is sufficiently moved by this evidence of her old
lover's devotion to marry him. Both "The Legend of Rabbi Ben Levi" and "Azrael" seem to go back to rabbinical
sources, but Longfellow is believed to have got "Ben Levi"
from his friend Emmanuel Scherb. The very old story of
"King Robert of Sicily" is told in the *Gesta Romanorum*
and other venerable sources, and one would also expect
Longfellow to have known Leigh Hunt's version of it, "A
Jar of Honey from Mt. Hybla."[15] Samuel Laing's 1844
translation of the *Heimskringla* of Snorri Sturleson was the
principal source of "The Saga of King Olaf," but
Longfellow was probably also influenced by Tegnér's
Frithiof's Saga.[16] "Torquemada," the dreadful tale of the
fanatical hidalgo whose "sole diversion was to hunt the
boar," attend the bullfight,

> Or in the crowd with lighted taper stand,
> When Jews were burned, or banished from the land,

and who, having learned that his daughters are heretics,
not only betrays them to the Inquisition but begs the
privilege of lighting their death pyre with his own hand,
comes from De Castro's *Protestantes Españolas.*

In Part Second "The Bell of Atri" was taken from
Gualteruzzi's *Canto Novelle Antiche.* Longfellow's feeling
for animals here is akin to that displayed in "The Birds of
Killingworth," for the poor horse whom the greedy knight

has turned adrift tugs at the vines of briony attached to the bell which the lord of Atri had installed so that even his humblest subjects might ring for justice and be heard. The poet got "Kambalu" (which Poe might have handled very differently in the vein of "The Pit and the Pendulum") from Marco Polo and "The Cobbler of Hagenau," an amusing but not entirely fair or accurate account of indulgences, from D'Aubigné's *History of the Reformation.* "Lady Wentworth" came from C. W. Brewster's *Rambles about Portsmouth* and the story of "The Baron of Saint Castine," who takes an Indian bride, from Williamson's *History of Maine.* [17] Jeremy Taylor supplied "The Legend Beautiful," in which a monk to whom Christ has appeared in his cell deserts the Beatific Vision to minister to the poor at the convent gates, not sure of anything except that he must do his duty and leave the rest to God, and learns that "Hadst thou stayed, I must have fled!"

Part Third, which opens with "Azrael," contains two stories about Charlemagne. The first, which is called simply by his name, is based on the chronicle, *De Factis Caroli Magni,* as quoted by Cantù in *Storia degli Italiani,* [18] and is of little interest, but "Emma and Eginhard" is more noteworthy. [19] If, as has been suggested, it is inferior to Alfred de Musset's version in *"La Neige,"* it still seems something of a changeling in Longfellow's oeuvre. I once playfully remarked that it was a wonder it had not caused the *Tales* to be "banned in Boston," and it still seems odd to me that he should have been able to present the situation so completely free from moralizing or that his having done so should apparently have been passed by with so little comment. What *was* profoundly characteristic of him, however, was that the emphasis should have fallen so completely not on the daughter's transgression but on the father's charity. The Quaker tale "Elizabeth" was derived from "The Youthful Emigrant," a story by Lydia Maria Child which Longfellow read in a Portland paper, but he also had access to a pious book, *A Call to the Unfaithful Professors of Truth,* which had been written by the hero of the story, John Estaugh, and contained a preface by his widow. "The Monk of Casal-Maggiore" comes from a collection of Italian stories by Michele Colombo; "Scanderberg" is ascribed tentatively to "the old chronicler Ben Meir" in the interlude that follows its telling; "The Mother's Ghost" is a translation of a Danish ballad in Grundtvig's great collection.

"The Rhyme of Sir Christopher," one of the most light-hearted of the tales, deals with much the same kind of material that Hawthorne used in "The Maypole of Merry Mount." There is a certain slyness involved in Longfellow's presentation of the rascal who is the hero of this tale, which may remind us that the establishment is not treated with excessive reverence in "The Cobbler of Hagenau" or the frolicsome and extravagant "Monk of Casal-Maggiore" either; these stories could hardly be more different than they are from such touching, pious pieces as "The Legend Beautiful" and "King Robert of Sicily." For that matter, no clerical sycophant could have created the Parson in even so tender a story as "The Birds of Killingworth":

> The Parson, too, appeared, a man austere,
>   The instinct of whose nature was to kill;
> The wrath of God he preached from year to year,
>   And read, with fervor, Edwards on the Will;
> His favorite pastime was to slay the deer
>   In Summer on some Adirondac hill;
> E'en now, while walking down the rural land,
> He lopped the wayside lilies with his cane.

Such a passage may remind us that there is an underlying consistency of character or temperament manifesting itself through all the variety of these tales, so that we ought not to be surprised upon finding that "Torquemada," a tale

in which devils themselves might well take lessons from
the pious, should also call forth some of Longfellow's
strongest expressions of sympathy:

> O pious skies! why did your clouds retain
> For peasants' fields their floods of hoarded rain?
> O pitiless earth! why open no abyss
> To bury in its chasm a crime like this?

Though nobody would pretend that the *Tales of a
Wayside Inn* can sustain serious comparison with *The Canterbury Tales,* it is still our best American poetic story
book, and the intensive reading to which it has been subjected during its long history has no doubt sufficiently
sorted out its more significant tales from those that may
safely be passed over quickly. Yet there is still room for the
discriminating reader to find personal favorites that other
readers may have overlooked. Sometimes, even, over-
familiarity may have dulled appreciation, as notably with
"Paul Revere's Ride." It is much, no doubt, that
"through the gloom and the light. / The fate of a nation
was riding that night," but there is more to the poem than
patriotic fervor or "the hurrying hoof-beats of that steed"
as they echo through it. Many a poet who could have com-
passed the hoof-beats would have been quite incapable of
the Gothic vision of the *Somerset* in Boston harbor,

> A phantom ship, with each mast and spar
> Across the moon like a prison bar,
> And a huge black hulk, that was magnified
> By its own reflection in the tide.

Surely Revere's friend is impressive as he climbed

> the tower of the old North Church,
> By the wooden stairs, with stealthy tread,
> To the belfry-chamber overhead,

where he

> startled the pigeons from their perch
> On the sombre rafters, that round him made
> Masses and moving shapes of shade,—
> By the trembling ladder, steep and tall,
> To the highest window in the wall,
> Where he paused to listen and look down
> A moment on the roofs of the town,
> And the moonlight flowing over all.

And certainly the passage which follows is pure vintage Longfellow:

> Beneath, in the churchyard, lay the dead,
> In their night-encampment on the hill,
> Wrapped in silence so deep and still
> That he could hear, like a sentinel's tread,
> The watchful night-wind, as it went
> Creeping along from tent to tent,
> And seeming to whisper, ''All is well!''

This may not be the best poetry ever written, but there is not much better in kind, and generations of elocutionists have not succeeded in spoiling it. Nor is it exactly what one expects to encounter in an action poem.

On the other hand, ''The Ballad of Carmilhan'' seems to me to have received considerably less acclaim than it deserves; Saintsbury's dismissal of it as ''sham 'silly sooth' '' is itself quite as silly as his fire-eating condemnation of ''The Arsenal at Springfield'' as ''a piece of mere claptrap'' and ''merely an instance of a cant common at the time.'' Though it is only a cadet in the company commanded by ''The Rime of the Ancient Mariner,'' ''Carmilhan'' is surely no unworthy recruit. The ''jolly skipper,'' cut from the same fool cloth as him of the *Hesperus,* who would like to see the ''ship of the Dead'' that is "called the Carmilhan," and who swears that should he do so,

> He would run her down, although he ran
> Right into Eternity!

is a classic case study of hubris, and the Klaboterman as clearly one of the most considerate of all malign spirits. He makes a surprisingly strong impression upon the reader in view of how little we see of him, and he endears himself to us because he spares the cabin boy, who, like Ishmael in *Moby-Dick* alone survives the wreck. This "simple country lad" is out of place on the *Valdemar,* and when he hears the sailors blaspheme,

> He thought of home, he thought of God,
> And his mother under the churchyard sod,
> And wished it were a dream.

This is not lost on the Klaboterman,

> Who saw the Bible in his chest,
> And made a sign upon his breast,
> All evil things to ban.

But if this is vintage Longfellow, what shall be said of "The Saga of King Olaf"? It may not be what Newton Arvin called "incomparably the most successful of all the tales in the *Wayside Inn*" (certainly it has not been the most popular), but there can be no question about the technical virtuosity Longfellow displays in the astonishing variety of verse forms and measures he employed in it. The difficulty is posed by what Arvin himself called "its sustained celebration of the virtues, and even the vices, of an age of warlike action." Succumbing for once to Freudian balderdash, Arvin ascribed this to the "con-

tradictory streak of imaginative violence'' buried in
Longfellow's own quiet and kindly makeup.

Whether it be ascribed to Longfellow's own complexes
or to his mastery of his medium in a poem which sought to
recapture the spirit of the sagas, there can be no question
that the violence is there. The hero is the tenth-century
Viking who ''christianized'' the North, apparently without ever having succeeded in christianizing himself or even
finding out what Christianity is.

> ''Choose ye between two things, my folk,
> To be baptized or given up to slaughter!''

He sets out to preach the gospel with his sword or be
brought back in his shroud. His drunken priest,
''swaggering Thrangbrand,'' is the right lieutenant for
him, and one stubborn heathen who remains unattracted
by the ''White Christ'' is forced to swallow an adder. Nor
do the women fare much better than the men. Olaf wishes
to marry Queen Sigrid, but when she refuses to forsake her
ancestral faith, he calles her a ''faded old woman, a
heathenish jade'' and strikes her in the face with his glove.
Only in the last canto, ''The Nun of Nidaros,'' which, like
the introduction, ''The Challenge of Thor,'' stands apart
from the rest of the poem, is there any true Christian
feeling.

> ''The dawn is not distant,
> Nor is the night starless;
> Love is eternal!
> God is still God, and
> His faith shall not fail us;
> Christ is eternal!''

IX

Later Poems

All Longfellow's collections of short poems, up to and including *The Seaside and the Fireside* (1850) were considered in Chapter IV of this volume. The present chapter concerns itself with those that followed.

The most substantial of these was "Birds of Passage," which, like *Tales of a Wayside Inn*, was published in parts, appearing in five "flights," as Longfellow fancifully called them. The first flight was made in 1858 in the same volume with *The Courtship of Miles Standish;* the second in 1863 with the first part of the *Tales* themselves; the third in 1873, along with "Part Third" of the *Tales*, in *Aftermath;* the fourth in *The Masque of Pandora and Other Poems* (1875); and the last in *Kéramos and Other Poems* (1878). The "Birds of Passage" will be considered together here, as they appear in the collected editions.

The first flight was by far the most sustained, covering twenty-four poems. There are only seven in the second, nine in the third, and eight in the fourth, but the fifth was up again to sixteen.

It should go without saying that Longfellow's metrical skill was manifested again in these poems and in the fullness of its development. He was much freer in admitting variations than many persons believe him to have been and in some instances rather startlingly anticipative of innovations supposedly introduced by later poets who often thought of themselves as in rebellion against his kind of poetry, and he did not always write so that he who runs may read.

By all means the most famous poem in the first flight is the almost universally admired "My Lost Youth," which supplied Robert Frost with the title for his first book, *A Boy's Will,* and which is certainly one of the most successful of all American poems of reminiscence. It is old Portland that Longfellow is remembering—"the beautiful town / That is seated by the sea," "the shadowy lines of its trees," "the sheen of the far-surrounding sea,"

> the black wharves and the slips,
> And the sea-tides tossing free;
> And Spanish sailors with bearded lips,
> And the beauty and mystery of the ships,
> And the magic of the sea,

as well as

> the bulwarks by the shore,
> And the fort upon the hill;
> The sunrise gun, with its hollow roar,
> The drum-beat repeated o'er and o'er,

to say nothing of "the sea-fight far away," which "thundered o'er the tide," in which both the captain of the American *Enterprise* and he of the British *Boxer* were slain in 1813, to be brought into the town by the victorious Americans and buried there "o'erlooking the tranquil bay." Best of all, however, he remembers

> the breezy dome of groves,
> The shadows of Deering's Woods;
> And the friendships old and the early loves,

which form

> the gleams and glooms that dart
> Across the school-boy's brain;
> The song and the silence in the heart,
> That in part are prophecies, and in part
> Are longings wild and vain.

It is this above all else that makes "the strong heart weak, /And bring[s] a pallor into the cheek," and into his mind the words of the old Lapland song that he repeats at the end of each stanza:

> "A boy's will is the wind's will,
> And the thoughts of youth are long, long thoughts."

Longfellow found it in Herder's translation:

> *Knabenwille ist Winderwille,*
> *Jünglings Gedanken lange Gedanken.*[1]

The only possible question about the complete success of the poem must be whether ten refrains do not make for a certain monotony.

At least three of the poems in "Flight the First" are definitely occasional: "The Warden of the Cinque Ports," a memorial tribute to the Duke of Wellington, which comes rather unexpectedly from the generally pacifistic Longfellow, especially so late as 1852; "The Fiftieth Birthday of Agassiz," which is interesting for its personifiction of nature and the poet's obvious focusing upon the spiritual significance of nature study rather than those aspects that a scientist would think of first of all; and "Catawba Wine," which was occasioned by a gift from the Ohio Valley vineyards of the contemporary Nicholas Longworth, and which is perhaps Longfellow's only really chauvinistic utterance. For if,

> The revel of the ruddy wine,
> And all occasions of excess

deserve the castigation he gives them in "The Ladder of
St. Augustine," then surely it is nonsense to condemn
"the Borgia wine" and the foreign vintages

> To rack our brains
> With the fever pains,
> That have driven the Old World frantic,

only to praise the Catawba, "pure as a spring," simply
because it is American. In a sense, "Santa Filomena,"
which presents Florence Nightingale as the "Lady with a
Lamp" of the Crimean War, was occasional also, but the
title and the implied identification of its heroine with the
saint came from Mrs. Jameson's *Sacred and Legendary Art*;
"the palm, the lily, and the spear" of the final stanza are
in a picture of the saint in the church of San Francisco at
Pisa. "Santa Filomena" gains a certain extrinsic interest
from having been Longfellow's first contribution to the
Atlantic Monthly, where it appeared in the very first number, November, 1857.

There are four straight narrative poems in the first series.
"The Phantom Ship" and "The Discoverer of the North
Cape" came from Longfellow's reading, the first from a
passage in Cotton Mather's *Magnalia Christi* and the
second from Orosius. "The Emperor's Bird's-Nest" is a
curious and rather tender story about an oddly humane
whim of "the Emperor Charles of Spain" on a campaign
in Flanders, and "Victor Galbraith" (Longfellow's "Dan-
ny Deever") is a bloody narrative, derived from a
newspaper paragraph, about a soldier shot before Mon-
terey for some unspecified breach of discipline. In form,
"Sandolphon," an old Jewish story which has an affinity
with the Spanish Jew's narratives in *Tales of a Wayside
Inn,* [2] is a narrative poem also, but this time the interest

inheres less in the story itself than in "the beautiful, strange superstition" that "haunts" and "holds" the poet and inspires a "frenzy and fire" in his brain and which the closing stanzas do not quite seem to account for.

All the rest are in one way or another reflective poems. "Prometheus" and "Epimetheus," both about poetry, describe the painful contrast between the ecstasy of creation and the inevitable following disappointment over what has actually been achieved. Longfellow makes it clear that for him it is only through the efforts of "the Poet, Prophet, Seer" that nations are made "nobler, freer," and that life can come to its flowering, but he also realizes, as did Goethe, that

> Only those are crowned and sainted
> Who with grief have been acquainted,

and that even the efforts doomed to disappointment are worth making. Another poem, "Oliver Basselin," written to praise the fifteenth-century poet of "the Valley of the Vire," is in harmony with this. "His songs were not divine," nor did they belong to that "high art" which finds "an answer in each heart," but Longfellow's feeling that he is nevertheless worth remembering is in harmony with the views he expresses elsewhere, notably in the early poem, "The Day Is Done," which has already been quoted, and in the somewhat Wordsworthian "Children," in itself a kind of poem about poetry, which concludes,

> Ye are better than all the ballads
>   That ever were sung or said;
> For ye are the living poems,
>   And all the rest are dead. [3]

Neither of the two churchyard poems have anything in common with the sickish verses of the "graveyard school"

that had still not quite outlived its popularity in
Longfellow's time. ''The Jewish Cemetery at Newport'' is
primarily a denunciation of anti-Semitism, showing the
poet in agreement with George W. Cable's view of the
Jews as ''a race to which the Christian world owes a larger
debt of gratitude incurred from the days of Abraham until
now, and from which it should ask more forgiveness than
to and from any other people that ever trod the earth.''
These words were occasioned by the death of the American
poet Emma Lazarus, who objected to Longfellow's poem,
though recognizing his sympathy, because he seemed to
assume that there was no future for Judaism. This view is
largely explained, however, by the fact that the Touro
synagogue, which adjoins the Newport cemetery, was inac-
tive in Longfellow's time. And it is for this reason too that
even Emma Lazarus's own poem, ''In the Jewish
Synagogue at Newport,'' has much the same tone.[4] ''In
the Churchyard at Cambridge,'' a considerably odder and
more original poem, is a meditation over the grave of
Madame Vassall, the original owner of what is now the
Longfellow House, in the graveyard adjoining Christ
Church, who was said to have been buried with one slave
at her head and another at her feet. Was this ''foolish
pomp'' and worldly vanity, the poet asks, or was it
''Christian charity,'' illustrating the equality of all God's
children in death, but he considers even the question
''rude'' and exhorts the reader not to expect the mystery to
be cleared up at the Judgment, but to occupy himself instead with what may be revealed concerning his own
''secret sins'' on that day, a characteristically humane
ending.[5]

A number of other poems are concerned with death.
''The Two Angels'' (representing death and life) was inspired by the fact that the first Mrs. James Russell Lowell
died in Cambridge at about the same time that Edith
Longfellow was born. More striking is ''Haunted Houses,''
a piece startlingly anticipative of Thomas Hardy.

> All houses wherein men have lived and died
>> Are haunted houses. Through the open doors
> The harmless phantoms on their errands glide,
>> With feet that make no sound upon the floors.

"We have no title-deeds to house or lands" and "the spirit-world around this world of sense / Floats like an atmosphere," from which the conclusions that Longfellow draws, though partly moralistic, are more metaphysical. "Haunted Houses" is not the only poem in the first flight that bears traces of the moralizing that moderns deplore in Longfellow, but only "The Ladder of St. Augustine," an exposition of the saint's view

> That of our vices we can frame
> A ladder, if we will but tread
> Beneath our feet each deed of shame!

is primarily didactic. One stanza ranks among Longfellow's most frequently quoted lines:

> The heights by great men reached and kept
>> Were not attained by sudden flight,
> But they, while their companions slept,
>> Were toiling upward in the night.

Finally, "Daybreak," which begins with a personified wind that "came up out of the sea," achieves a brief roll call of earthly activities. Though not primarily concerned with death, it does have a rather macabre ending:

> It crossed the churchyard with a sigh,
> And said, "Not yet! In quiet lie."

It is possible, however, that Longfellow may have intended this to be religious rather than macabre.

Both "The Ropewalk" and "The Golden Milestone" are developed much like "The Arsenal at Springfield." "The Golden Milestone" (the Roman *millerium aureum*)

is a man's own hearth, and Longfellow permits it to
suggest the various types of human experience, both good
and bad, that center around it. "The Ropewalk" connects
with "My Lost Youth" in that both are remembrances of
Portland. Here the poet's imagination conjures up the different uses to which ropes may be put—a swing for girls,
support for an aerialist in a circus, means for a coun-
trywoman to draw up water for a well, equipment for a
bellringer or a fisherman and for ships dragging their an-
chors. Surely Longfellow's vision of the circus girl does not
focus on the aspect that most men would think of first:

> Then a booth of mountebanks,
> With a smell of tar and planks,
>   And a girl poised high in air
> On a cord, in spangled dress,
> With a faded loveliness,
>   And a weary look of care.

And, however this may be, certainly the use of the rope in
the prison-yard scene testifies still more eloquently to his
humanity:

> Ah! it is the gallows-tree!
> Breath of Christian charity,
> Blow, and sweep it from the earth!

There is much of what later came to be known as imagism
in this poem, and Amy Lowell, who was once reported as
having taken it as her mission to rid the world of
Longfellow, might well herself have been proud of the first
stanza of "Daylight and Moonlight":

> In broad daylight, and at noon,
> Yesterday I saw the moon
> Sailing high, but faint and white,
> Like a school-boy's paper kite.

The brief second flight of the "Birds of Passage" opens with "The Children's Hour," which has been set to music, but with an unfortunately abbreviated text, by Charles Ives.[6] The last poem in the collection, "Weariness," is likewise concerned with "little feet," "little hands," "little hearts," and "little souls," soon destined to bear such burdens as now oppress the writer, though at the end, his emphasis shifts, moralistically, to the contrast between the whiteness of their souls and the sad condition of his own. Weariness weighs down the penultimate poem, "Something Left Undone," even more than the one so denominated, and though the children are not specifically mentioned in it, they obviously had their share in causing it. "A Day of Sunshine," however, despite its weak ending, is one of the most ardent pieces of Longfellow ever wrote:

> Through every fibre of my brain,
> Through every nerve, though every vein,
> I feel the electric thrill, the touch
> Of life, that seems almost too much.

There is plenty of zest too, though of a different kind, along with an unusual stanza form, in the Civil War poem, "The Cumberland," celebrating the "brave hearts that went down in the sea" and congratulating the "brave land" that possessed "hearts like these" when the sloop was sunk by the *Merrimack* off Newport News, on March 8, 1862, rather than surrender. Perhaps Longfellow was thinking of the uncle for whom he had been named, who died under comparable circumstances in Tripoli harbor.

As for the other two poems, "Snow-Flakes" opens quite as imagistically as "Daylight and Moonlight," but then takes off into a somewhat forced parallelism between nature and human emotions. "Enceladus" is a more ambitious poem inspired by Longfellow's sympathy with the

Italian struggle for freedom, and its earnings were
dedicated to relief purposes. Enceladus is the giant imprisoned in Mount Aetna, but he is also the country
struggling to be free; the double symbolism leaves the
reader feeling uncomfortably that he is expected to look
forward to the eruption of a volcano as a blessing.
Longfellow's incorrigible bookishness comes out
everywhere, even in his domestic poems. When "grave
Alice, laughing Allegra, and Edith with golden hair" raid
his study in "The Children's Hour," he thinks "of the
Bishop of Bingen / In his Mouse-Tower on the Rhine!"
and in "Something Left Undone," he cannot even think
of domestic chores without seeing himself

> Like the dwarfs of times gone by,
> Who, as Northern legends say,
> On their shoulders held the sky.

Except for "The Challenge" there is nothing very new
in "Flight the Third," and there is certainly nothing
metrically startling, but all eight of the comparatively
minor pieces included are entirely successful on their own
terms. Three are concerned with poetry, one of them only
by implication. The first, "Fata Morgana," deals with the
elusiveness and capriciousness of poetic inspiration; the
poet compares it to a mirage in the desert, which can be
glimpsed but not seized upon; he might with equal ap-
propriateness have compared it to the mystical experience.
"Vox Populi" begins with a journey during which every
region traversed has its own heroes.

> Camaralzaman is famous
> Where Badoura is unknown.

Only in the last of the three stanzas are we told that the
fame of poets is localized also, though this is obviously the
aspect of the matter that concerned Longfellow most. And

in the last poem, "Aftermath," which gave its title to the volume in which the "flight" under consideration first appeared, the poet pleases his modern admirers by simply describing the last harvest of "the rowen mixed with weeds" rather than "upland clover bloom," leaving the application to the reader and never spelling it out for him that the aging poet is a late harvester too.

Advancing years figure importantly also in three other poems that have nothing to do with poetry. "The Meeting" describes the mingled pleasure and pain involved in meeting with old friends after a long separation, while "Change" deals with the alteration time has wrought not in people but in a place, in this instance a Portland locale. "The Haunted Chamber" has its affinity with "Haunted Houses" in the first flight. It is tempting to identify the woman who sits at the window in the moonlight with Fanny Longfellow and "the little child, / Who died upon life's threshold" with the child the Lt ngfellows lost, but this is conjecture.

If ghosts and memories are the past, children are the future, and "The Castle-Builders" has its obvious affinity with "The Children's Hour" (one little boy now taking the place of the three little girls in the other poem), but this time the father looks forward to the accomplishments of the coming years, not, as in "Weariness," to their burdens.

> There will be other towers for thee to build:
> There will be other steeds for thee to ride.

"The Brook and the Wave," one of the earliest pieces in the collection, simply describes, briefly and perfectly, the meeting of the waters.

But it is "The Challenge"which, as I have already suggested, challenges the reader as well as the adversaries

in the poem. It does not wholly break with the traditional
style of the Longfellow of the past, for it begins with

> a vague remembrance
> Of a story, that is told
> In some ancient Spanish legend
> Or chronicle of old.

What is challenging is that King Sanchez and the "great
lord of the army," Don Diego de Ordonez, who are
besieging Zamora, challenge as traitors "all the people of
Zamora," the born and the unborn, the living and the
dead, and that the challenge is issued in the name of "the
poverty-stricken millions" who extend their "wasted
hands" in the "cold and darkness, / And hunger and
despair" to "catch the crumbs that fall" from the banquet
tables in "the lighted hall." At the end it is neither King
Sanchez nor Don Diego but "Christ, the great Lord of the
army" who "lies upon the plain." Newton Arvin found in
the "startlingly bitter final note" of this poem "the interest of being a literally unique expression, among the
New England poets of that generation, of something like
socialist protest." But the conclusion is a straight deduc-
tion from Christ's "Inasmuch as ye have done it unto one
of the least of these . . . ." Are only socialists interested in
the dispossessed? If so, the outlook is bleak indeed.

The fourth flight of the "Birds of Passage" is the least
distinguished. Five of its eight items are travel poems;
Longfellow was much preoccupied at the time these poems
were written with his gigantic anthology, *Poems of Places,*
and "Travels by the Fireside," which expounds how and
why the aging poet now preferred books to travel, was written as an introduction to this series of volumes. "Cadenab-
bia," "Monte Cassino," and "Amalfi" all draw upon
memories of the author's last visit to Italy during the
1868–69 excursion to Europe, and all gain in interest

through the many references they make to great figures of days gone by—Saint Benedict, Saint Thomas Aquinas, Dante, Boccaccio.

> The conflict of the Present and the Past,
>   The ideal and the actual in our life,
> As on a field of battle held me fast,
>   Where this world and the next world were at strife.

In "Amalfi" the sympathetic reference to the "sunburnt" peasant girls bearing heavy burdens—

> What inexorable fate
> Dooms them to this life of toil?—

recalls the mood of "The Challenge." "Songo River," the remaining travel poem, if one may call it that, harks back to Maine, and at the end the river itself catches the nineteenth-century poet's habit of moralizing:

> "Be not like a stream that brawls
> Loud with shallow waterfalls,
> But in quiet self-control
> Link together soul and soul."

Two of the other three poems derive from reading. "The Sermon of Saint Francis" retells a familiar story, with a rather weak ending:

> He knew not if the brotherhood
> His homily had understood;
> He only knew that to one ear
> The meaning of his words was clear.

"Belisarius" ranges further afield to take up Justinian's great general and accepts the legend that in his old age he became an outcast, reduced to begging his bread. The remaining poem is "Charles Sumner," a memorial tribute

to the Massachusetts senator and opponent of slavery who
was probably Longfellow's closest friend. The first four
stanzas are devoted to praising Sumner, and the poem
might have ended at this point. Instead it takes an abrupt
turn, and the last five stanzas comprise reflections on
death in general, its relation to greatness, what it destroys
and what it spares.

> Were a star quenched on high,
>   For ages would its light,
> Still travelling downward from the sky,
>   Shine on our mortal sight.
>
> So when a great man dies,
>   For years beyond our ken,
> The light he leaves behind him lies
>   Upon the paths of men.

The sixteen poems in "Flight the Fifth" travel far and
wide for their inspiration. Only three are wholly
American. "Delia," a tender little piece, written for the
daughter of a neighbor, a friend of Edith Longfellow's,
who died in her teens, is the only true elegy, for although
"The Herons of Elmwood," a perfect poem, has a rather
elegiac tone, James Russell Lowell, in whose honor it was
written, was not dead but merely absent at the time. The
poet pauses by Elmwood on a warm, still summer night,
when nothing can be heard but "the chirp of crickets, /
And the cry of the herons winging their way," to send him
a friendly greeting and to reflect that

> The surest pledge of a deathless name
>   Is the silent homage of thoughts unspoken.

"The Revenge of Rain-in-the-Face" is quite different in
tone, for it deals with Sitting Bull's vengeance upon
General Custer at the Battle of the Little Big Horn. In ad-

dition to these poems, "A Ballad of the French Fleet," which was written as part of the campaign to save the Old South Meeting House from threatened destruction, is partly American; it deals with the ill-starred French expedition of 1746 against British possessions in the new world, including Boston.

Seven poems are purely European in their inspiration, three derive from Oriental sources, and one—"The Three Kings"—from the New Testament. Unfortunately this last is a wholly uninspired retelling of Saint Matthew's story, with none of the individualizing touches of Goethe's "Epiphanias," Heine's *"Die heiligen drei Könige aus Morgenland,"* or T. S. Eliot's "Journey of the Magi." Two of the Oriental pieces are slight but neat. "King Trisanku," which is from the *Ramayana,* concerns an Indian king who finds himself, like human hearts, suspended "midway between earth and heaven," and the more purely reflective "Haroun al Raschid," which has *Arabian Nights* associations, establishes the transience of worldly fame and possessions. The other Oriental piece, "The Leap of Roushan Beg"—more accurately the leap of the good steed Kyrat, which carries the robber-hero across the chasm where he must otherwise surely have perished—is a quite successful action piece, yet its best touch is wholly pictorial:

> Flash of harness in the air
> Seen a moment like the glare
>   Of a sword drawn from its sheath;
> Thus the phantom horseman passed,
> And the shadow that he cast
>   Leaped the cataract underneath.

Among the European pieces, "To the River Yvette" was written because it was needed for *Poems of Places*. "The Emperor's Glove," where the point is a play on words, is an anecdote of the Duke of Alva's campaign in Flanders. Dr. Johnson, likewise conjured up for *Poems of Places,* is "A Wraith in the Mist" on "the green little island of Inchkenneth," and Peter the Great is not much more substantial in "The White Czar." "Castles in Spain," however, recaptures all "the colors of romance" of that "Aladdin's palace of delight," the Alhambra, that enthralled Longfellow upon his early visit to Spain. "All was a dream to me," he says, even though "something sombre and severe" reigned "o'er the enchanted atmosphere," and ghosts of Philip II and Torquemada could not be completely exorcised. "Vittoria Colonna" brings up a different kind of ghost in a poem which constitutes a noble tribute to a great lady and poet whom we shall meet again in *Michael Angelo,* and "A Dutch Picture" creates a rich Rembrandt-like atmosphere.

I have spoken of "The Leap of Roushan Beg" as an action piece. It must be evident from what I have written that action is important too in a number of the other pieces in this "flight," and that it is not only Roushan Beg who might seem an unlikely hero for our poet, especially during his declining years. In "The Revenge of Rain-in-the-Face," to be sure, he does debate the rights and wrongs of the matter, but his sympathy with the Indians never wavers.

> Whose was the right and the wrong?
> Sing it, O funeral-song,
>   With a voice that is full of tears,
> And say that our broken faith
> Wrought all this ruin and scathe,
>   In the Year of a Hundred Years.

But it would be hard to find a moral in "A Dutch Picture," whose hero is a Dutch buccaneer who had singed the King of Spain's beard and committed many depredations. It is true that we see him only in his retirement, in a house richly crammed with beautiful loot, but he is still dreaming of further adventures, and he does not express any remorse on his own account nor does the poet do it for him.

In 1867 Longfellow published *Flower-de-Luce,* the first volume in seventeen years he had devoted exclusively to short poems. It is a little book rich in beauty. The finest single achievement contained in it is the sequence of six sonnets on *The Divine Comedy,*[7] but there are other things too that no lover of poetry should miss.

Though "The Bells of Lynn," which describes what the poet heard at his summer place in Nahant and what this suggested to him has its admirers, it seems to at least one reader somewhat monotonous, and though the title poem has a fine personification of the dragonfly, one suspects that "lin" and "run" were used because the poet needed the rhymes rather than because of their meaning, nor does the piece as a whole quite succeed in achieving singleness of effect. "Noël," written in French as an 1864 Christmas present for Louis Agassiz is essentially an interesting novelty. On the other hand, hardly any praise could be too high for "Hawthorne," which is equally happy in its suggestion of the subject's personality and in the way it invokes the healing beauty of Concord on the day of his funeral:

> How beautiful it was, that one bright day
>   In the long week of rain!
> Though all its splendor could not chase away
>   The omnipresent pain.

Much the same might be said of "Killed at the Ford," one of the best of Civil War poems, in which the senseless uselessness of slaughter is skillfully suggested not only by what is said but by the use of an irregular rhyme scheme and many variations in meter. At the end, direct observation is characteristically supplemented by imaginative sympathy in the description of the effect of the young soldier's death upon others who are not present on the scene. There is no moralizing, and the situation speaks for itself more effectively than anybody could speak for it.

What is most impressive and most moving in the *Flower-de-Luce* volume however is the atmosphere of melancholy and mortality that broods over it. In "Palingenesis" the poet remembers his youth and those he has lost, but the memory brings only pain, for the resurrection of forms of which the old alchemists dreamed does not apply to human beings, and he can only try to reconcile himself to his increasing age ("the glow / Of sunsets burning low") and to whatever the present and the future may still hold for him, even if it should take the form of "temptations in lone wildernesses," "famine in the heart," or "pain and loss / The bearing of what cross." In "The Bridge of Cloud" the hearth plays a role analogous to that of the sea in "Palingenesis," but, alas, "wizard Fancy" no longer "builds her castles in the air" but only constructs "bridges / Over many a dark ravine," and even though "the land forbidden" may still hold "its vanished charm,"

> Naught avails the imploring gesture,
>   Naught avails the cry of pain!

Worse still, in "The Wind Over the Chimney," time devours even the wisdom of the past, with books themselves having become the mere "sepulchres of thought," so that at the end no comfort is left save the grim conviction that "no endeavor is vain." It is true that "Christmas Bells" opens on a note of comfort:

> I heard the bells on Christmas Day
> Their old, familiar carols play,
>   And wild and sweet

> The words repeat
> Of peace on earth, good will to men!

But the poem was written on December 25, 1864, with the cannons still thundering in the south, and though the poet's despair is rebuked in the last stanza by the bells themselves—

> "God is not dead; nor doth he sleep!
>   The Wrong shall fail,
>   The Right prevail,
> With peace on earth, good will to men!"—

there is somehow an uncomfortable suggestion of whistling in the dark about it all.

Three poems by Longfellow, of moderate length, seem to call for separate treatment. These are "The Hanging of the Crane," "Morituri Salutamus," and "Kéramos."

"The Hanging of the Crane" first appeared in *The New York Ledger,* whose publisher, Robert Bonner, paid Longfellow three thousand dollars for it, the highest price he ever received for a poem. The Harpers paid him a thousand dollars each for the other two poems and even held up an isue of *Harper's Magazine* in order to print "Morituri Salutamus" as soon as possible after the poet had read it at the fiftieth-anniversary reunion of his Bowdoin College class in 1875. "The Hanging of the Crane" was published by itself in an illustrated edition in 1874 and "collected" the next year, along with the "Morituri Salutamus" and othe materials in *The Masque of Pandora and Other Poems.* "Kéramos" too appeared first in an illustrated edition in 1877 and then in *Kéramos and Other Poems* in 1878.

Longfellow visited the Thomas Bailey Aldriches early in their married life in the house at 84 Pinckney Street in Boston and, as he was about to leave, said to his host,

"Ah, Mr. Aldrich, your small round table will not always be closed. By and by you will find new young faces clustering about it; as years go on, leaf after leaf will be added until the time comes when the young guests will take flight, one by one, to build nests of their own elsewhere. Gradually the long table will shrink to a circle again, leaving two old people sitting there alone together. This is the story of life, the sweet and pathetic poem of the fireside. Make an idyll of it. I give the idea to you."[8]

He had outlined the whole structure of "The Hanging of the Crane." Since Aldrich did not use the idea, he himself returned to it, and the result was the most elaborate of all his domestic poems.

In 1907 Houghton, Mifflin and Company chose to celebrate the Longfellow centenary by bringing out an elaborate edition of "The Hanging of the Crane," with illustrations by Arthur I. Keller and decorations by Florence W. Swan, both based upon the backgrounds and treasures of the Longfellow House, which was issued in three different forms, of which the most elaborate was priced at twenty dollars, a very high price for a book in 1907. With contemporary readers so desperately afraid of "sentimentality' as they are, one could hardly expect a publisher today to make a similar choice. It *is* a bit trying to have the first child of the young couple in the poem described as "a little angel" whom they have entertained unawares, but the baby's behavior, as Longfellow describes it, is certainly more realistic than angelic, and I do not see why we should gag at "the very pattern girl of girls" for his little sister if we accept "Queen rose of the rosebud garden of girls" from Tennyson. These, however, are largely matters of taste, with no positive right or wrong about them, though there is no denying that, as poetry—compared to either of the other two poems, but especially to "Morituri Salutamus—" "The Hanging of the Crane" is rather commonplace.

It is divided into seven sections, and to mark his transitions from scene to scene, the poet employs a showman's magic lantern at a village fair.

> Again the tossing boughs shut out the scene,
> Again the drifting vapours intervene,
>   And the moon's pallid disk is hidden quite.

The note of mortality is sounded, as in so much of Longfellow's poetry at this period, when the climax draws nearer:

> The meadow-brook, that seemeth to stand still,
> Quickens its current as it nears the mill.

But the ending is cheerful, with the crowded, happy celebration of the golden wedding.

"Morituri Salutamus" takes its title from the gladiators' greeting, 'O Caesar, we who are about to die / Salute you!'' which seems to have been recalled to Longfellow's mind by Gêrome's famous painting. His dislike of writing occasional poetry was surpassed only by his horror of public speaking, and his first reply to the request that he produce a poem and read it at the class reunion had been negative. He did it nevertheless, and the result was by all means his most elaborate and successful ode.

The opening saluation to the "familiar scenes" that have lived in the poet's memory since his college days is quickly dismissed ("Ye do not answer us! ye do not hear!''). From it he turns quickly to his old teachers, one living, the others "all gone / Into the land of shadows," where indeed many of Longfellow's classmates have followed them.

> And ye who fill the places we once filled,
> And follow in the furrows that we tilled,
> Young men, whose generous hearts are beating high,

> We who are old, and are about to die,
> Salute you; hail you; take your hands in ours,
> And crown you with our welcome as with flowers!

Compared with these, his successors, Longfellow places himself with the old men who sat with Priam on the walls of Troy, for the poem echoes the Bible, the classics, Dante, and Spenser.

> Write on your doors the saying wise and old,
> "Be bold! be bold!" and everywhere, "Be bold;
> But not too bold!" Yet better the excess
> Than the defect; better the more than less;
> Better like Hector in the field to die,
> Than like a perfumed Paris turn and fly.

Looking back over the fifty years that have passed since his graduation, Longfellow acknowledges that

> "Whatever hath been written shall remain,
> Not to be erased nor written o'er again;
> The unwritten only still belongs to thee:
> Take heed, and ponder well what that shall be."

But, less comfortable with this thought than was Omar Khayyám, he turns next to "a tale of wonder, with enchantment fraught," which he retells at length from the *Gesta Romanorum,* in what is perhaps the only passage in the poem that is not wholly effective. Yet its relevance is clear, for it explores the conflict between learning and the world: "The endless strife / The discord in the harmonies of life!" He rejects out of hand

> The market-place, the eager love of gain,
> Whose aim is vanity, and whose end is pain!

giving all his allegiance instead to

> The love of learning, the sequesterd nooks,
> And all the sweet serenity of books.

Nor will he grant that such reflections have no relevance "to men grown old," for

> nothing is too late
> Till the tired heart shall cease to palpitate.
> Cato learned Greek at eighty: Sophocles
> Wrote his grand Oedipus; and Simonides
> Bore off the praise of verse from his compeers,
> When each had numbered more than fourscore years,
> And Theophrastus, at fourscore and ten,
> Had but begun his Characters of Men.
> Chaucer, at Woodstock with the nightingales,
> At sixty wrote the Canterbury Tales:[9]
> Goethe at Weimar, toiling to the last,
> Completed Faust when eighty years were past.

Old age, to be sure, is

> the waning, not the crescent moon;
> The dusk of evening, not the blaze of noon;
> It is not strength, but weakness; not desire,
> But its surcease; not the fierce heat of fire,
> The burning and consuming element,

yet for Longfellow and those who heed his counsel, as for Tennyson's Ulysses,

> The night hath not yet come; we are not quite
> Cut off from labor by the failing light;
> Something remains for us to do or dare; . . .
> And as the evening twilight fades away
> The sky is filled with stars, invisible by day.

There are no rose-colored spectacles here, no evasion, no Pollyanna optimism. But there *is* courage, the courage a man needs to face the inevitable conditions of human life.

Kéramos is the Greek word for pottery, and the sources of Longfellow's "Kéramos" lie not only in his memories of

the place in Portland where, as a boy, he used to stop to
watch the potter at his work but probably also in recent
books occasioned by the revival of interest in ceramics. It
has also been suggested, and not unreasonably, that *The
Rubáiyát of Omar Khayyám,* "Rabbi Ben Exra," and
Saint Paul's Epistle to the Romans may have contributed.
Essentially, or ostensibly, "Kéramos" is a poem about
potters and pottery, but the potter is a type figure for the
artist, who in turn figures forth the Creator. The text is
divided between the narrative portions, which describe the
poet's far-ranging vision, and the potter's song,
printed in italic type, which from time to time breaks in
upon it. Both are in tetrameter, with an abundance of
imagery and somewhat irregular rhyme. The poet's imagination carries him far beyond what is seen, over the world
to wherever pottery is made: Holland, France, Spain, Italy,
Egypt, India, China, and Japan; as he says, he is

> Wrapped in my visions like the Seer,
> Whose eyes behold not what is near,
> But only what is far away.

In this aspect, the poem becomes a virtual guidebook.
Raphael, della Robbia, and others enter the Italian section; the latter's "forms so wondrous fair" are happily
described as

> These choristers with lips of stone,
> Whose music is not heard, but seen.

Particularly interesting passages recall *The Arabian Nights,*
which seems never to have been far from Longfellow's
mind, and, in sharp contrast between the exotic and
familiar, "the willow pattern that we knew" in childhood
among "the coarser household wares" and

> The tiles that in our nurseries
> Filled us with wonder and delight,
> Or haunted us in dreams at night.

There is no summarizing reflection about art until close to
the end, where we read,

> Art is the child of Nature; yes,
> Her darling child, in whom we trace
> The features of the mother's face,
> Her aspect and her attitude;
> All her majestic loveliness
> Chastened and softened and subdued
> Into a more attractive grace,
> And with a human sense imbued.
> He is the greatest artist, then,
> Whether of pencil or of pen,
> Who follows Nature. Never man,
> As artist or as artisan,
> Pursuing his own fantasies,
> Can touch the human heart, or please,
> Or satisfy our noblest needs,
> As he who sets his willing feet
> In Nature's footprints, light and fleet,
> And follows fearless where she leads.

When Paul Elmer More celebrated Longfellow's centenary by an article in *The Nation,* he called for a collected
volume of the sonnets, but before his piece could be
reprinted in the Fifth Series of his *Shelburne Essays,* Ferris
Greenslet had gratified him, [10] as he was obliged to indicate in a footnote. The sonnets appeared originally in
various places and collections (two of the most personal,
"Mezzo Cammin" and "The Cross of Snow," never indeed until Samuel Longfellow's biography of his brother
was published), and since even those who do not greatly
admire Longfellow's work in general have never ventured
to deny his quality as a sonneteer, it was important that

they should be brought together. So too they shall be considered here before we proceed to Longfellow's two last books of verse. Exclusive of the appendix he entitled "Experiments and Translations," Greenslet arranged the sonnets in three goups: Personal Sonnets (twenty-one); Nature (seventeen); and The Life of Letters (twenty-four). He also supplied an introduction in which he said almost everything that needs to be said about the sonnets collectively. To him the ensuing discussion gladly avows its indebtedness.

Most of Longfellow's sonnets were the product of his later years. The earliest was "Mezzo Cammin" (1842), followed three years later by "Dante" and "The Evening Star," and four years after that, by "On Mrs. Kemble's Readings from Shakespeare." The "Divina Commedia" sequence came along in 1864–67. Between 1872 and 1876 Longfellow composed thirty-one sonnets and thereafter he continued to turn out sonnets from time to time until the end.

Greenslet's considered judgment was that

Longfellow's work in this kind is upon a more even and a higher level than any other similar body of sonnets that can readily be found. There is no single sonnet so fine and memorable as many of Shakespeare's, as a few of Milton's and Wordsworth's, and as sundry fortunate sonnets by other hands that are among the choicest treasures of English poetry. The best of Longfellow's never have quite the intensity, the *unforgetableness,* of these greatest sonnets. Yet their average is incomparably high. They exhibit very notably the dignity and repose of mood which are essential to sustained success in sonnet-writing. In grave, nobly impassioned language, adorned with stately or vivid imagery, often pointed with some quaint and telling conceit, they express with completeness and beauty the pensively shadowed, tender, and generous spirit of one of the most sincere of poets.

Of course Greenslet's divisions do not indicate watertight compartments. There is nature in the personal sonnets, and personal references find their way into the nature division. Moreover, Longfellow being Longfellow, there are literary references everywhere and a preoccupation with the poet's own task. Nothing, for example, could be more characteristic of him than that he should apply to "President Garfield" Dante's "I came from martydom unto this peace!"

Nobody has ever doubted that in the first of the personal sonnets, "Mezzo Cammin," which was written at thirty-five and which has been quoted in its entirety in Chapter IV, Longfellow is speaking directly for himself. The "care that almost killed" was of course the death of his first wife. But he seems equally direct and sincere in "Sleep," where he presents himself as "weary" and "overwrought"

> With too much toil, with too much care distraught,
> And with the iron crown of anguish crowned,

and in "Shadow," where he worries about what would happen to his children if he were to die. "Three Friends of Mine" is a series of sonnets about Felton, Agassiz, and Sumner; its most memorable passage comes at the end of the Sumner section:

> Thou hast but taken thy lamp and gone to bed;
>   I stay a little longer, as one stays
>   To cover up the embers that still burn.

"A Nameless Grave" is interesting in its expression of the shame which a non-combatant, however conscientious his motives, must always be tempted to feel before the thought of one who has endured something he has not endured himself and paid a price he was not called upon to pay. If it seems odd that Longfellow as a sonneteer should so largely have ignored the subject to which, above all others, sonneteering has been dedicated—that is, sexual or

romantic love—it is even more odd that in the one where
he came closest, "The Evening Star," he should have
described the second Mrs. Longfellow disrobing for bed!
The most touching, by far, is his memorial tribute to her,
"The Cross of Snow."

> In the long sleepless watches of the night,
>   A gentle face—the face of one long dead—
>   Looks at me from the wall, where round its head
>   The night-lamp casts a halo of pale light.
> Here in this room she died; and soul more white
>   Never through martydom of fire was led
>   To its repose; nor can in books be read
>   The legend of a life more benedight.
> There is a mountain in the distant West
>   That, sun-defying, in its deep ravines
>   Displays a cross of snow upon its side.
> Such is the cross I wear upon my breast
>   These eighteen years, through all the changing scenes
>   And seasons, changeless since the day she died. [11]

Greenslet placed in his "Nature" section four poems
which reflect Longfellow's European travels: "Venice,"
"Giotto's Tower," "Boston" (in Lincolnshire), and "To
the River Rhone." Any of the others he could have written
without ever leaving America. In "The Harvest Moon" he
tells us that

> All things are symbols: the external shows
> Of Nature have their image in the mind,

and no idea could possibly have been more characteristic of
him. Since he was nearly always at his best in writing of the
sea, it is not surprising that both "The Tides" and "The
Sound of the Sea" should image the poet's inspiration in
terms of the incoming tide. "A Summer Day by the Sea"
domesticates "light-house gleams" rather charmingly as
"the street-lamps of the ocean." But perhaps the very

finest sonnet in this section is the last and most general, which is called simply ''Nature'' and consists of one sentence developing an Homeric simile:

> As a fond mother, when the day is o'er,
>   Leads by the hand her little child to bed,
>   Half willing, half reluctant to be led,
>   And leave his broken playthings on the floor,
> Still gazing at them through the open door,
>   Not wholly reassured and comforted
>   By promises of others in their stead,
>   Which, though more splendid, may not please him more;
> So Nature deals with us, and takes away
>   Our playthings one by one, and by the hand
>   Leads us to rest so gently, that we go
> Scarce knowing if we wish to go or stay,
>   Being too full of sleep to understand
>   How far the unknown transcends the what we know. [12]

In the third division, ''The Life of Letters,'' stands the sequence of six sonnets. ''Divina Commedia,'' in which the great poem is presented as a Gothic cathedral:

> Oft have I seen at some cathedral door
>   A laborer, pausing in the dust and heat,
>   Lay down his burden, and with reverent feet
>   Enter, and cross himself, and on the floor
> Kneel to repeat his paternoster o'er;
>   Far off the noises of the world retreat;
>   The loud vociferations of the street
>   Become an indistinguishable roar.
> So, as I enter here from day to day,
>   And leave my burden at this minster gate,
>   Kneeling in prayer, and not ashamed to pray,
> The tumult of the time disconsolate
>   To inarticulate murmurs dies away,
>   While the eternal ages watch and wait.

Of the six sections, two are named for each division of the

Comedy, but the first, which has just been quoted, is a general introduction, not concerned with the "Inferno" in particular, and in the last Longfellow forsakes both the "Paradiso" and Dante to express his hopes for contemporary Italy. The violation of unity involved here may perhaps be judged a fault; if so, it is the only one that appears. Surely nothing could be more beautifully integrated than the invocation of the murmurs that arise from the confessionals in one of the "Purgatorio" sonnets,

> From the confessionals I hear arise
>   Rehearsals of forgotten tragedies,
>   And lamentations from the crypts below,

nor the association of the reunion of Dante and Beatrice with the elevation of the Host and the glories of "Christ's Triumph" in the Rose window. Nor, probably, has any poet ever more adequately described the work of a greater than Longfellow described the *Comedy* when he wrote,

> Ah! from what agonies of heart and brain,
>   What exultations trampling on despair,
>   What tenderness, what tears, what hate of wrong,
> What passionate outcry of a soul in pain,
>   Uprose this poem of the earth and air,
>   This mediaeval miracle of song!

Chaucer, "the poet of the dawn," Shakespeare, Milton, and Keats all receive sonnet tributes, but Tennyson was the only living poet to be thus honored. Certainly Chaucer's quality could not have been more happily indicated than in

> as I read
> I hear the crowing cock, I hear the note
>   Of lark and linnet, and from every page
>   Rise odors of ploughed field or flowery mead.[13]

Shakespeare, "the Poet paramount, / Whom all the
Muses loved, not one alone," is quite as happily imaged in

> A vision as of crowded city streets,
> With human life in endless overflow.

As a matter of fact, Shakespeare gets two sonnets, though
he must share one with Fanny Kemble.

> O happy Reader! having for thy text
>   The magic book, whose Sibylline leaves have caught
>   The rarest essence of all human thought!
> O happy Poet! by no critic vext!
>   How must thy listening spirit now rejoice
>   To be interpreted by such a voice!

Moving to America, "In the Churchyard at Tarrytown"
catches the gentle spirit of Washington Irving, and the
Quaker valuation on silence made it suitable that Whittier
should be praised, at his seventieth-birthday celebration,
by "The Three Silences of Molinos."

> Hermit of Amesbury! thou too hast heard
>   Voices and melodies from beyond the gates,
>   And speakest only when thy soul is stirred.

"The Burial of the Poet" (Richard Henry Dana I) is a charming winterscape, and in "My Books" Longfellow, only a
year before his death, takes touching leave of the tools of
his trade, like a knight saying farewell to his arms. The
other sonnets in this section deal with poetry in a less personal way.

Ultima Thule (1880) was the last book Longfellow
published and judging by its title the last he expected to
publish. Excluding the sonnets, it comprises fifteen items,
of which the author called nine "Poems" and four "Folk-
Songs," the "Dedication" and "L'Envoi" being set
apart. After his death, the verses he had not yet collected

were brought together in *In the Harbor* (1882), which is made up of twenty-four poems, six of them sonnets. If there is little or nothing startingly new in these collections, it is more noteworthy that they should indicate no decline in either Longfellow's skill or charm and that though a number of poems reveal a preoccupation with age and mortality, he should still be reaching out for subjects and interests in many directions.

The "Dedication" of *Ultima Thule* to George Washington Greene recalls nostalgically the days when the two friends "sailed for the Hesperides" and acknowledges that now "the ocean streams" have swept both far from their "lost Atlantis" or "land of dreams" and that the time has come when both must rest for awhile in the harbor of "Ultima Thule! Utmost Isle!" If there is aspiration here, there is more resignation. "Bayard Taylor"—

> Dead he lay among his books!
> The peace of God was in his looks—

and "The Chamber Over the Gate" are out-and-out elegy, and the new exercise in hexameters, "Elegiac," is in the same mood:

> Dark is the morning with mist; in the narrow mouth of
>   the harbor
> Motionless lies the sea, under its curtain of cloud;
> Dreamily glimmer the sails of ships on the distant horizon,
>   Like to the towers of a town, built on the verge of the sea.

It is a little surprising that "The Chamber Over the Gate," which takes its title from David's mourning over Absalom, should be the more poignant of the two poems, for it was written for the Bishop of Mississippi, whom the poet scarcely knew, and it mourns the sacrificial death of the bishop's son, whom Longfellow may never have seen at all, during a yellow fever epidemic. In the cry,

> "Would God I had died for thee,
>   O Absalom, my son!"

it is surely not fantastic to hear the voice of the writer's own passionate fatherhood.

Two of the poems in *Ultima Thule* are occasional. "The Iron Pen" was a letter of thanks to a Maine lady who had given the poet a pen made of a bit of iron from Bonvard's prison at Chillon, with a wooden handle taken from "Old Ironsides," and "From My Armchair" thanks the children of Cambridge for having presented him with a chair made from the wood of the Village Blacksmith's "spreading chestnut tree," sitting in which he could "roll back the tide of Time" and recapture his lost youth.

Three poems take their direct inspiration from reading, while a fourth blends literature with life and memory. "Old Saint David's at Radnor" was a real church, but its charm for Longfellow was due partly to its reminding him of "Herbert's chapel at Bemerton"; both weariness and resignation appear strongly in this poem. Longfellow catches the spirit of "Robert Burns" unerringly:

> I see amid the fields of Ayr
> A ploughman, who, in foul and fair,
>   Sings at his task
> So clear, we know not if it is
> The laverock's song we hear, or his,
>   Nor care to ask.

Being a moralist, he cannot but refer to Burns's weaknesses, but being a Christian gentleman, he charitably makes the best case he can for him. What disarms him most is that though Burns's "voice" was sometimes "harsh," it was not harsh "with hate," and he closes with hearty acceptance:

> His presence haunts this room to-night,
> A form of mingled mist and light
>   From that far coast.
> Welcome beneath this roof of mine!
> Welcome! this vacant chair is thine,
>   Dear guest and ghost!

But it is the other two poems in this collection that are the finest. ''Jugurtha'' is short enough to be quoted entire:

> How cold are thy baths, Apollo!
>   Cried the African monarch, the splendid,
> As down to his death in the hollow
>   Dark dungeons of Rome he descended,
>   Uncrowned, unthroned, unattended;
> How cold are thy baths, Apollo!
>
> How cold are thy baths, Apollo!
>   Cried the Poet, unknown, unbefriended,
> As the vision, that lured him to follow,
>   With the mist and the darkness blended,
>   And the dream of his life was ended;
> How cold are thy baths, Apollo!

Jugurtha was a king of Numidia, captued by Sulla in 106 B.C. and imprisoned in Rome, where he died two years later. Longfellow's second stanza registers his conviction that it is as tragic for the poet to outlive his inspiration as for the monarch his freedom and his throne. According to Plutarch, what Jugurtha exclaimed as he descended into his dark prison was '''O Hercules! how cold your bath is!'' and ''Hercules'' was an interjection or exclamation, not the invocation of a god. It is impossible to be sure whether Longfellow misremembered his Plutarch or made the change deliberately. [14]

''Helen of Tyre'' is a complement to the last division of the ''Second Passover'' section of ''The Divine Tragedy,'' one of the most original of the series. Simon Magus is the sorcerer we meet in the eighth chapter of the Book of Acts, whom Justin Martyr makes the father of the Gnostic heresy in Rome during the reign of Claudius. Simon represented himself "both as God and the Word, . . . stressing the fact that a female principle, whom he identified with the prostitute Helen, had shared in the creative process, naming her his Ennoia, or the first conception of his mind."[15] She had gone through various incarnations. "Helen of Tyre" mentions Queen Candace and Helen of Troy; in "The Divine Tragedy" she is also identified with Rahab, the Queen of Sheba, Semiramis, Jezebel, and "Sara of seven husbands." What Simon promises is to rescue her from this bondage of reincarnation and "restore her to eminence as the First Thought of his Divine Intelligence." The most interesting thing about Longfellow's presentation is his wholly sympathetic treatment of her, as victim, not vampire.

> For the famished heart believes
> The falsehood that tempts and deceives,
>   And the promise that betrays.

When the poet directly exhorts his reader to "stoop down and write / With thy finger in the dust," he is plainly echoing one of the tenderest passages in the Gospels, Christ's treatment of the woman taken in adultery, whom he saved from death by commanding him among her accusers who was himself without sin to cast the first stone at her.

In the Harbor finds Longfellow still preoccupied, perhaps even obsessed, with the problem of the poetic inspiration (in "Becalmed" he tries expressing it in terms of nautical imagery again) and with age (as in "Sundown," "Autumn Within," and "Loss and Gain," where he does not seem much better satisfied with his achievements than in "Mezzo Cammin," so long ago). "The Poet's Calendar," "Mad River," and "The Four Lakes of Madison"

are nature poems, and "Decoration Day" is a modest little
tribute to those who died in the Civil War, but "To the
Avon" is basically an encomium to Shakespeare, and in
"Moonlight" the real interest lies in the transforming
power of the imagination that the effect of the moonlight
suggests.

The longest of the poems derived from history is "The
Children's Crusade," which never quite made up its mind
where it was going and consequently, not surprisingly,
never got itself finished. The most characteristic passage is
that in which the poet expresses his pity for the children so
tragically betrayed by their own faith and zeal:

> Passed they into lands unknown,
> Passed to suffer and to die.

Much more successful is the poem about the part legendary, part divine "Hermes Trismegistus," which reveals
much the same kind of imagination we have seen at work
in "Belisarius," "Jugurtha," and especially "Helen of
Tyre." From one point of view it is a lament for the tran-
sitory nature of fame. More significantly, the sympathetic
comprehension of something quite alien to the poet that
has been noted in "Helen of Tyre" shines out here in a
totally different aspect:

> Who shall call his dreams fallacious?
>   Who has searched or sought
> All the unexplored and spacious
>   Universe of thought?
> Who, in his own skill confiding,
>   Shall with rule and line
> Mark the border-land dividing
>   Human and divine?

There is an elegy for the publisher James T. Fields,
"Auf Wiedersehen," interesting among other things as

another expression of faith in survival. "Elegiac Verse" appears again, and once more in hexameters, but this time in the form of fourteen unconnected observations, more preoccupied with poetry than with death. Faith appears once more in the very last poem in the book, "The Bells of San Blas," which was suggested by an article about Mexico in *Harper's Magazine* and was the last thing Longfellow wrote, only a few days before his death. The final stanza declares that

> Out of the shadows of night
> The world rolls into light;
>   It is daybreak everywhere.

This, however, was an afterthought, and the bells are themselves aware that the age of faith, as they understand faith, has passed its crest.

X

Dramatic Works

Longfellow's failure to achieve success as a dramatist was not caused by any lack of interest in the dramatic form. During his junior year at Bowdoin he produced "The Poor Student, A Dramatic Sketch,"[1] whose consumptive hero works himself to death. Seymour loves and is loved by one Gertrude, who tells him, "Thy thoughts dwell too much on the mournful grave, / Dear Seymour!" Though this is undeniable, she is in a weak position to reproach him, for after his death she comes to his grave on the bank of a stream, hears "a mournful voice none else may hear" and sees "a spectral form that beckons me!" whereupon she cries, "It points me to the grave! Seymour, I come," and in the closing immortal stage direction, her corpse "is precipitated over the waterfall," and the "Second Peasant," watching, cries, " 'Tis she! 'tis she!"

Young Longfellow considered other dramatic works, among them a play about Toussaint L'Ouverture,[2] but the only dramatic work he published during his early writing career was *The Spanish Student,* which came closer to being capable of production in the legitimate theater than anything he was to turn out later; indeed it was acted, in German translation, at the Ducal Court Theater, Dessau, on January 28, 1855.

We first hear of the play early in 1840, when his passion

for Lope de Vega inspired a resolve to "write a comedy, 'The Spanish Student'!'" At the end of the year he told his father he had written it and was inclined to look upon it "with some self-complacency," though he admitted he could not estimate it dispassionately until after "the glow of composition" had worn off. At different times he thought of it as fit and unfit for the stage; once he was so discouraged by the lack of enthusiasm his friends showed for it that he threatened to burn it, an act of which he seems to have been incapable with any manuscript. But when, in 1842, *Graham's Magazine* offered him $150 for it, his hopes rose again. It ran in *Graham's* through the September, October, and November numbers, and he soon found himself eager for book publication also. The book appeared in the year of his second marriage, 1843, and between then and the spring of 1857, thirty-eight thousand copies were sold.[3]

Longfellow's preface to the book attributes the subject to "the beautiful tale of Cervantes, *La Gitanilla*," carefully adding that to his source he was "indebted for the main incident only, the love of a Spanish student for a Gypsy girl, and the name of the heroine, Preciosa." He notes further that in Spain this subject has been twice handled dramatically; first by Juan Perez de Montalvan, in *La Gitanilla*, and afterwards by Antonio de Solis y Riverdeneira in *La Gitanilla de Madrid* and in English by Thomas Middleton in *The Spanish Gypsy,* who also drew upon another story by Cervantes, "La Fuerza de la Sangre."[4] Considerable music is called for in *The Spanish Student,* and except that the dates would be wrong, the modern reader would surely be tempted to suspect that Longfellow had been hearing *Il Trovatore* before writing the scenes in the gypsy camp!

Poe's summary of the argument of this play is so well done that I find it impossible to resist the temptation to enlist him as a collaborator in this chapter:

Preciosa, the daughter of a Spanish gentleman, is stolen, while an infant, by Gypsies; brought up as his own daughter, and as a dancing-girl, by a Gypsy leader, Cruzado; and by him betrothed to a young Gypsy, Bartolomé. At Madrid, Preciosa loves and is beloved by Victorian, a student of Alcalá, who resolves to marry her, notwithstanding her caste, rumors involving her purity, the dissuasions of his friends, and his betrothal to an heiress of Madrid. Preciosa is also sought by the Count of Lara, a *roué*. She rejects him. He forces his way into her chamber, and is there seen by Victorian, who, misinterpreting some words overheard, doubts the fidelity of his mistress, and leaves her in anger, after challenging the Count of Lara. In the duel, the Count receives his life at the hands of Victorian; declares his ignorance of the understanding between Victorian and Preciosa; boasts of favors received from the latter; and to make good his words, produces a ring which she gave him, he asserts, as a pledge of her love. This ring is a duplicate of one previously given the girl by Victorian, and known to have been so given by the Count. Victorian mistakes it for his own, believes all that has been said, and abandons the field to his rival, who, immediately afterwards, while attempting to procure access to the Gypsy, is assassinated by Bartolomé. Meanwhile, Victorian, wandering through the country, reaches Guadarrama. Here he receives a letter from Madrid, disclosing the treachery practised by Lara, and telling that Preciosa, rejecting his addresses, had been, through his instrumentalitty, hissed from the stage, and now again roamed with the Gypsies. He goes in search of her; finds her in a wood near Guadarrama; approaches her, disguising his voice; she recognizes him, pretending she does not, and unaware that he knows her innocence; a conversation of equivoque ensues; he sees his ring upon her finger; offers to purchase it; she refuses to part with it; a full *éclaircissement* takes place; at this juncture a servant of Victorian's arrives with "news from court," giving the first intimation of the true parentage of Preciosa. The lovers set out, forthwith, from Madrid, to see the newly discovered father. On the route, Bartolomé dogs their steps; fires at Preciosa; misses her; the shot is returned; he falls; and "The Spanish Student" is concluded.[5]

The sweetest tribute ever paid to *The Spanish Student* was that of William Dean Howells, who, as a boy in Ohio, found a copy of it in a loft in the log cabin where his family was temporarily housed and devoured it eagerly. He fell "in love with the heroine . . . and went about with the thought of her burning in [his] heart as if she had been a real person," and the play in which she figured became one of his passions, "a minor passion, not a grand one, like *Don Quixote* and the *Conquest of Granada,* but still a passion." By the time he wrote *My Literary Passions,* however, even he admitted that "I should dread a little to read the piece now, lest I should disturb my old ideal of its beauty." As for Poe, who was never quite sane on the subject of plagiarism, he made himself ridiculous by arguing that Longfellow had stolen one scene from his own *Politian,* but, barring his unpleasant tone of rather malignant carping, he was dead right in his analysis of the defects of *The Spanish Student* as drama. It is one of the multitudinous nineteenth-century romantic plays written in dutiful imitation of the Elizabethans (Chispa talks prose like a Shakespearean clown), and except for the generally superior quality of its verse, there is little to distinguish it from the rank and file. "Stars of the summer night," to be sure, is a charming serenade,[6] and there are lines like

> Hark! how the loud and ponderous mace of Time
> Knocks at the golden portals of the day!

that might easily pass muster with any of the Elizabethans. But Lara is an unshaded melodramatic villain; irrelevant materials are included (the scene in which Preciosa dances before the Cardinal and the Archbishop accomplishes nothing); much of the dialogue is stilted; and important developments are awkwardly handled or passed over with inadequate emphasis. Finally, as to the revelation of Preciosa's irreproachable lineage at the close, not only was this kind of thing in fiction and drama being laughed out of court as early as Fielding's time but in this instance it makes nonsense of Victorian's love as being strong enough to overleap the barriers of caste, which we had thought we were expected to admire.

According to C. C. Felton, the publication of the play occasioned some lifting of eyebrows in Boston.

Sally Lowell was at first a good deal troubled and shut herself up several days. Since then she has emerged into the daylight, and is now doing as well as can be expected. Several old women have laid it under ban and forbidden their daughters to read it. This only makes the daughters the more earnest to get hold of it, and they have been not a little disappointed to find it no worse.

Actually what Preciosa's virtue is used for is to test the decency of men. The villainous Count of Lara asks,

> And would you persuade me
> That a mere dancing-girl, who shows herself
> Nightly, half-naked, on the stage, for money,
> And with voluptuous motions fires the blood
> Of inconsiderate youth, is to be held
> A model for her virtue?

But Don Carlos replies,

> That woman, in her deepest degradation,
> Holds something sacred, something undefiled,
> Some pledge and keepsake of her higher nature,
> And, like the diamond in the dark, retains
> Some quenchless gleam of the celestial light!

And our hero, who has good reason to know that "degradation" has not touched Preciosa until he is, not too convincingly, disillusioned about her, sees her as

> a precious jewel I have found
> Among the filth and rubbish of the world,
> I'll stoop for it; but when I wear it here,
> Set on my forehead like the morning star,
> The world may wonder, but it will not laugh.

So far, so good. But, unfortunately for the success of the play, the action forces the girl into situations where, the limitations of Longfellow's art as a dramatist being what they were, she must prate of her virtue in stilted, priggish, wholly unconvincing language. All in all, while *The Spanish Student* might well have made an acceptable libretto for such a Victorian operetta as *Maritana* or *The Bohemian Girl,* which latter does indeed go back to the same source in Cervantes, it could hardly be expected to qualify as a really actable poetic drama of quality.

The Masque of Pandora appears prominently in Longfellow's letters of 1875. In February he tells George Washington Greene that he has sketched out half of it but does not believe it will come to anything, but by July he has finished "The Legend of Prometheus" and is planning to deliver it to the printer next day. In August he tells James T. Fields that he prefers "The Masque of Epimetheus" ("I never had so many afterthoughts about a title"), but ten days later he has settled upon the title we know. By early December *The Masque of Pandora and Other Poems* (the others were "Morituri Salutamus," "The Hanging of the Crane," Flight the Fourth of the "Birds of Passage," and a group of sonnets) had sold five thousand copies, and a second printing was in press.

It will be noted that in the title of the book he had simply classified his composition as a poem without involving the muse of dramatic art in any form. By taking the Elizabethan masque rather than the Elizabethan drama as his general model, he had freed himself from many requirements and consigned his operations to areas where he felt more at home. Nevertheless Alfred Cellier did compose music for *The Masque of Pandora,* and on January 10, 1881, when Longfellow had only little more than a year to live, it was produced as a kind of opera at the Boston Theater, with his friend and admirer Blanche Roosevelt as Pandora. Longfellow had been unhappy when an English composer had wished to make an opera out of *Evangeline,* for he said he hated English music, but his dislike of Bolton Rowe's adaptation of the *Pandora* text seems excessive for him; Rowe had made no more changes than stage presentation required. Unfortunately the production was plagued by a series of mishaps and was not a success. [7]

The masque is in eight scenes, and the doings of the characters are commented upon by choruses of Graces, Fates, Eumenides, Birds, Reeds, Dryads, Oreads, Waters, Winds, Forests, Dreams from the Ivory Gate, and Dreams from the Gate of Horn. The story is the Greek myth told in Hesiod's *Works and Days,* relating how Pandora was created by Hephaestus and offered first to Prometheus, who scornfully refused her and all other gifts from the gods. Unfortunately for himself and for mankind, his brother Epimetheus was more trusting:

> O my brother!
> I am not as thou art. Thou dost inherit
> Our father's strength, and I our mother's weakness:
> The softness of the Oceanides,
> The yielding nature that cannot resist.

Like another Eve or Bluebeard's wife, Pandora opens the forbidden chest, persuading herself that a voice has spoken to her in sleep:

> "Do not delay; the golden moments fly!
> The oracle hath forbidden; yet not thee
> Doth it forbid, but Epimetheus only!"

thus forfeiting for herself and her descendants all life's comforts except hope.

Yet she is lovingly handled. Epimetheus blames himself rather than her:

> Mine is the fault, not thine. On me shall fall
> The vengeance of the Gods, for I betrayed
> Their secret when, in evil hour, I said
> It was a secret; when, in evil hour,
> I left thee here alone to this temptation.
> Why did I leave thee?

Courageously he sets to work

> To build a new life on a ruined life,
> To make the future fairer than the past,
> And to make the past appear a troubled dream.

But the last word of the Eumenides makes it clear that this will not be easy:

> Never by lapse of time
> The soul defaced by crime
> Into its former self returns again;
> For every guilty deed
> Holds in itself the seed
> Of retribution and undying pain.
>
> Never shall be the loss
> Restored, till Helios
> Hath purified them with his heavenly fires;
> Then what was lost is won,
> And the new life begun,
> Kindled with nobler passions and desires.

The foremost admirer of *The Masque and Pandora* was Newton Arvin, who commented admiringly on the "lyrical grace . . . and even something firmer and closer-knit than that, in some of the choruses," especially in Scene VI, where he found "a kind of energy in its use of dynamic imagery from nature—driving snows, tempests of wind, hurrying streams, flying clouds—that is not wholly unworthy of the great parallel that suggestss itself." The parallel is to the Chorus of Elves and the speeches of Ariel in *Faust,* Part II, Scene 1. "No one would seriously compare the two choruses for lyric splendor, but it is of Goethe that Longfellow manages, without utter absurdity, to remind us."

Christus: A Mystery was Longfellow's "Tower of Song," that

loftier strain, the sublimer Song whose broken melodies have for so many years breathed through my soul in the better hours of life, and which I trust and believe will ere long unite themselves into a symphony not all unworthy the sublime theme, but furnishing "some equivalent expression for the trouble and wrath of life, for its sorrow and its mystery."

The idea first entered his mind on the evening of November 8, 1841 "to undertake a long and elaborate poem by the holy name of CHRIST; the theme of which would be the various aspects of Christendom in the Apostolic, Middle, and Modern Ages." The next year, at Marienburg, he made this entry in his notebook:

> CHRISTUS, a dramatic poem in three parts:
>   Part First. The Times of Christ. (Hope.)
>   Part Second. The Middle Ages. (Faith.)
>   Part Third. The Present. (Charity.)

Through the years external circumstances combined with what must have been a certain inner uncertainty to postpone the execution of his plan and to thrust other works into his agenda ahead of it, and when he did return to it, he came very close to writing it backwards. Various stages in the writing of the second part, *The Golden Legend,* can be traced through his journal for 1850–51. It was published by itself very late in 1851, without any indication that it was destined to be part of a larger whole, and three-thousand-five-hundred copies were sold immediately. Yet the third part, *The New England Tragedies,* did not follow until 1868, even though the first of these, "John Endicott," had been written in prose as early as 1857[8] and put aside in favor of *The Courtship of Miles Standish.* In March 1868 Longfellow told Charles Sumner that he had rewritten "Endicott" and composed "Giles Corey of the Salem Farms" out of hand. Late in 1870 he turned at last to the first part, *The Divine Tragedy,* and produced the bulk of it during the opening weeks of 1871. While he was working on it it absorbed him completely, but after it was finished, he was sure of nothing but that it had been "written with great sincerity and simplicity." Published in December, it immediately sold ten thousand copies.

Only writers like George Moore (*The Brook Kerith*) and D. H. Lawrence *(The Man Who Died)* who are willing, and sometimes eager, to shock their readers can feel entirely free in dealing with material drawn from the Four Gospels; others, like Longfellow here, must choose between merely paraphrasing the King James Version and attempting to present it in combination with other materials with which it may sometimes be reluctant to blend. Longfellow's Jesus enters the poem as a

> youth with dark azure eyes,
> And hair, in color like unto the wine,
> Parted upon his forehead, and behind
> Falling in flowing locks.

He is the

> Most beautiful among the sons of men!
> Oft known to weep, but never known to laugh,

and his "serene" aspect is "manly yet womanly." His magnetism is so great that Mary Magdalene, having but glimpsed him in passing, finds herself overwhelmed

> With a mysterious power, that streamed from him,
> And overflowed me with an atmosphere
> Of light and love,

and possessed by an imperious need to "find him / And follow him, and be with him forever!" Longfellow draws his materials from the Synoptists and the Fourth Gospel with fine impartiality, showing no awareness of any contradictions between the different accounts, nor, as must go without saying, of any of the critical problems to which modern New Testament scholars have called our attention, and dividing his work into three parts corresponding to the three Passovers suggested by the Synoptists. Though he does paraphrase at times, this causes less difficulty than the fact that many of his scenes are too short to have the impact the author must have desired. Moreover the effect of this brevity is less cinematic than suggestive of the lantern slides with which Longfellow's contemporaries were familiar.

The story of the Temptation includes material original with Longfellow, and the episode dealing with the marriage at Cana draws freely upon the Song of Songs. We overhear Caiaphas conferring with the Pharisees and Gamaliel recalling Christ's visit to the Temple at the age of twelve:

> I can remember, many years ago,
> A little bright-eyed school-boy, a mere stripling,
> Son of a Galilean carpenter,
> From Nazareth, I think, who came one day
> And sat here in the Temple with the Scribes,
> Hearing us speak, and asking many questions,
> And we were all astonished at his quickness.

But the old man is less pleased with Christ's activities in the Temple now:

> Oh, had I here my subtle dialectician,
> My little Saul of Tarsus, the tent-maker,
> Whose wit is sharper than his needle's point,
> He would delight to foil this noisy wrangler!

The blind Bartimeus episode is treated more originally here than in the separate poem, and the scene in Herod's palace has no parallel in Scripture except for Salome's dance and the demand that follows it, from which all the dramatic tension has been filtered out:

> For mine oath's sake, then. Send unto the prison;
> Let him die quickly. Oh, accursed oath![9]

Such characters as Judas Iscariot, Pontius Pilate, Mary Magdalene (obviously derived from legendary as well as Biblical elements), Barabbas, Manahem the Essenian (perhaps suggested by Manaen in Acts 13), and of course Simon Magus and Helen of Tyre are developed at some length and assigned long speeches. Menahem's musing over the three crosses is a good piece of verse, quite capable of standing alone, and the soliloquy of Judas Iscariot, before he kills himself, is one of the best things in the entire *Christus.* "How I loved, / Yet hated Him!''

> I know I am not generous, am not gentle,
> Like other men; but I have tried to be,
> And I have failed. I thought by following Him
> I should grow like Him; but the unclean spirit
> That from my childhood up hath tortured me
> Hath been too cunning and too strong for me.
> Am I to blame for this?[10]

Longfellow was pondering the idea of Part II, *The*

Golden Legend, generally considered the most successful part of the *Christus,* as early as 1839: "Cotton Mather? or a drama on the old poetic legend of Der Arme Heinrich? The tale is exquisite. I have a heroine as sweet as Imogen, could I but picture her so. I think I must try this." *Der Ar-me Heinrich* (Poor Henry) was the work of a twelfth-century German poet, Heinrich von der Aue, and was included in Mailáth's *Altdeutsche Gedichte* (1809). Here Longfellow found the leprous prince who was told that he could be cured only by the blood of a virgin, freely offered for his healing, which he found in the peasant girl Elsie. Thinking the leprosy too revolting, Longfellow changed it to a mysterious, undefined malady,[11] and the journey of the prince and the girl to Salerno, where the healing is to take place, affords an opportunity for a wide-ranging panorama of medieval scenes and activities of which the poem takes full advantage. The girl, who has won her parents over to acceptance of what she considers her mission, is obsessed with the idea of dying for her prince, who struggles with his conscience at some length, trying to make up his mind whether or not to accept the offered sacrifice. At the last possible moment, he overcomes his temptation, saves the girl, and is healed by a miracle, after which, we gather, he will make her his bride. The climax is deliberately muffed, however; it occurs "off stage" or between sections, and we do not learn what happened until the news is reported to Elsie's parents.

In the notes he prepared for *The Golden Legend* Longfellow declared that his source surpassed "all other legends in beauty and significance. It exhibits, amid the corruptions of the Middle Ages, the virtue of disinterestedness and self-sacrifice, and the power of Faith, Hope, and Charity, sufficient for the exigencies of life and death." He does not seem always to have been of this mind however, for when he read *The Saint's Tragedy* by Charles Kingsley, he regretted, at least momentarily, that he had not used the Elizabeth of Hungary story instead. As for Elsie being as sweet a heroine as Imogen, she falls as far short of Imogen in vividness and intensity as Longfellow's dramatic poetry falls short of Shakespeare's, but her most serious limitation in enlisting the reader's full sympathy is the almost suicidal note involved in her self-sacrifice.

> The Saints are dead, the Martyrs dead,
> And Mary, and our Lord, and I
> Would follow in humility
> The way by them illumined!

But in doing so, as she is well aware, she may gain more than she gives up.

> Why should I live? Do I not know
> The life of woman is full of woe?
> Toiling on and on and on,
> With breaking heart, and tearful eyes,
> And silent lips, and in the soul
> The secret longings that arise,
> Which this world never satisfies!
> Some more, some less, but of the whole
> Not one quite happy, no, not one!

Not only is this sickish and repellent in itself, but if life is not worth anything to Elsie anyway, the admiration she is expected to awaken through her willingness to give it up for her prince must be seriously undercut. Nor is he, nor the reader's response to him, unaffected by all this, for it is he who reminds her (who surely needed no such reminder) that

> This life of ours is a wild aeolian harp of many a
>   joyous strain,
> But under them all there runs a loud perpetual wail,
>   as of souls in pain,

and in the inn at Genoa he certainly comes pretty close to
suggesting that they commit suicide together:

> Ah, yes! the sea is still and deep.
> All things within its bosom sleep!
> A single step, and all is o'er,
> A plunge, a bubble, and no more;
> And thou, dear Elsie, will be free
> From martyrdom and agony.

Der Arme Heinrich however is far from being the only
source of *The Golden Legend.* The Lucifer who weaves in
and out of it in many disguises has no counterpart in the
principal source, but derives rather from Goethe's *Faust,*
whose hero Prince Henry himself closely resembles in the
opening scene. Lucifer seems to me considerably more
than the minor romantic poet he has been called, but it is
certainly true that he has much less vitality and variety
than his Goethean counterpart. [12] The varied materials included episodically naturally involve a variety of other
sources. Thus the story of Christ and the Sultan's
Daughter is from *The Boy's Wonder-Horn;* Father Cuth-
bert's appalling sermon is an actual discourse by Fra
Gabriella Barletta, a fifteenth-century Dominican; and
that little gem, the Nativity miracle play, a very successful
imitation of medieval drama, is based, as the author himself pointed out, on "The Apocryphal Gospel of James
and The Infancy of Christ." But the *Legenda Aurea,* written in Latin by a thirteenth-century Dominican, Jacobus
de Voragine, and translated into French by Jean de Vigny
and into English by Caxton, was apparently not seen by
Longfellow until after his poem had been completed.

Though there is believable and lifelike dialogue in such
scenes as those between Elsie and her parents at the farm in
the Odenwald and that in which the abbot receives Prince
Henry and Elsie at the convent of Hirschau, *The Golden
Legend* is a dramatic poem, not a drama. It is more like a

vast, indefinitely unrolling panorama of shifting and ever-varied scenes; only the figure would be more accurate if the panorama were painted not upon canvas but on stained glass through which the light brings out every possible variation of color. [13] Not only do we see the medieval church in almost every aspect, good and bad—learned scholastic disputations and appalling coarse popular preaching; monks wallowing drunken at the convent in the Black Forest and Father Pacificus, the pious illuminator, humanized by his innocent pride in his art; to say nothing of the Abbess Irmingard's long narrative to Elsie of her youthful love for Walter of the Vogelweid, their attempt to elope, and how she was apprehended and consigned to the cloister because her father was determined that she must marry a prince or nobody—but the vast, teeming life of the Middle Ages looms up behind it in manifold aspects, reminding us of Chesterton's observation that "how high the sea of human delight rose in the Middle Ages, we know only by the colossal walls they built to keep it within bounds." In addition to all this we have a number of charming interpolated stories in various measures, with good poetry everywhere.

> O gladsome light
> Of the Father immortal,
> And of the celestial
> Sacred and blessed
> Jesus, our Saviour!

> Now to the sunset
> Again thou hast brought us;
> And, meeting the evening
> Twilight, we bless thee,
> Praise thee, adore thee!

> Father omnipotent!
> Son, the Life-giver!
> Spirit, the Comforter!
> Worthy at all times
> Of worship and wonder!

Ruskin saw Longfellow as having "entered more closely into the temper of the monk, for good and for evil, than ever yet theological writer or historian, though they may have given their life's labor to the analysis," and though Saintsbury admitted that the author of *The Golden Legend* had not "gone very deeply into any medieval sentiment," he quickly modified his statement:

It was not his way to go very deeply or to *appear* to go very deeply (which is perhaps a different thing), into anything. . . . But . . . his "superficiality," as it seems to some folk, has a curious quality of not being so very superficial after all. His etching is not deeply bitten; his colour is but a sort of preliminary wash. But somehow both are right as far as they go, and both give to the spectator on effect much more trustworthy than some far more heavily treated plates and pictures.

The New England Tragedies, which make up the last third of the *Christus, are* plays in blank verse after the Elizabethan manner, and, with reasonable adaptation, they could be acted on the stage, although they never have been. "John Endicott" deals with the persecution of Quakers in Boston and "Giles Corey of the Salem Farms" with the witchcraft madness. Both are brief and sparsely developed, but when the publisher Fields wished to describe them as sketches, Longfellow objected. They were not sketches, he insisted; he had deliberately worked for simplification. Newton Arvin overstates the case for the inferiority of the second play, but there is point to his objection that Longfellow's close concentration upon the Coreys gives no idea of the extent of the Salem delusion, and the last two scenes are so brief as to suggest that the writer had tired of his work and put it out of the way as quickly as possible. In the theater certainly both would fail to achieve the effect he intended.

"John Endicott" was conceived much earlier than the "Giles Corey" play, which was written later and apparently much more hurriedly. Emmanuel Scherb suggested "Endicott" in March 1856, and Longfellow considered calling its first prose version "The Old Colony" or "Scourged in Three Towns" and then settled upon "The New England Tragedy." Though this version was never published, Longfellow had ten copies struck off in 1860 and the manuscript still exists. It was not until 1868 that he turned it into verse, first calling it "Wenlock Christison," but it was "John Endicott" when it appeared together with "Giles Corey" in *The New England Tragedies* that same year. [14]

For the Boston background, Longfellow used Caleb Snow's *History of Boston,* Charles W. Elliott's *The New England History,* and Samuel Gardner Drake's *The History and Antiquities of Boston.* His most important Quaker source was Joseph Besse's *A Collection of the Sufferings of the People Called Quakers for the Testimony of a Good Conscience from the Time of Their Being First Distinguished by That Name in the Year 1650, to the Time of the Act, Commonly Called the Act of Toleration, Granted to Protestant Dissenters in the First Year of the Reign of King William the Third and Queen Mary, in the year 1689,* especially Book II, Chapter 5. On the Quaker side, he also read George Fox, Bishop's *New England Judged,* and, on the side of their opponents, Norton's *Heart of New England Rent.*

Longfellow's prologues to the two plays tell the reader exactly what attitude is expected to be taken toward the material presented. In "Giles Corey" the poet commits himself from the first line:

> Delusions of the days that once have been,
> Witchcraft and wonders of the world unseen,
> Phantoms of air and necromantic arts
> That crushed the weak and awed the stoutest hearts,—
> These are our theme to-night.

But though he admits that his Puritan ancestors "ruled their little realm with iron rod / Less in the love than in the fear of God," he would not have his reader be

> too swift in casting the first stone,
> Nor think New England bears the guilt alone,
> This sudden burst of wickedness and crime
> Was but the common madness of the time,
> When in all lands, that lie within the sound
> Of Sabbath bells, a Witch was burned or drowned.

The "John Endicott" prologue adds justification for the poet's use of such unpleasant themes "for the lesson that they teach: / The tolerance of opinion and of speech" and begs that the historian may not

> blame the Poet here
> If he perchance misdate the day or year,
> And group events together, by his art,
> That in the Chronicles lie far apart.

Setting his action in 1665, Longfellow had been obliged to misdate a number of events which did not actually occur in that year: King Charles II's order, which put an end to the persecution of Quakers in New England, for example, was actually issued in 1661, when, having been apprised that a vein of blood had been opened in his dominions, the restored Stuart promptly replied, "But I will stop that vein."

Longfellow uses Governor Endicott and the Reverend John Norton to represent the Puritan state and church respectively; the Quakers are represented by Wenlock

Christison and his daughter Edith. The father is an historical character; of the five Quakers who had been condemned to death, he was the only one whom the King's mandamus came in time to save. His daughter Edith is the poet's own creation, however, as is the governor's son, young John Endicott, for whom the play was finally named and who opposes his father's policy and of course falls in love with the girl.

The play is as hard on Norton as was Besse himself; he is a man of blood with no shadow of turning and therefore not particularly interesting as a dramatic character. Longfellow's Endicott however is a human being, fearful of shedding innocent blood and never quite sure he is right, though desperately wanting to be.

> Bellingham,
> I did not put those wretched men to death,
> I did but guard the passage with the sword
> Pointed toward them, and they rushed upon it!
> Yet now I would that I had taken no part
> In all that bloody work.

Between his duty as a magistrate and his love for his son, who believes that

> In the sight of God,
> Perhaps all men are Heretics. Who dares
> To say that he alone has found the truth?

he suffers something like a tragic conflict, and the modern reader will be more likely to see his death as the result of this than a deliberate judgment of God upon him. Nor is the Puritan community over which he rules wholly devoid of humane, sensible people. Walter Merry absents himself from meeting when he feels like it to worship God "sitting in silence here at my own door" and shelters the Quakers at considerable risk to himself. Considerably farther from

center and less close to the community is the sea captain
Simon Kempthorn, who has brought Quakers into Boston
and who must put in his time in the pillory, which he takes
with amused tolerance:

> In this town
> They put sea-captains in the stocks for swearing,
> And Quakers for not swearing.

But there is no frivolity, even if there is a touch of
seaman's superstition, in his attitude toward Edith:

> I tell you, Goodman Cole, that Quaker girl
> Is precious as a sea-bream's eye. I tell you
> It was a lucky day when first she set
> Her little foot upon the Swallow's deck,
> Bringing good luck, fair winds, and pleasant weather.

The hurried death of all the persecutors at the end,
however, is now more likely to awaken mirth than awe.
Like many characters in Elizabethan tragedy, they may be
said to "die of the fifth act."

In "Giles Corey of the Salem Farms" Mary Walcot, who
seems both hysterical and malicious, alone represents the
afflicted children, as the Coreys represent the accused.
Tituba, despite the rationalism of the prologue, is presented as certainly guilty, at least in intent, and, one
would think, as more frank in describing herself as a witch
than she could have dared to be at the time, so that one
must wonder why she was not molested. Cotton Mather is
made more important in the anti-witchcraft activity than
he was in fact, but Longfellow is accurate in representing
him as unwilling to credit "spectral evidence" when un-
supported by independent testimony:

> May not the Devil take the outward shape
> Of innocent persons? Are we not in danger,
> Perhaps, of punishing some who are not guilty?

He is sure that

> It were indeed by far more credulous
> To be incredulous than to believe.
> None but a Sadducee, who doubts of all
> Pertaining to the spiritual world,
> Could doubt such manifest and damning proofs!

At the same time one must

> Be careful. Carry the knife with such exactness,
> That on one side no innocent blood be shed
> By too excessive zeal, and, on the other
> No shelter given to any work of darkness.

Only his closing observation that the dead Corey "hereafter will be counted as a martyr" is unbelievable in its historical context.

The contrast between Martha Corey's rationalism and her husband's credulity is effectively drawn. Act II, Scene I, is an amusing altercation between the two, possibly influenced by the Hotspur scenes in *King Henry IV*. It is irony indeed that the believer and the sceptic fare alike at the hands of the superstitious and that both meet the same horrible death. By the same token, Scene 2, which follows, presents a pretty convincing demonstration of how, in an atmosphere of panic, perfectly baseless charges against innocent people can be advanced so as to seem convincing to the ignorant, the frightened, and the credulous. If Longfellow ever wrote anything that suggests the eloquence of Shakespeare, let Martha Corey's defense in the court scene recall Hermione's defense in *The Winter's Tale:*

> Give me leave to speak.
> Will you condemn me on such evidence,—
> You who have known me for so many years?
> Will you condemn me in this house of God,

> Where I so long have worshipped with you all?
> Where I have eaten the bread and drunk the wine
> So many times at our Lord's Table with you?
> Bear witness, you that hear me; you all know
> That I have led a blameless life among you,
> That never any whisper of suspicion
> Was breathed against me till this accusation.
> And shall this count for nothing? Will you take
> My life away from me, because this girl,
> Who is distraught, and not in her right mind,
> Accuses me of things I blush to name?[15]

Bayard Taylor placed the "Introitus" to *The Divine Tragedy,* and consequently to the *Christus,* at the peak of Longfellow's achievement: "I know nothing else of yours that equals it. The music of the lines is to me like that of some unknown instrument, as weird and variable as a windharp, yet with the strength of an organ." Longfellow's heart must have been warmed, for the *Christus* was by far his most ambitious and aspiring work, and in spite of all the good things in it, neither the critics nor the public have ever rated it an unqualified success.

Yet in no other work has Longfellow displayed such metrical virtuosity as here. Howard Mumford Jones remarks of *The Golden Legend* that "it includes some of the finest blank verse that Longfellow, a master craftsman, ever wrote."[16] He originally composed the opening scene in blank verse, then rewrote it as it now stands. His use of the octosyllabic couplet, varied by alternate rhyme, probably shows the influence of Goethe, and he also used dimeter and trimeter in the *Faust* manner. But his line length and his rhyming are both characteristically irregular, and he sometimes approaches, and even achieves, free verse.

As has already been pointed out, the *Christus* often fails to achieve the intensity it needed for the effect Longfellow was trying to secure in passages where such intensity was indispensable; aside from this, its principal general fault is that, as Howells observed, its parts are *"welded,* not *fused,* together"—in other words, it is not really a unit. The Epilogue to *The Divine Tragedy* does not even versify the Apostles Creed (which Longfellow, a Unitarian, can hardly be supposed to have believed),[17] but merely divides up its various clauses among the disciples. The Second Interlude, showing Martin Luther composing his great hymn, *"Ein Feste Burg,"* in the Wartburg, might have provided a suitable transition between the Catholic Middle Ages *(The Golden Legend)* and the Protestant modern period *(The New England Tragedies),* but if the intention here was to indicate progress, why such heavy emphasis upon Luther's intolerance? But, for that matter, ending with the tragedies undercuts the whole plan of illustrating Christianity in ancient, medieval, and modern times, for if modern Christianity expresses itself in hanging Quakers and ferreting out witches, it certainly represents the most appalling anticlimax in history. In a vague sort of way, Longfellow must himself have felt this, for he pondered the possibility of attempting "to harmonize the discord of *The New England Tragedies* and thus give a not unfitting close to the work" by writing another piece about the Moravians of Bethlehem. This, however, remained among his many unwritten works.

Nevertheless where he intended the emphasis of his work to fall is quite clear. If the prophet Habakkuk being borne through the air by an angel seems an odd introduction to a poem about Christ, the emphasis upon charity in the "Introitus" *does* strike the right keynote at the outset. One may reasonably object that the Abbot Joachim's exposition of the plan of salvation in the First Interlude fails to find adequate embodiment in the body of the poem, but it is not possible to fault it as an eloquent expression of the spirit of the work.

> For Hate is death; and Love is life,
> A peace, a splendor from above;
> And Hate, a never-ending strife,
> A smoke, a blackness from the abyss
> Where unclean serpents coil and hiss!
> Love is the Holy Ghost within,
> Hate the unpardonable sin!
> Who preaches otherwise than this,
> Betrays his Master with a kiss!

This is completely in harmony with the prologue to "John Endicott," where we are told that "the errors of an age long passed away" are being dragged again "into the light of day"

> "For the lesson that they teach:
> The tolerance of opinion and of speech,
> Hope, Faith, and Charity remain—these three:
> And greatest of them all is Charity."

More importantly, however, it is in harmony with Saint John's valedictory at the close of the *Christus:*

> Poor, sad Humanity
> Through all the dust and heat
> Turns back with bleeding feet,
> By the weary road it came,
> Unto the simple thought
> By the great Master taught,
> And that remaineth still:
> Not he that repeateth the name,
> But he that doeth the will!

This, to be sure, comes after the saint's observation:

> But the evil doth not cease;
> There is war instead of peace,
> Instead of Love there is hate;
> And still I must wander and wait,

> Still I must watch and pray,
> Not forgetting in whose sight
> A thousand years in their flight
> Are as a single day.

To poor, short-lived mortals this is not precisely exhilarating. Moreover, its sad, unblinking realism harmonizes with the tone of much of Longfellow's other later poetry. It is clear, nevertheless, that insofar as *Christus* has a theology, it is, as Howard Mumford Jones declared, a theology illuminated by love, as befitted a lover of Dante. "It is a plea to rise above anti-Catholicism and anti-Protestantism into a universe where the soul of man can live in *l'amor che muova il sole a l'altre stelle.*"

"Judas Maccabaeus," the last dramatic work Longfellow ever completed, was as tiny an enterprise as the *Christus* had been vast. It occupies only a little over sixty-one pages in the Craigie Edition, and the double-columned, illustrated Household Edition gets it into nineteen, pictures and all. Add to this the fact that it is divided into five acts and fourteen scenes and one gets some idea of how much opportunity for development the poet allowed himself.

The theme is the struggle of the Jews against the fanatical Syrian Hellenizer Antiochus Epiphanes in the second century B.C., the second great heroic age of Hebrew history, with Judas himself, the great military hero of the Old Testament Apocrypha, as its central figure. Longfellow first thought of writing the play in 1850, but he did not begin the first draft until December 10, 1871, and finished it eleven days later. He thought the subject tragic enough and "the collision of Judaism with Hellenism" very "striking," but he was not sure that his work possessed proper unity and a catastrophe. It was derived from the First and Second Books of Maccabees and the *Antiquities* of Josephus and was first published in *Three Books of Song* in May 1872.

Act I opens upon Antiochus discussing with Jason, the renegade Jew, his plans to Hellenize the Jews through the establishment of multiple gods ''and goodness besides'' in addition to

> hippodromes, and games, and baths,
> Stage-plays and festivals, and most of all
> The Dionysia.

Antiochus is, in his way, the same kind of fanatic as Norton in ''John Endicott.'' In the second scene, Samaritan ambassadors warm his heart by bringing him a request to be allowed to rename their temple after ''Jupiter Hellenius,'' but Jason warns him that

> The tribe of Judah
> Is of a different temper, and the task
> Will be more difficult,

to which he adds that

> Hundreds have fled already to the mountains
> Of Ephraim, where Judas Maccabaeus
> Hath raised the standard of revolt against thee.

In Act II, Antiochus attempts to persuade ''The Mother of the Seven Sons'' whom he is prepared to torture to death, to urge her sons to give up their religion and save their lives, but she does just the opposite. Judas himself is not introduced until Act III—''The Battle-Field of Beth-Horon''—and we are told nothing about his background nor given any explanation of why he should have become the leader of his people. He refuses Nicanor's plea that he make peace with Antiochus and prepares for battle, which takes place between Acts III and IV. In Act IV we find the triumphant hero in the outer courts of the Temple at Jerusalem, where

> Nicanor's severed head, a sign of terror,
> Blackens in wind and sun.

Jason is captured but banished, not killed. The last act shifts to "The Mountains of Ecbatana," where Antiochus languishes in utter desolation, all his plans to defeat Judas having failed, and ends with his death. His disappointment is real enough; it even has a touch of pathos. But one cannot believe that he would acknowledge his "pride and arrogance," wish his Jewish subjects "joy, prosperity, and health," and even promise to become a Jew himself and

> declare
> Through all the world that is inhabited
> The power of God!

Except for this obviously false and forced ending, there is nothing much wrong with "Judas Maccabaeus" except that it needed fuller development. As it stands, the second act, devoted to the heroism of the mother and her seven sons, is the most impressive.

On the very day he completed "Judas Maccabaeus" Longfellow recorded that "a new subject comes to my mind." On February 26, 1872, the subject was defined as a dramatic poem about Michael Angelo. He turned first to Hermann Grimm's life of the great artist and on March 2 noted that he was reading Vasari, Cellini, and Mrs. Jameson's *Lives of the Italian Painters*. On March 4, he complained that the subject was difficult to treat dramatically because of the absence of action and plot, but by March 15 he had not only written one act and the epilogue and sketched others but made up his mind that he was in no hurry to finish his work, preferring to keep it instead for "a long and delightful occupation." Before he really settled it with himself to leave *Michael Angelo* unfinished however, and wrote "A Fragment" on the first page of his manuscript, he had read other biographies, and on May 18 he even supposed he had finished a first draft, though he knew other scenes would still be intercalated. Probably it was after he had reconciled himself to leaving the work unfinished that he discarded the scene describing his hero's death, no doubt now thinking this too definite a conclusion for a "fragment." The manuscript was found in his desk after his death and published in the *Atlantic Monthly* in January, February, and March, 1883, and as a book in the autumn.

The definitive study of the sources of *Michael Angelo* is that of Emilio Goggio,[18] who writes:

Longfellow borrowed very freely from various authors, quoting, paraphrasing, or adapting their material. In spite of all this, however, it would be wrong to consider *Michael Angelo* a mere compilation of facts gathered from different sources. . . . In it Longfellow has vividly presented to us certain phases of that fascinating and most interesting age known as the Italian Renaissance. He has touched upon the life, character, the personal experiences and outstanding achievements of some of the most eminent artists of that period, such as Michael Angelo, Titian, Sabastiano del Piombo, Vasari, Cellini, Ghiberti, Giotto, Ghirlandajo, Tintoretto, and Brunelleschi; he has given us a glimpse of court life as was then prevalent in many cities in Italy, in all its pomp and magnificence, its enormous wealth of distinguished scientists and men of letters, of beautiful and learned women; he has described the tyranny and oppression which was then practiced by the Italian rulers upon their subjects, and the brave and noble efforts made by certain patriots to gain their political freedom; he has depicted the corruption and abuses of the Catholic church at that time, and the general revolt against it which led to the Reformation.

Since *Michael Angelo* was neither completed nor designed for the stage, it escapes many of the tests to which it would otherwise be subjected. For what it is, a gigantic fragment, it is, without qualification, splendid.

As Gay Wilson Allen has said, it contains "as excellent
blank verse, technically, as can be found in nineteenth-
century American poetry." More importantly, it embraces
some of the most eloquent expressions we have of
Longfellow's maturest musings about art and life. And
this time, surely, the poet has allowed himself ample scope
for everything he wished to say.

It may be that Michael Angelo himself is somewhat
idealized in this poem. To the noble Vittoria Colonna, apparently the only woman who means anything to him and
whom he loves for her spiritual qualities alone, he is

> A lion all men fear and none can tame;
> A man that all men honor, and the model
> That all should follow; one who works and prays,
> For work is prayer, and consecrates his life
> To the sublime ideal of his art,
> Till art and life are one; a man who holds
> Such place in all men's thoughts, that when they speak
> Of great things done, or to be done, his name
> Is ever on their lips.

But surely he is not unbelievable. His brusqueness and his
pride in his descent from the Counts Canossa are clearly
human weaknesses, and his austerity is at least a
limitation. He has no sense of mirth and shuns social
gatherings.

> To me what you and other men call pleasure
> Is only pain. Work is my recreation.

He thinks of himself as old and crumbling into ruin like
Rome itself, his countenance "like Laocöon's, full of
pain" and his forehead "a ploughed harvest-field." His
brain and hand are "dull and torpid," and he feels that he
has accomplished little of what he planned and hoped for.
To him life has become

> An empty theatre,—its lights extinguished,
> The music silent, and the actors gone,

while he sits alone, "musing on the scenes / That once
have been," and in such moods he feels that "to die
young is best," and can only comfort himself by trying to
believe that

> The happiness of man lies in pursuing,
> Not in possessing; for the things possessed
> Lose half their value.

Yet for all that, there is still

> The fever to accomplish some great work
> That will not let us sleep. I must go on
> Until I die.

His humanity nowhere shows more attractively than in
his attitude toward his fellow artists, especially Benvenuto
Cellini, whose virtues and vices he sees with equal clarity,
trying always, with no suggestion of priggish superiority,
to nurture the first and discourage the second, and to
foster the production of great art, not mere ornamentation, however beautiful it may be. Cellini bears
much the same relationship to Michael Angelo that Julia
Gonzaga bears to Vittoria Colonna. Julia is the friend of
the worldly, luxurious, and generous and apparently not
vicious, young Cardinal Ippolito, and is torn and confused
between the world of sense and that of spirit: "There are
too many week-days for one Sunday."

Since Michael Angelo lives for his art—or, rather for the
expression of life and the interpretation of life's meaning
in art—it is natural that much of his eloquence should be
devoted to describing his artistic faith and aspirations. It
was not unfitting that Longfellow should have placed the
most frequently quoted passage on this subject not in his
mouth but in Vittoria's, for she, after all, is his other self:

> Art is the gift of God, and must be used
> Unto His glory. That art is highest
> which aims at this.

But he himself says it quite as clearly when he declares that art is

> All that embellishes and sweetens life,
> And lifts it from the level of low cares
> Into the purer atmosphere of beauty;
> The faith in the Ideal.

If he must rank the arts in their order of greatness, he sees them as architecture, sculpture, painting.

> Painting and sculpture are but images,
> Are merely shadows cast by outward things
> On stone or canvas, having in themselves
> No separate existence. Architecture,
> Existing in itself, and not in seeming
> A something it is not, surpasses them
> As substance shadow.

By the same token,

> Sculpture is more than painting. It is greater
> To raise the dead to life than to create
> Phantoms that seem to live.

It has been remarked as curious that Longfellow should have told us so much more about Michael Angelo's aesthetic beliefs than his Christian faith, and in a sense this is true, but perhaps the artist would have said that the two were one, and perhaps Longfellow would have agreed with him. Perhaps even for both men, they were. And how could a poet better die than to leave behind him an unfinished work of such magnitude as to suggest that it could no more have been completed than life itself?

XI

The Man

Longfellow was of medium height and slight of figure. His eyes were blue, his somewhat aquiline nose prominent, and his mouth large. His hair was first brown, then gray, and finally snowy white, and his complexion delicate and comparatively colorful. Though his face gained in authority in middle life, he long retained a comparatively youthful appearance, and he moved rapidly, almost jauntily, as long as he lived. Perhaps because his mouth was not handsome, the bearded portraits of his later years are more attractive than the earlier ones—when Dickens saw him again after many years in 1867–68, he thought him "infinitely handsomer" than when he had been younger—but this does not mean that he had not been admired before. The eyes clearly could flash, they could also "sparkle and bubble over with fun," and they could radiate tenderness. His voice, "a very deep baritone without a trace of harshness," was "veiled and reserved," says Bret Harte, "as if he had never parted entirely from it." Elizabeth Peabody called it "an *organ voice*," and Oliver Wendell Holmes says nobody who heard it was ever able to forget it.

He was careful to enhance his appearance with suitable and becoming attire, and in his early days he was often

considered a dandy, as a Hasty Pudding jingle remains to
testify:

> Just twig the Professor dressed out in his best,
> Yellow kids and buff gaiters, green breeches, blue vest;
> With hat on one whisker and an air that says go it!
> Look here! the Great North American poet.

That he was capable of getting to the point of such ribbing
seems attested by his making the Baron in *Hyperion* tell
Paul Flemming that his gloves are "a shade too light for a
strictly virtuous man." But he continued to be careful,
though not dandified, in his attire as long as he lived.
Never, even at home, says his daughter Alice, did he appear "in anything that was at all untidy or unattractive";
neither would he allow any other member of his household
to do so.

He obviously had enough stamina to support his body
through seventy-five years, but there was no lack of
illnesses. He suffered from a seriously infected foot in
childhood, a severe attack of rheumatic fever when he was
in Rome, and rheumatism and lumbago in later life. As
student and teacher he was often plagued by a vaguely
described "swimming and aching in my head—a fulness
and heaviness—I hardly know what to call it" which was
apparently never diagnosed and which he was, quite un-
scientifically, inclined to attribute to mental work. "This
pulling by the head (as oxen do in some countries) is not
conducive to health, I am persuaded." Even more
mysterious was what he called the "partial blindness" that
came upon him suddenly in 1844 and lasted at least until
1848, causing him to scrawl the first draft of *Evangeline* in
pencil before the fire, without looking at his pad. This,
along with insomnia, dyspepsia, and, from the 1850s on,
frequent visitations from "goddess Neuralgia" (his
terrible toothaches may have been a part of this, though he
does not say so) were, healthwise, the real plagues of his

life. Sometimes he calls himself a hypochondriac, and at this distance it is of course impossible to say whether or not there may have been a psychosomatic element in his illnesses. He was not fanatically attached to any medical theory, but insofar as he had any convictions in this area he was a homeopath who also had great faith in hydropathy. But he tried everything he thought of or anybody suggested to him, all the way from getting up at six o'clock to swallow an egg in a tumbler full of milk before going out for a short walk to wearing a medicated belt "of wash-leather, lined with fine red flannel," coupled with "a small breast-plate of the same make and materials, and a vial of homeopathic pellets" which "a mysterious stranger" had brought to the door.

As a boy, Longfellow seems to have enjoyed many childish sports and games, but carefully excluded all blood sports. As a man he even objected to the shooting of crows until he was persuaded that they preyed on song-birds. Once he thanked a correspondent for a poem about fox-hunting, "beautiful notwithstanding its subject, for which I have no sympathy." The only thing that surprises me in this connection is his strangely tolerant attitude toward the bullfight in Spain. This atrocity is condemned in *The Spanish Student* and by implication in "Torquemada," but there is no outright condemnation in *Outre-Mer* nor in the poet's letters and journals.

In 1858, for the first and only time in his life, he saw a little "sparring," which he says was quite enough to satisfy him. As a man he took little exercise. From time to time he went in for walking, skating, rowing, gardening, the use of a gymnastic apparatus, once even boxing as health measures, but only bathing seems ever to have taken any hold upon him. There is one rapturous description of "a magnificent bath" at evening in the river, "the sunset seeming to mingle with the water." By the time Richard Henry Dana became his son-in-law, not even this tempted him greatly however, nor did he care for sailing, driving, or riding, though he was probably not entirely serious when he told Howells "that one got a great deal of exercise in putting on and off one's overcoat and overshoes." Longfellow played whist at the Nortons' and there are a number of references to billiards and bowling, but he cared so little for them that it seems appropriate that one summer he and Tom Appleton should have played billiards "at the Lunatic Asylum" in Brattleboro.

The board at Craigie House would seem to have been lavish by modern dietary standards, but Longfellow does not appear to have partaken of its treasures to excess, and the most ecstatic food passage in his journals sings the praises of bread and butter as the only passion that goes with us from the cradle to the grave. Alice says that as he grew older, he veered more and more away from meat-eating and became more doubtful of its legitimacy, and when Wyatt Eaton visited him, he took oatmeal and milk for both breakfast and lunch.

There is a passage in Emerson in which Longfellow appears as something of a sybarite: "If Socrates were here, we could go and talk with him; but Longfellow we cannot go and talk with; there is a palace and servants, and a row of bottles of different colored wines and wine glasses, and fine coats." But though the cellar at Craigie House was undoubtedly well stocked, this is somewhat misleading. Longfellow saw fine wine as an important part of a good dinner, but Alice insists that he disapproved of hard liquors, and he never fails to condemn excess. His Michael Angelo loves not wine and avoids the banquet where it is to be served, and "The Revel of Earl Sigvald," which was finally excluded from "The Saga of King Olaf," includes the lines:

> Feasts kill more than fighting;
> Drinking more than smiting;
> Swords are sharp, but sharper
>   Is the Drinking Horn!

In the Robin Goodfellow play Longfellow projected but never wrote, alcoholic beverages were to appear among the curses that afflict mankind.

Tobacco, however, seems to have tempted him more than either food or drink, and there is one passage in which he points to the bottle, not the weed, as the fellow that does the mischief. The lethal effects of tobacco were less well understood in his time than they are today, but smoking was no less filthy a habit then than it is now, and Longfellow does show, on a number of occasions, that he was aware it was doing him no good. From time to time he swore off, but he always backslid. There were a few occasions also when coffee or tea interfered with his nerves—or he thought they did.

There may, however, have been a closer connection between his health and his temperament, the most interesting aspect of which was the strange, apparently irreconcilable combination in it of ardor and eagerness on the one hand and, on the other, a holding back which at its best might be called serenity but at its worst deserved no better name than lethargy. He disliked extremes of all sorts, says his son Ernest, and "always thought it best not to do a thing." He closed his shutters at the approach of a thunderstorm, and even in literature he found tragedy almost unbearably painful and was thankful when he got through the "Inferno" portion in his translation of *The Divine Comedy*. He was peculiarly dependent upon congenial surroundings not only for happiness but for effective functioning. Nothing could have been more untrue than his statement that he did not "care a fig" for the weather. He was unusually sensitive to cold, and though he thought fog romantic—"mysterious, transfiguring all things"—he was oppressed, overwhelmed, sometimes even nauseated by snow. Unfortunately, however, it was not only bad weather that lowered his resistance, wore him out, and made him incapable of writing; sometimes good weather had the same effect. Summer in general was bad for his muse. Like Milton, he always expected a revival of power in the autumn—perhaps this is why October was his favorite month—but his hopes were not always realized. Whatever the cause, it is clear that he was often overcome by a dull apathy, which could develop into a positive, active misery, and sometimes this even produced a kind of mystical terror and foreboding. Not even his completely happy marriage seems to have been able to maintain abiding good spirits in him.

No doubt all this is true of many men. But it does not often coexist with the eagerness, optimism, and friendliness of what Longfellow himself called "my rather effervescent nature" and "such an ardent nature as mine"; as he says, he was "at one and the same time listless and restless." To make it all still more complicated and difficult to understand, he was not lacking in a great deal more of that wonderful safety valve humor than many persons have given him credit for. This appears in more than his fondness for "making harmless puns and small witticisms," recording chitchat, and relishing oddities; he had also that capacity for detached observation of himself and his concerns that marks the comic spirit at its best. When his face is swollen with the toothache he reminds himself of Henry VIII, and when his head throbs he feels a sewing machine inside it "turning out any amount of ready-made clothing." Even after Fanny Appleton has seemingly quite rejected him, he can still speak of his late serious accident in Beacon Street.

Paradox appears again in Longfellow's social life. He was friendly, kindly, and affectionate, but he was also intensely reserved. Even in his college days, one of his classmates speaks of him as "rather disinclined to general intercourse," and we are told that in Cambridge "he was Longfellow to the friends who were James and Charles and Wendell to each other." Once a friend, disappointed at being unable to draw some information from him, remarked, "Yet you confessed to me once." "No," replied Longfellow, with a laugh, "I think I never did." And the characteristic, highly unusual note in all this is that there was never anything furtive about it.

During his early years in Cambridge, he was very much the society man, but his interest fell off notably after Fanny's death, and during his last years he was increasingly disinclined to go anywhere. The highest society was open to him, not only here but in Europe—the latter somewhat surprisingly at the beginning when he went there with letters of introduction—but he was so little snob that he was quite capable of going to the door to invite somebody he saw looking at his house to come inside, and though he was neither a gifted conversationalist not a brilliant host, he does not seem to have been ovewhelmed in any gathering. "He did not talk much himself," says Howells, "and I recall nothing that he said. But he always spoke both wisely and simply, without the least touch of pose, and with no intention of effect, but with something that I must call quality for want of a better word." Those who asked help received it if it was at all within his power to give ("Why, Charles," he once gently rebuked Norton, "who will be kind to him if I am not?"), and he was as much intruded upon by cranks and fanatics and impostors as any man of his time. Sarah Bernhardt once remarked that all the crazy people in the world seemed attracted to her, and Longfellow might well have said the same. Some of them were literally crazy, and there is no lack of anecdotes concerning their contacts with him, some hilarious, some maddening, and all surely exasperating. He handled everything with divine patience but without setting aside either honesty or frankness. Once when he was asked if he had not been greatly bored, he replied that he had but added that it was a small matter since he had been bored so often.

Charles Sumner was probably the closest of his friends, but if he cared more for him than for the others, we may be sure the others never found it out. Looking back over thirty years of friendship with Longfellow, Lowell rejoiced that there had never been a clash between them; "if there had been," he added, "it would certainly have been my fault and not yours." Dickens would seem to have been the only one of the British lions with whom Longfellow established really close relations,[1] but the warmth of the mutual affection which subsisted between him and the German poet Ferdinand Freiligrath was never cooled by either time or distance. The difficult George Washington Greene was undoubtedly the friend for whom Longfellow did the most, even to the extent of taking him into his house, where he humored all his vagaries and performed even physical services for him as patiently as a nurse with a fretful child. And this he did quite without failing or pretending to fail to recognize his friend's shortcomings. "Pray don't let those unpleasant thoughts haunt and torment you," he begs him. "Not the wrongs done to us harm us, only those we do to others." There is abundant evidence to prove that his clear-sighted wife was not blinded by affection when she spoke of "his almost angelic disposition, his strength under trial and constant consideration of the happiness of others."

If he was considerate of his friends, he was all the more so toward those whom, in the narrower sense of the term, he loved. Of his capacity for love we have already seen something in connection with his long wooing of Fanny Appleton. He combined extreme susceptibility to the beauty and charm of women with an unfailingly high-minded attitude toward them. "You were ever an admirer of the sex," wrote an early acquaintance, "but they seemed to you something enshrined and holy—to be gazed at and talked with and nothing further," and his brother adds that it might have been said of him as of

Villemain that "whenever he spoke to a woman it was as if he were offering her a bouquet of flowers." Yet he was not a prude. If sexual imagery in his poetry is not extensive, what there is seems beautiful and unblushingly appropriate; there are examples in "The Evening Star," in "Chrysaor," and in "The Building of the Ship," where the ocean is the lover and the ship the bride who leaps to his embrace. In *Outre-Mer* the change from spring to summer is expressed in terms of the changes in a ripening girl, and whenever he deals with sexual situations and problems, he faces them honestly.

Outside of his personal affairs (if, indeed, they deserve to be exempted), it was the arts that interested Longfellow most, but this does not mean that he lived insulated from the practical concerns of life. It pleased him, for example, to think of himself as a financial innocent who never "dealt with any other figures than figures of speech" and did not know the difference "between a bank-note and a greenback." This may well be true in substance so far as the science of money is concerned, but he was an excellent businessman for all that. Though he was always generous with money, he knew that you must have it before you can give it away, and he never proposed to be cheated. No author of his time was more canny in his negotiations with publishers. In view of the widespread impression that his fortune was nearly all derived from his second wife, it is interesting to observe, as William Charvat has pointed out, that "during the first ten years of marriage only once was his wife's income larger than his, and that in three of those years his income from writings alone was larger than hers from investments."[2] After her death, each of her children inherited their share of her considerable fortune, and during his later years their father spent a good deal of his time and energy looking after their financial affairs. His books, which I have examined, were scrupulously kept, and the success of the investments made proves that he did his work well. When he died in 1882, his estate was officially appraised at $356,320, which included $75,000 for the Craigie House and its grounds, but by the time the last surviving child, Alice, died in 1928, she left $1,500,000.

The science of politics as such did not interest Longfellow much more than the science of money, but he did not lack convictions on public policy. Like his mother before him, he was opposed to capital punishment. He rejoiced in the revolutions of 1848 in Europe. At home he was an antislaveryman always, though not an abolitionist. He favored Elihu Burritt's plan of compensated emancipation, and once at least he called Garrison a traitor. Daniel Webster's Seventh of March speech shocked him, and he was horrified by the Fugitive Slave Law. When the slave-hunters came to Boston, he hoped they would be imprisoned, and when Massachusetts men broke the law in opposing them, he approved. "The government must not pass laws that outrage the sense of right in the community." And despite all his reluctance to engage in personal controversy, he could not contain himself when a Florida judge argued that "Do unto others" simply meant that you must treat your slaves as you would like to be treated if you were a slave. "If you were a slave," Longfellow replied bluntly, "the thing you would wish most of all would be your freedom. So your Scripture argument for Slavery is knocked into a cocked hat."

When the antislavery cause identified itself with the war cause, a conflict in Longfellow's sympathies appeared. He was not a pacifist in the doctrinaire sense of the term like the Quaker Whittier, yet Whittier made more provocative statements during the Civil War crisis than did Longfellow. He opposed appeasing the South from the beginning, believed in Lincoln from his nomination, and grew sterner in his attitude between the election and the inauguration. He thought the Inaugural Address "conciliatory and yet firm," but it is impossible to tell on the basis of available evidence whether or not he had by this time accepted the idea of war to preserve the Union. Thereafter he hoped and suffered. Several of Lincoln's appointments disappointed him, but he rejoiced in the Emancipation Proclamation, found the Gettysburg Address admirable, and breathed more freely when the president had been reelected. He also grew very bitter against "John Bull" for putting "Civilization and Barbarism" on a plane of equality. But the martial spirit and war sermons sickened him ("A 'truce of God' once a week is pleasant. At present the north is warlike enough, and does not need rousing"), and he kept Ernest out of the army and would have kept Charley out too if he had been able. After the war he supported Sumner's Reconstruction policies and had harsh things to say about Andrew Johnson. Later the scandals of the seventies depressed him deeply, but he refused to follow Sumner in deserting Grant for Greeley.

Certainly nobody could have believed more than Longfellow did in American institutions nor cherished more the American heritage. As a lover of arts and letters, he did indeed feel powerfully the lure of Europe. But even during his first journey thither, his attitude was by no means one of unmodifed eager response. If he capitulated completely to Spain, he was at the outset decidedly unsympathetic toward France, Italy experienced marked ups and downs in his affections, and he was very critical toward the Scandinavian countries. French villages could not hold a candle to New England villages. The Rhine was "a noble river, but not so fine as the Hudson," and the Arno was only "a stream of dirty water, almost entirely dry in summer." There is a difference in tone between such statements and the judgments of matters European entered by Mark Twain in *The Innocents Abroad,* but the difference is less marked than has commonly been supposed.

The ardent, passionate side of Longfellow's complex

nature reveals itself best in connection with his response to art and beauty in all its forms and most clearly of course in connection with the art that he himself practiced and toward which he aspired. But the primary, elemental source of beauty in the world, toward which most of us respond before we become aware of art, is of course the beauty of nature, and like most nineteenth-century poets Longfellow responded to it warmly. The praise of spring runs all through his writings and journals, but if possible he loved autumn, especially October, even more. The birds and the flowers were important elements in this charm, though he knew nothing about either scientifically, but above all he loved the sea—"a never-ending delight," he calls it—and none of his other nature poems quite reach the level of those that deal with water. But though he sometimes reads ineffable meanings into it and makes natural phenomena the symbols of human and spiritual reality, he never sacrifices man to nature nor makes nature worship a surrogate for religious faith; neither did he believe that nature can be counted upon to sympathize with men. "I love the works of Nature—but even more the works of man, 'the masterpieces of her own masterpiece'—as Goethe has said." For, "after all, what are . . . [the glories of nature] but the decorations and painted scenery in the great theater of human life? What are they but the coarse materials of the poet's song? Glorious indeed is the world of God around us, but more glorious is the world of God within us." Thus Longfellow escapes the Romantic fallacy and enrolls himself in the great Christian-humanist tradition.

Aside from his comments on the spiritual meaning of the Gothic, Longfellow says little about architecture beyond calling it the greatest of the arts. There is more about painting and sculpture. Like Michael Angelo, he seems to have considered the latter the nobler of the two, and he declined to go along with those who awarded the

Greeks supremacy over the moderns in this art. On the other hand, he disliked pictures of modern life, finding "our fatal broadcloth" ill adapted to the painter's brush, and Blanche Roosevelt says he thought his son's Japanese collection "more comical than beautiful."

With music he was familiar from childhood and learned to play both the flute and the piano, the latter, Alice says, by ear. He did not care much for "noisy oratorios." In opera he probably loved *Don Giovanni* and *The Marriage of Figaro* most, but he found *Martha* charming, thought *Fidelio* "simple and beautiful, and old-fashioned" and found *Rigoletto* wild, mad, and stirring but *A Masked Ball* "new and null." When he first heard Wagner's music in concert he thought it "strange, original, and somewhat barbaric," but by 1877 he was enthusiastic about *Lohengrin.* He loved *Pinafore* but considered *The Beggar's Opera* only a period piece.

Like most intellectuals in his time, he was completely captivated by Jenny Lind, but, unlike some of Lind's admirers, he did not disparage her great rival, Giulia Grisi, whom indeed he called "the Queen of the Lyric Drama"; in 1855 he found himself going to hear her and Mario every night. Whitman's great operatic love, Marietta Alboni, captured him also, and he admired Christine Nilsson, Etelka Gerster, and, among the Americans, Clara Louise Kellogg. When he first heard the sixteen-year-old Adelina Patti in *The Barber of Seville* in 1860, he thought her "crude, but full of promise" though "too young to appear on the stage," but two weeks later he admitted he had never seen a better Amina. Among the instrumentalists he praises Schlesinger, de Meyer, Thalberg, and Ole Bull. I get the impression that Longfellow's interest in instrumental music increased during his later years but that his greatest enthusiasm was always reserved for singers. Once he speaks appreciatively of a concert of chamber music, and once he finds an organ recital of Bach preludes and fugues "learned and, I am afraid, to unlearned ears, decidedly heavy." Though there are two admiring references to Beethoven's Ninth, his son-in-law declares that he never cared greatly for symphonies.

Opera is theater of course as well as music. There was little theater in Portland during Longfellow's youth, but there was no feeling against it in the Longfellow family. As a youngster Longfellow relished the circus and the minstrel show. In his maturity he thought Rachel the greatest actress he ever saw and admired Modjeska, Adelaide Neilson, and Mary Anderson, but was cold toward New England's own Charlotte Cushman ("I like less acting better"). In his reminiscences, Ernest Longfellow records the legend that when Sarah Bernhardt came to see his father, she gave him a kiss but refuses to vouch for its authenticity. Among the actors, he admired Salvini and Edwin Booth, though he blames the latter for his mutilation of *The Taming of the Shrew.* Charles Kean he admired as a man but not as an actor. He agreed with Dickens as to the merits of Charles Fechter's somewhat unconventional Hamlet but disagreed with him about the Shakespeare readings of his friend Fanny Kemble, which Dickens thought fantastically bad and which Longfellow admired so much that he hardly thought it worth while to go to see any play of Shakespeare's acted after having heard her read it. Rather surprisingly, he seems to have sympathized with the burgeoning realistic movement in the drama during his later days, for he laughed at his daughter for her raptures over *The Lady of Lyons* and warmly applauded Howells's efforts in behalf of a more "natural" type of play. When Lawrence Barrett produced *A Counterfeit Presentment,* Longfellow entertained both the author and the actor.

Longfellow's interest in literature was that of a scholar as well as a creative writer. The Student in *Tales of a Wayside*

Inn was obviously suggested by Chaucer's Clerk, but he is also a self-portrait.

> Books were his passion and delight,
> And in his upper room at home
> Stood many a rare and sumptuous tome,
> In vellum bound, with gold bedight,
> Great volumes garmented in white,
> Recalling Florence, Pisa, Rome.

Longfellow did an immense amount of reading in various languages, though, oddly enough, for so gifted a linguist, he sometimes read foreign literature in translation. His Latin seems to have been better than his Greek, but he calls Horace his favorite classic, as he should have been, since, as we have seen, Horace got his Bowdoin professorship for him and saved him from the law. As to his scholarship one can do no better than quote the judgment of Stanley T. Williams, who called Longfellow "one of our first great scholars in Romance languages and one of the most learned men of his time." He "helped to found the tradition of American scholarship in Spanish literature," and the idea that his scholarship was "incidental and meagre" compared to Ticknor's is an "illusion," for though he had less learning than Ticknor and less history than Prescott, he "surpassed them both in his intimate knowledge of many Spanish men of letters."[3]

Longfellow's recorded comments on Anglo-Saxon literature are mainly those of the professional scholar. Barring a few not very significant references to Chaucer, he does not, as a reader, have very much to say about the pre-Elizabethans, nor, for that matter, about the Elizabethans themselves, except for Shakespeare, most of his references to whom were made in connection with the performances he witnessed of his plays. On the other hand, his understanding and appreciation of Donne was considerable for his time. About Tennyson he was enthusiastic but not

undiscriminating. Lawrance Thompson credited Scott with
a large influence upon him not only in diction and
vocabulary but also in the way of directing his attention to
balladry and awakening his interest in European romance.
Among the Victorian novelists, Dickens was more important than all the others together and the only one who
can be suspected of having exercised any influence upon
his own writing. The American writers of whom he came
closest to considered evaluation are Emerson and Hawthorne, but Irving and Bryant were the ones who had the
largest influence upon him. Among his younger American
contemporaries, he appreciated and encouraged, in
varying degrees, Sidney Lanier, Thomas Bailey Aldrich,
Richard Watson Gildel, William Dean Howells, George
W. Cable, and Elizabeth Stuart Phelps.

Among the European literatures, Longfellow's preoccupation with Dante gave the Italian a special importance
for him. Victor Hugo is probably the French writer he
praises most warmly, but, though he enters some reser-
vations, as might have been expected, upon moral
grounds, George Sand is the one he refers to most often.
He had considerable difficulty too with Goethe, but, in
the long run, he did not fail to appreciate his greatness. He
delivered the first lectures on Goethe ever heard in
America, and O. W. Long, who studied the matter in
detail, called him "the first important interpreter in this
country of [Goethe's] genius and fame." [4]

The most interesting aspect of Longfellow's use of his
reading in his own writing is not his quotations, in which
he was always sparing, but the way he uses literature to
clarify life. As Carl Johnson once remarked, he was "quick
to see parallels between his own feelings and experiences
and those described in literature." A real storm becomes
more real to him when it reminds him of a storm in the
"Inferno" and a real woman because she recalls the
Blessed Damozel. He saw the approach of the Civil War in

terms borrowed from Greek tragedy, and in *The Courtship of Miles Standish* he even lent his own knowledge of European legendry to John Alden, who applied to Priscilla a comparison which, in her milieu, she can hardly have been expected to understand:

> "Truly, Priscilla," he said, "when I see you spinning
>   and spinning,
> Never idle a moment, but thrifty and thoughful of others,
> Suddenly you are transformed, are visibly changed in
>   a moment;
> You are no longer Priscilla, but Bertha the Beautiful
>   Spinner."

On his seventy-fourth birthday he saw himself surrounded by roses and lilies

> And that which should accompany old age,
> As honor, love, obedience, troops of friends,

and even in his last illness he writes of himself, "I know not whether I shall pull through, but I have as much hope as had the old bishop of Salamanca."

I am not aware that anybody has ever accused Longfellow of thinking of himself more highly than he ought to think. His judgment of his own work varied greatly from time to time, and he seems to have felt at least a normal need of reassurance from others as to his worth. But he did manifest a reasonable self-assurance and reliance upon his own judgment, never more so than when he chose to travel on a pioneering road for his non-literary occupation and went off to Europe all by himself as a youngster to prepare himself for it.

He tried to avoid personal publicity, burned his first wife's journal, and objected to having his private conversation reported in print. Yet, though he thought of critics as "a wretched race of hungry alligators," he saved even bad reviews and kept elaborate records, knowing well that ultimately many of his papers would find their way into print, and he knew too that an author reveals himself pitilessly in his work and tells the world secrets he would not confide even to his nearest and dearest.

In the beginning, he admits that the desire for fame was strong within him. Sometimes he seems to have believed that this longing died with his first wife. To do good work regardless of the response it awakened and "to oppose error and vice, and make mankind more in love with truth and virtue"—this he saw as "a far higher motive than mere literary ambition." Yet as late as 1854 he is wondering "what poetic victories, if any, will be won this year. In that direction," he admits, "lie my hopes and wishes, nay, my ardent longings." In his later years he could not long for fame, since he already had it, but he still knew that

> The surest pledge of a deathless name
> Is the silent homage of thoughts unspoken,

nor would he have had it otherwise.

But there was one other thing in life that was very important to Longfellow, and that was religion. His daughter Alice said that he was "born a Unitarian and remained one all his life. He never changed." But the Unitarianism on which he was reared was early Unitarianism, in which Christ, though not coexistent with the Father, was still a Divine Being, and not "mere man." Certainly there was nothing denominational about Longfellow's religious spirit. "I know of no poet who has written so little that is professedly Christian," says Augustus H. Strong, "and whose poetry is notwithstanding so shot through with the Christian spirit."[5] During his early life at least, he was not quite incapable of the kind of doubts that tormented Melville, but he possessed that basic essential in religion, the will to believe, and realizing that "that way madness lies," he resolutely held his doubts away from him. In systematic theology he had little interest, and even E. J. Bailey, who credits him with faith in "the three important fundamental doctrines, the goodness of God, the divinity of Christ, and the immortality of the soul," admits that "the theological concept of the Trinity" does not seem to have interested him. But if he was not in the habit of discussing religious problems with others, it must be remembered that he treated everything else that was very close to him in much the same way.

He was quite unperturbed when, in 1879, his daughter Edith told him she had decided to leave the Unitarian for the Episcopal Church, but he seems pretty consistently to have identified Calvinism with religious intolerance. His first contacts with Catholic services and ceremonies were made in Europe, and though he did not always admire, the majesty and aspiration of the Catholic service soon began to move him, and it was not long before he found himself responding to the devotional literature of Spain, even in its most Spanish and Catholic aspects. Though Martin Luther still has a place of honor in the *Christus,* there is an 1838 lecture in which Longfellow grants that it was the Reformation that set the tide in the direction of the modern unbelief with which he had no sympathy. There is a friendly picture of the Catholic missionaries at the close of *Hiawatha,* and such passages as the scene in *Christus* called "A Covered Bridge at Lucerne" in which the pope appears as "the chief builder and architect of the invisible bridge that leads from earth to heaven" make it easy to understand why Father Hickey, though he does not attempt to make Longfellow a Catholic, still credits him with a knowledge of Catholic lore "of vast range and variety" and calls him "the first American Protestant to make serious efforts to enter fully into the spirit of the life and practice of Catholicism."

The Spanish Jew in the *Tales of a Wayside Inn* is learned, romantic, exotic, and luxurious, but Longfellow's most considered utterance on Jewish matters is in the poem "The Jewish Cemetery at Newport." Of the fringe religious movements that flourished in his time, he seems most sympathetic to spiritualism, partly perhaps because he himself had some degree of psychic sensitiveness and certainly because he was anti-materialist in his convictions and human survival was very important to him.

Yet, in the last analysis, Longfellow never pretended to be able to explain the mystery of life. Like his own Theologian, he was

>   still perplexed
> With thoughts of this world and the next.

But for this very reason he thought faith indispensable. The purpose of our being we may not know, "but I do know—for in such things faith is knowledge—that my being has a purpose in the omniscience of my Creator, and that all my actions tend to the completion, to the full accomplishment of that purpose." His spirit was essentially a devotional spirit, and it fed on all it looked upon. He tells us that a sense of "peace . . . which passeth all understanding" came over him when he walked past St. John's Memorial Chapel on the way from his house to Harvard Square. He felt the nearness of God in both nature and human life, and it was because God informed it and manifested Himself through it that life was sacred to him. Art itself he valued most highly when, as with Albrecht Durer, and his own Michael Angelo, it was informed with the spirit of religious devotion.

During his later years Longfellow was one of the most famous men in the world, and it would be difficult to exaggerate either his vogue or the love that went out to him from both high and low, not only here but in Europe,[6] an affection inspired, it is quite clear, as much by the man as the writer. Taking his cue from the senile Emerson's remark at Longfellow's funeral that the gentleman being buried had a beautiful soul though he could not remember his name, Gamaliel Bradford, who admired Longfellow as a man though not as a poet, ended his portrait study of him by declaring that "It is a great thing to have a beautiful soul. It is a far, far greater thing to leave that soul as an eternal possession and example and inspiration to millions of one's fellow-men." But perhaps the very finest thing ever said about Longfellow as a man was said by Howells: "All other men I have known, besides, have had some foible . . . , or some meanness, or pettiness, or bitterness; but Longfellow had none, nor the suggestion of any."[7]

Appendix: Translations
and Anthologies

The collected editions of Longfellow's writings run to eleven volumes. Of the nine volumes devoted to poetry, over three and one-half consist of translations. Even allowing for the fact that his translation of *The Divine Comedy of Dante Alighieri* fills three of these volumes, the proportion of translated material in his output is still high. His first published book, in 1833, was his translation of *Coplas de Don Jorge Manrique,* with Spanish and English texts on facing pages, and seven Spanish sonnets appended, and there were times during his early career when he devoted himself more to translation than to independent composition. Indeed, it was Andrew Hilen's opinion that until "his sensitive mind had . . . received the compelling stimulus of deep personal emotion . . . he remained an imitative author who practiced primarily with verbal skills and borrowed passions."[1]

In the collected editions, where, except for the Dante, all the translations have been gathered together from the different volumes in which they first appeared, the different headings are Spanish, Swedish and Danish, German, Anglo-Saxon, French, Italian, Portuguese, "Eastern Sources," and Latin. In his 1902 biography of Longfellow in the American Men of Letters series, Thomas Wentworth Higginson attempted a more detailed analysis:

The list includes thirty-five versions of whole books or detached poems in German, twelve in Italian, nine each in French and Dutch, seven in Swedish, five in Danish, five in Polish, three in Portuguese, two each in Spanish, Russian, Hungarian, and Bohemian, with single translations in Latin, Hebrew, Chinese, Sanskrit, Marath, and Judea-German, yielding one hundred versions altogether, extending into eighteen languages, apart from the original English.

Even though Longfellow did not know all these languages at first hand, we are obviously dealing here with a writer who could not have functioned as he did without considerable linguistic prowess.

At the outset he made translations for his classes, an unavoidable procedure in a day when much of the material he was teaching was simply unavailable. There were some translated poems in his scholarly articles in *The North American Review* also and in *Outre-Mer* and *Hyperion,* as well as his anthologies. But these things do not supply a complete raison d'être for what may seem his more than normal interest in translation. He clearly used it to furnish examples for his own writing and to stimulate his poetic powers, and he showed how clearly he recognized this when he wrote the German poet Ferdinand Freiligrath that translating was "like running a ploughshare through the soil of one's mind; a thousand gems of thought start up . . . which might otherwise have lain and rotted in the ground."

One need not go along with Poe's charges of plagiarism against Longfellow to be frank in admitting that he was not one of the most original of poets. If from "A Psalm of Life" on he looked in his heart to write, it was still a heart that had been steeped in literature. He himself said that one could hardly strike a spade into the soil of Parnassus nowadays without disturbing the bones of a dead poet, and nobody was more mindful of the dependence of the individual talent upon tradition. As a professional scholar,

Longfellow read far more widely than most poets do; it would have been strange indeed if he had never echoed his reading in his writing. Margaret Fuller, who, though she criticized him severely, acquitted him of the charge of plagiarism, said that "nature with him, whether human or external, is always seen through the windows of literature," and Horace E. Scudder too admitted that his "vision and faculty divine . . . was directed toward the reflection of the facts of nature and society, rather than toward the facts themselves" and that he was essentially a "composer," who "saw his subjects in their relations rather than in their essence." Finally, George L. White, who, in his discussion of Longfellow's translations from the Scandinavian, went at this whole matter more systematically than either of the earlier writers, saw him as "using a deliberately planned method to provide inspiration for his muse." In him we find "the picture of a man who is determined to keep his experiences fresh through intelligent study of foreign languages and literatures."[2]

He had his own decided views about translation and adhered to them religiously. In his preface to the *Coplas* he wrote:

The great art of translating well lies in the power of rendering the words of a foreign author while at the same time we preserve the spirit of the original. But how far one of these requisites of a good translation may be sacrificed to the other—how far a translator is at liberty to embellish the original before him, while clothing it in a new language, is a question which has been decided differently by persons of different tastes. . . . As there are certain beauties of thought and expression in a good original, which cannot be fairly represented in the less flexible material of another language, [the translator] . . . at times may be permitted to transgress the rigid truth of language, and remedy the defect, so far as such defect can be remedied, by slight and judicious embellishment.

By this principle I have been guided in the following translations. I have rendered literally the words of the original, when it could be done without injuring their spirit, and when this could not be done, I have occasionally used the embellishment of an additional epithet, or a more forcible turn of expression. How far I have succeeded in my purpose, the reader shall determine.

As he grew older, he bacame more doubtful of the propriety of "embellishments," and by the time he arrived at *The Divine Comedy* he had adopted as his motto these words of Spenser's:

> I follow here the footing of thy feete,
> That with thy meaning so I may the rather meete.

So, in the third sonnet of his "Divina Commedia" sequence, he tells Dante that he strives "to make my steps keep pace with thine," in other words, to translate line by line.

In theory, then, the two aims of a good translation had now achieved a compatible marriage. "The only merit my book has," he wrote Robert Ferguson, "is that it is exactly what Dante says, and not what the translator imagines he might have said if he had been an Englishman," and to John Neal he was even more emphatic:

A great many people think that a translation ought not to be too faithful; that the translator should put himself into it as well as his original; that it should be Homer and Co., or Dante and Co.; and that what the foreign author really says should be falsified or modified, if thereby the smoothness of the verses can be improved. On the contrary I maintain . . . that a translator . . . should hold up his right hand and swear to "tell the truth, the whole truth, and nothing but the truth."

Even here, however, one sacrifice or adjustment had to be made. Dante wrote in terza rima, a verse form in which the second line of each tercet rimes with the first and third lines of the tercet that follows. This is much more difficult in English than it is in Italian, where rhymes are easier to come by, and Longfellow found that he could not use it without being compelled to sacrifice meaning to meter. He wrote his translation, therefore, in blank verse, sacrificing "the beautiful rhyme that blossoms all along the lines like honeysuckle on a hedge" so that he might "retain something more precious than rhyme, namely, fidelity, truth,—the life of the hedge itself."

Longfellow's first translations from *The Divine Comedy* were made for his classes at Harvard and printed as "The Celestial Pilot," "The Terrestrial Paradise," and "Beatrice" in *Voices of the Night.* It is surprising that these selections were all from the "Purgatorio," the most "human" part of the *Comedy,* which was his favorite (he found the "Inferno" almost unbearably painful).[3] Writing a few lines every day after breakfast ("the morning prayer—the keynote of the day," he calls it) he completed sixteen cantos of the "Purgatorio" during the spring and summer of 1843. Then, for some reason, he set the work aside and did not return to it until February 1, 1853:

> In weariness of spirit and despair of writing anything original, I turned again to-day, to dear old Dante, and resumed my translation of the "Purgatorio" where I left it in 1843. I find great delight in the work. It diffused its benediction through the day.

On his forty-sixth birthday, February 27, he finished Canto 31, and, the college term beginning, said farewell to both Dante and "the ease of vacation." He adds, "I have not been wholly idle; let the completed 'Purgatorio' answer for me."

He did not return to his task until after Fanny Appleton's death, when he seems to have used it as a kind of desperate refuge from grief and loss. "All the past week," he wrote on March 18, 1862, "I have been pretty busy upon Dante,—quite absorbed," and, later, "Another week gone. All given to Dante." For thirty-four successive days he translated a canto a day. His work was completed on April 16, 1863, the "Inferno" having been left for the last, but revision and copying the "Purgatorio" occupied him until March 1864. Ten copies of the "Inferno" were struck off in time for half of them to be sent to Florence in May 1865 *"in commemorazione del secentessimo anniversario della nascita di Dante Alighieri,"* but Longfellow did not finish correcting the last proofs of his very extensive illustrations and notes until the beginning of 1867. The three-volume work appeared in May 1867, and there was a slightly revised edition three years later.

While the manuscript was going though the press, Lowell and Charles Eliot Norton were sometimes joined by other friends of Longfellow's in his study on Wednesday evenings, to go over the proof sheets and suggest alterations and corrections (making alterations in proof was a less expensive undertaking in those days than it is now). As Norton wrote afterwards:

We paused over every doubtful passage, discussed the various readings, considered the true meaning of obscure words and phrases, sought for the most exact equivalent of Dante's expression, objected, criticised, praised with a freedom that was made perfect by Mr. Longfellow's absolute sweetness, simplicity, and modesty, and by the entire confidence that existed between us.[4]

In a sense, the Dante Society, which was formed in 1880–81, which Longfellow served as its first president, and which still exists, was an outgrowth of these meetings.

Obviously no translation of a poetical work into another language can ever be completely successful. Gamaliel Bradford felt this so strongly that he committed himself to the proposition that poetry should never be translated and that those who cannot read it in the language in which it was written had better leave it alone. So far as lyrical poetry is concerned, he may very well have been right. This would be very unfortunate, however, in the case of a writer like Dante whose admittedly incompletely translatable lyrical quality is matched by profundity of thought and depth of characterization, for such things do not defy translation. By the same token, however, it must be equally clear that, granting the need for translation, no given attempt can be equally satisfactory to all readers. Norton, who himself afterwards produced an excellent prose translation of the *Comedy*, wrote:

> The directness and simplicity of Dante's diction require of the translator like directness and simplicity. The difficulty of presenting these qualities in a rhymed version is such as to make such a version practically impossible; and the sympathy of the translator is shown by his discarding rhyme for the sake of preserving the more important elements of style. . . . The method of translation which Mr. Longfellow has chosen is free alike from the reproach of pedantic literalness and of unfaithful license.

There have been those, however, who have complained that Longfellow was unimaginative and mechanical or that he was too gentle a spirit to catch the fire and power of Dante. Odell Shepard thought he "blurred and emasculated" not only Dante but Heine and Jean Paul Richter, and even Howells complained that he translated Dante "into the English dictionary rather than the English language." When all allowances for these views have been made however, it still remains true that Longfellow's translation of the *Comedy* has held an honorable place for a long time now, and one may doubt that it would be possible to secure unanimity of opinion on any one of his successors having driven him from the field. All this, however, takes us into an area where only an Italian scholar could enter anything like a definitive opinion.[5]

The difficulties multiply indefinitely when it comes to entering an opinion concerning the quality of Longfellow's translations in general. Naturally, then, most of the competent judgments that have been entered in this area concern single languages and sometimes even single poems. The great Swedish poet Esaias Tegnér called the quotations from his *Frithiof's Saga* that Longfellow included in his essay on that poem the best translations he had seen in English and wished that the American would translate the entire poem. Daniel Kilham Dodge also accords Longfellow high praise as a translator from the Scandinavian, not merely for his knowledge of the language itself but also for his feeling for the life and literature of the Scandinavian countries. Contrariwise, John Leighly has devoted a whole article to the ''inaccuracies'' in Longfellow's translation of ''The Children of the Lord's Supper'': ''Longfellow's knowledge of Swedish was plainly more deficient than critics have realized.'' Similarly, Walter Silz dissents from the general appreciation of the translation from the German of one of Goethe's night songs: ''One can say for Longfellow's poem that it conveys an approximate idea of the content and structure of Goethe's. But the magic of Goethe's utterance is not in it.'' Silz does not blame Longfellow for this however but instead concludes generously, ''That so accomplished a linguist and so skilled a poet . . . could do no better proves that great lyric poetry is simply untranslatable.'' On the other hand, though Carl Hammer, Jr. does not seem sure that he can accept without reservation James Taft Hatfield's ''all but unconditional praise'' of Longfellow's translations from the German, he does find that he displays ''a high order of proficiency in reproducing the substance and spirit'' of the poems he selects and that when he is inaccurate, he usually compensates for this with ''a touch of genius.'' ''While one may take exception to individual translations, his aptitude in general and his astonishing versatility remain beyond all doubt,'' and this is probably about as close as we can hope to come to a fair overall evaluation of Longfellow's quality, essaying an impossible task in an imperfect world.[6]

If the consideration of Longfellow's translations must necessarily remain undefinitive in such a book as this, certainly no extended account of his anthologies can be called for. *The Poems and Poetry of Europe,* which drew upon ten languages, was published first in 1845 in an edition of 776 large pages and then added 340 pages more in the edition of 1871, through whose preparation the editor found himself ''altogether more entangled than I meant to be.'' *The Waif* came out in 1845 and *The Estray* in 1846, and the *Poems of Places* between 1876 and 1879.

Though it is surprising to find a writer of Longfellow's eminence devoting himself to anthologizing at all, one must admit that nobody in his America could have done *The Poems and Poetry of Europe* better than he did and that there were few who could have done it at all. As we examine the book now, we shudder for what it must have done to the eyesight of Longfellow's contemporaries, yet the fact remains that it was read and that it was one of the pioneering attempts to introduce Americans to European literature. W. P. Trent hardly exaggerated when he wrote that Longfellow ''was probably the most important link for almost two generations between the culture of the old world and that of the new.''[7] As a people, we are still quite ignorant enough of Continental writers, but something at least has been accomplished, and we owe some of this to Longfellow. He himself wrote some but by no means all the critical introductions and evaluations included in *The Poets and Poetry of Europe,* to which C. C. Felton also contributed largely.

The Waif and *The Estray* were both slender little volumes in which, as their titles suggest, Longfellow collected out-of-the-way fugitive pieces by unfamiliar poets.

Poe seems strangely not to have understood the titles, for while he called Longfellow's "Proem" by far the best poem in *The Waif,* he found the collection "infected with a *moral taint*" because the editor had excluded all those contemporaries whose claims to eminence might have infringed upon his own! The circumstances being what they were, it would of course have been an unforgivable insult to include them.[8]

The most amazing aspect of Longfellow's anthologizing, however, is that as late as the 1870s he should have taken the time to edit the thirty-one volumed *Poems of Places.* He worked on this over about five years, finding it expanding under his hands far beyond his expectations. Traveling in his easy chair was pleasant, but the "infinite detail" involved and "the lengthening chain" he found himself dragging behind him wearied him unspeakably as time ran on. Though the work was published in dainty, multi-colored volumes that still stand gathering dust in large libraries, William Sloane Kennedy, one of Longfellow's early biographers, says that the publishers lost money on them. They contain just what their name implies; the editor roams the world, place by place, collecting poems written about each locality, the result being a kind of poetical gazeteer. In some cases, where he could not find anything ready to his hand, Longfellow even produced original poems of his own. In one respect, however, the work was a "natural" for him, for he himself was as alive to place as the most sensitive cat who ever lived. Sometimes indeed he was even tempted to wish that he could inhabit all the places he had known simultaneously.

Notes

The following abbreviations are employed in bibliographical references in the Notes and Bibliography.

ABC	American Book Company
AL	*American Literature*
Bkm	*Bookman* (New York)
CLQ	*Colby Library Quarterly*
Col	*Colophon*
ESQ	*Emerson Society Quarterly*
Expl	*Explicator*
HM	Houghton Mifflin Company
HUP	Harvard University Press
HWL	Henry Wadsworth Longfellow
I	*Italica*
L	Longfellow
LG	Longmans, Greene & Co.
LSUP	Louisiana State University Press
M	Macmillan
MLN	*Modern Language Notes*
MP	*Modern Philology*
NEQ	*New England Quarterly*
NYFQ	*New York Folklore Quarterly*
OUP	Oxford University Press
PBSA	*Publications of the Bibliographical Society of America*
P-L	*Poet-Lore*
PMLA	*Publications of the Modern Language Association*

PPLCC   *Papers Presented at the Longfellow Commemorative*
         Conference, April 1–3, 1982 (National Park Service,
         Longfellow National Historical Park, n.d.)
PQ   *Philological Quarterly*
SSN   *Scandinavian Studies and Notes*
Okla   University of Oklahoma Press
YUP   Yale University Press

I: Biography

1 The family comprised Stephen, b. August 14, 1805, m.
   Marianne Preble, 1831, d. September 19, 1850: Henry
   Wadsworth; Elizabeth Wadsworth, b. August 14, 1808, d.
   May 5, 1829; Anne (or Annie), b. March 3, 1810, m. George
   W. Pierce, 1832, d. January 24, 1901; Alexander Wads-
   worth, b. May 20, 1814, m. Elizabeth C. Porter, 1851, d.
   February 14, 1901; Mary, b. June 28, 1816, m. James
   Greenleaf, 1839, d. December 3, 1902; Ellen, b. July 12,
   1818, d. August 12, 1834; Samuel, b. June 18, 1819, d. Oc-
   tober 3, 1892.

2 Stephen was the black sheep of the Longfellow family and a
   problem to his kinsmen until he died in 1850 after his own
   family had been broken up and reason itself had failed; their
   mother used to wonder how two sons of the same parents,
   brought up together, could have turned out so differently as
   Stephen and Henry. To make matters even worse, Stephen
   passed on his unfortunate characteristics to his son and
   namesake, who remained an anxiety to the poet even after
   the father had died. These facts are important for our purpose primarily because they help refute the popular but
   uninformed notion that Longfellow had an easy or un-
   troubled life. His relations with his brother Alexander were
   cordial and friendly, but I get the impression that he was
   closer temperamentally to Samuel, who became his
   biographer. Among the sisters, Anne (Mrs. Pierce), early
   widowed, seems to have been especially close to him.

3 See Carl L. Johnson, "HWL, Librarian," *College and Research Libraries,* 15 (1954), 425–29.

4 See Chapter III of the present volume.

5 Miss Goddard was soon recalled to America by the death of her father, but Miss Crowninshield remained with Longfellow to the end of the journey. *The Diary of Clara Crowninshield: A European Tour with L, 1835–36,* edited by Andrew Hilen (University of Washington Press, 1956) contains an invaluable record of this trip.

6 Speaking of Longfellow and Ticknor together, Carl L. Johnson writes, "They gave the first advanced instruction in modern languages. They opened the fields of modern literature and were the first language teachers to provide work above the level of basic grammar and elementary reading."

7 The children were Charles Appleton, b. June 9, 1844, d. April 13, 1893; Ernest Wadsworth, b. November 23, 1845, m. Harriet Spelman, 1868, d. November 24, 1921; Fanny, b. April 7, 1847, d. September 11, 1848; Alice Mary, b. September 21, 1850, d. December 7, 1928; Edith, b. October 22, 1853, m. Richard Henry Dana III, 1878, d. July 21, 1915; Annie Allegra, b. November 8, 1885, m. Joseph Gilbert Thorp, 1855, d. February 28, 1934. The second Mrs. Longfellow was a copious journal-keeper and letter-writer, and this material is liberally extracted in Edward Wagenknecht, ed., *Mrs. Longfellow: Selected Letters and Journals of Fanny Appleton Longfellow (1817–61)* (LG, 1956).

8 For a detailed account see Andrew Hilen, "Charley Longfellow Goes to War," *Harvard Library Bulletin,* 14 (1960), 59–81, 282–303.

9 The fullest and most sensible account of Longfellow's con-

tacts with Sherwood Bonner, including a bibliography, is in
Rayburn S. Moore, " 'Merlin and Vivien'? Some Notes on
Sherwood Bonner and L," *Mississippi Quarterly*, 28
(1974–75). 181–84. For Cornelia Fitch consult Volume 4 of
Andrew Hilen's definitive edition of Longfellow's *Letters*, in
which work will be found such of the poet's correspondence
with all the ladies he knew during his later years as the editor
was able to find. Longfellow's interest in Alice Frere was first
made known in Edward Wagenknecht's *L: A Full-Length
Portrait;* see pp. 282–88 for a documented account of the
available evidence.

II: Poetic Theory and Practice

1 George Arms, *The Fields Were Green* (Stanford University
   Press, 1953) finds in Longfellow's verses "a polished social
   tone, neither comic nor sentimental, but humanely ethical."
   He quotes I. A. Richards's comments on "In the Churchyard
   at Cambridge" as having "a social, urbane, highly
   cultivated, self-confident, temperate, and easy kind of
   humor." The poem is "not a grim warning, or an exhortation," which is what most nineteenth-century poets would
   have made of it, "but a cheerful realization of the situation,
   not in the least evangelical."

2 *HWL*, p. 191. Newton Arvin, *L, His Life and Work,* is very
   good on Longfellow's technique, especially his poetic experimentation, "free verse," etc. See especially p. 182,
   where he credits Longfellow with having anticipated the
   "sprung rhythm" of Gerard Manley Hopkins. In 1935
   Joseph Eugene O'Neill produced a Columbia dissertation on
   "Imagery in the Poetry of L." According to *Dissertation Ab-
   stracts,* 15 (1955), 2213, O'Neill found that Longfellow's
   imagery lacks "sharpness and precision," but that he "succeeds in panoramic effects, clear and vivid use of color, and
   effective contrasts of light and dark. Sound interests him
   more than sight and is used in surprising variety. Painful
   aspects of touch predominate, bitterness of taste is stressed,
   but pleasant odors outnumber unpleasant ones. Synesthesia
   appears, generally with imaginative effect." In *A History of*

English Prosody from the Twelfth Century to the Present Day (M, 1910),III, 487–89, George Saintsbury declared that "Longfellow represents, for America, the first and perhaps to this day, the greatest, of the verse-makers who . . . carried on during the whole of the nineteenth century the principles of prosodic variety and adaptation." But the standard and most detailed study of Longfellow's prosody is now that of Gay Wilson Allen in his *American Prosody,* ABC, 1935). Of particular interest is his observation that the great bulk of Longfellow's verse "is in paragraphs rather than stanzas, including not only his blank verse and heroic couplets but also four-stress couplets, the unrimed trochees of *Hiawatha,* and the several poems in hexameters."

3 For a fairly full account of the contents of the "Book of Suggestions," see my *L: A Full-Length Portrait,* Appendix A.

4 The most learned discussion of the hexameter problem in English in its relation to Longfellow is in C. C. Felton's review of *Ballads and Other Poems, North American Review,* 55 (1842), 114–44. See also E. C. Stedman, *Poets of America* (HM, 1885). pp. 195–99.

III: Longfellow's Prose Works

1 There are variations in content between the publications indicated, as also between the Harper edition and later editions, some of which are described in detail by Lawrance Thompson in *Young L,* where the portions of "The Schoolmaster" taken up into *Outre-Mer* are also indicated. It is interesting that while in Europe Longfellow should also have considered the possibility of doing a New England sketchbook, for which see Thompson's article, "L's Projected Sketch Book of New England," *Col.* Part XV (1933).

2 Longfellow expressed his affection for Irving in his remarks at a special meeting of the Massachusetts Historical Society, on December 15, 1859, commemorating Irving's death: "Every reader has his first book, I mean to say, one book, among all

others, which in early youth, first fascinates his imagination, and at once excites and satisfies the desires of his mind. To me, this first book was the 'Sketch-Book' of Washington Irving. I was a schoolboy when it was published and read each succeeding number with ever-increasing wonder and delight,—spell-bound by its pleasant humor, its melancholy tenderness, its atmosphere of revery; nay, even by its gray-brown covers, the shaded letters of its titles, and the fair, clear type,—which seemed an outward symbol of the style.'' There is a detailed commentary on Longfellow's imitation of Irving by William Charvat in Matthew J. Bruccoli, ed., *The Profession of Authorship in America, 1800–1870* (Ohio State University Press, 1969). For a dissenting view, see Thomas H. Pauly, "*Outre-Mer* and L's Quest for a Career," *NEQ,* 50 (1977), 3–52, which stresses the differences between *The Sketch-Book* and *Outre-Mer* rather than the resemblances.

3 *New Light on L,* Ch. 6, especially pp. 70–72, 77. The seduction of Emma is merely suggested as the book stands, but at one time the manuscript recorded that "in her death two beings perished."

4 Again Hatfield gives interesting details; see *New Light on L,* pp. 75–76. For Thompson, see *Young L,* p. 405, note 5. Martin L. Kornbluth, "L's *Hyperion* and Goethe's *Wilhelm Meister's Lehrjahre,*" *ESQ,* No. 31 (1963), pp. 55–59, attempts to show that "*Hyperion* may be considered Longfellow's version of *Wilhelm Meister.*" For detailed studies of the general subject indicated see Fred Lewis Pattee, "L and German Romance," *P-L* 17, Spring 1906, pp. 59–77, and Frederick Burwick, "L and German Romanticism," *Comparative Literature Studies,* 7 (1970), 12–42. See, further, J. Chesley Mathews, "Echoes of Dante in L's *Hyperion* and *Kavanagh.*" *Italica,* 28 (1951), 17–18.

5 See Lillian Faderman, "Female Same-Sex Relationships in Novels by L, Holmes, and James," *NEQ,* 51 (1978), 309–32.

6 "Voices of L: *Kavanagh* as Autobiography," *ESQ,* No. 58

(1970), pp. 3–14. William Charvat too thought "the frustrated Churchill . . . Longfellow's picture of the self he outgrew in the 1840's," Kavanagh "the leader with the will (unlike Churchill) to make his dream prevail," and Hawkins "a caricature of the Europeanized Longfellow of 1838" (see note 2).

7 Thus Clarissa Cartwright, the author of "Symphonies of the Soul, and Other Poems," which she has had bound in crimson velvet, who calls upon Churchill in Chapter XXIV to beg him to "look over" her manuscript, favor her with his "candid opinion," and, if he approves of her efforts, write her a preface, is clearly the young lady whose visit Longfellow himself reported in his journal on October 6, 1849. See Allaback's article, p. 13, note 13.

8 In *The Raven and the Whale* (Harcourt, Brace, 1956).

9 James Taft Hatfield, "An Unknown Prose Tale by L," *AL,* 3 (1931), 136–49.

10 See the very interesting and suggestive comment on realism and romance. "So long as truth is stranger than fiction, the elements of poetry and romance will not be wanting in common life. If, invisible ourselves, we could follow a single human being through a single day of his life, and know all his secret thoughts and hopes and anxieties, his prayers and tears and good resolves, his passionate delights and struggles against temptation,—all that excites, and all that soothes the heart of man,—we should have poetry enough to fill a volume." *Ulysses* seems just around the corner—does it not?

IV: Early Poems

1 In the volume in hand, all commentary on Longfellow's translations is reserved for the appendix.

2 "Hymn to the Night" left Poe with the "firm belief that a poet of genius had at length arisen amongst us." He thought

no poem had ever opened with more august beauty and that
the first five stanzas were nearly perfect. Had Longfellow
always reached this level, "we should have been tempted to
speak of him not only as *our* finest poet, but as one of the
noblest poets of all time." But the unsigned article, "L's
'Hymn to the Night.' " *Expl,* 1 (1942), Item 7, criticizes the
use of "Greek allusions" (epigraph?) and the personification
of Night "as a woman who by line 11 has inconsistently
become a palace."

3 "A Psalm of Life" has attracted considerable commentary;
   see W. A. Chamberlin, "L's Attitude toward Goethe," *MP,*
   16 (1918–19), 57–76; Carl L. Johnson, "Three Notes on L,"
   Harvard Studies and Notes in Philology and Literature, 14
   (1932), 249–71; William Charvat, " 'Let Us Then Be Up
   and Doing,' " *English Journal,* College Edition, 28 (1939),
   374–83; Robert S. Ward, "An Interpretation of 'A Psalm of
   Life' with References to Manrique's *Coplas,* " in Thomas B.
   Stroup and Sterling A. Stoudmire, eds., *South Atlantic
   Studies for Sturgis E. Leavitt* (Scarecrow Press, 1953) and
   "The Integrity of L's Philosophical Patterns," *The Carrell:
   Journal of the Friends of the University of Miami Library,* 1,
   December 1960, pp. 5–13; Daniel F. Littlefield, "L's 'A
   Psalm of Life,': A Relation of Method to Popularity,"
   Markham Review, 7 (1978), 49–51; Robert T. Cargo,
   "Baudelaire, L, and 'A Psalm of Life,' " *Revue de
   Littérature Comparée,* 54 (1980), 196–201 (Alfred G.
   Engstrom, "Baudelaire and L's 'Hymn to the Night,' "
   MLN, 74 [1959], 695–98, had already argued that
   Baudelaire used this poem also). Goethean influence has
   been well nigh universally accepted, the only important
   dissenter being Ward, who saw the psalm as rather a reaction
   against "the otherwordly view of life and literature" which
   he believed Longfellow had imbibed during his first
   European sojourn. The two views are not really irreconcilable; indeed Johnson had already brought Manrique into
   the picture in passing. Longfellow himself once pointed out
   that his first line resembled the beginning of a song in
   *Wilhelm Meisters Lehrjahre: "Singet nicht in Trauertonen /
   Von der Einsamkeit der Nacht,"* and Henry A. Pochmann,

in his *German Culture in America: Philosophical and Literary Influences, 1600–1900* (University of Wisconsin Press, 1957), pp. 419–20, 725, points out that Longfellow read "A Psalm of Life" to his class at Harvard at the end of the lecture on Goethe, also that "Art is long and time is fleeting" is very close to *"Die Kunst ist lang, and kurz ist unser Leben,"* as is "Let the dead past bury its dead" to *"Lass die Vergangene vergangen sein."* Iris Lilian Whitman, *L and Spain,* saw the psalm as a reply to Calderon's *Life Is a Dream* (see Thompson, *Young L,* pp. 406–408, note 15, for a general, informed, though unsympathetic, commentary on Longfellow's use of and relationship to the dream interpretation of life). Other sources invoked have been Emerson, Novalis *(Hymnen an die Nacht),* Chateaubriand *(Atala),* Beaumont and Fletcher *(The Humorous Lieutenant),* and even a poem on tobacco by Ralph Erskine in *Knickerbocker!* Littlefield interpreted Longfellow's poem as a pastiche of aphoristic counsel, like *The New England Primer* and *Poor Richard's Almanac.* Charvat is correct in reading it as interpreting the spirit of the times but makes Longfellow's indifference to politics seem much greater than it actually was.

4 Poe's notion that Longfellow had plagiarized Tennyson's "The Death of the Old Year" is absurd, and Thompson's argument *(Young L,* pp. 306–307, 416, note 4) that Longfellow's denial that he knew Tennyson's poem was untruthful because he owned a copy of the 1833 edition of Tennyson's poems is unconvincing; the fact that Longfellow had the book in his library does not prove that he had read it through, much less stolen from it. For further discussion, see Edward Wagenknecht, *Edgar Allan Poe: The Man Behind the Legend* (OUP, 1963), pp. 132–35.

5 See Henry Beston, "The Real Wreck of the Hesperus," *Bkm,* 61 (1925), 304–306; Charles A. Huguenin, "The Truth about the Schooner Hesperus," *NYFQ,* 16 (1960), 48–53. For other important references to contemorary Boston newspapers, see my *L: A Full-Length Portrait,* p. 58, note 2.

6 George Arms, "*Moby-Dick* and 'The Village Blacksmith,' "
   Notes and Queries, 192 (1947), 187–88, suggests interestingly that Melville was supplying a satirical or
   burlesque commentary upon Longfellow's poem in his
   Chapter CXII—"The Blacksmith."

7 Hilen, *Letters,* Vol. II, pp. 500–501. In another letter (Vol.
   VI, p. 129) Longfellow explains and defends his Latin. See
   the Craigie Edition of Longfellow, Vol. I, pp. 358–65, for a
   very detailed account of the changes made in "Excelsior"
   during the period of composition.

8 Edward Thorstenberg, " 'The Skeleton in Armor' and the
   Frithiof Saga," *MLN,* 25 (1910), 189–92, pointed out
   resemblances between the two works and argued
   Longfellow's indebtedness. Hilen believed that the Tegnér
   work contributed many details but thought Longfellow's
   hero more like the warriors in the *Heimskringla.* He added
   that the meter came from Drayton's "The Battle of Agin-
   court," that the invocation to the "fearful guest" begins
   with words taken from Longfellow's own translation of
   Uhland's "*Der schwarze Ritter,*" that both Campbell's
   "Lord Ullin's Daughter" and Shelley's "The Fugitives"
   may have been drawn upon for the account of the flight, and
   that the idea of the marginal notes (when the poem appeared
   in *Knickerbocker's)* probably came from "The Rime of the
   Ancient Mariner." See his "Longfellow and Scandinavia
   Revisited" in *PPLCC.*

9 Longfellow described the poem to Samuel Ward as "a
   funereal chant . . . full of ghastly images, which I shall not
   publish at all, as I hate grave-yards, and would like to be
   burned, not *buried.*" Hilen, *Letters,* Volume II, p. 337.

10 For the personal relations between Longfellow and Dickens,
   see Edward Wagenknecht, "Dickens in L's Letters and Journals," in *Dickens and the Scandalmongers: Essays in
   Criticism* (Okla, 1965). Other sources and influences are
   suggested by A. H. Applemann, "L's *Poems on Slavery* in
   their Relationship to Freiligrath," *MLN,* 30 (1915),

101–102, and Robert Haywood Morrison, "An Apparent Influence of Thomas Moore on L," *PQ*, 35 (1956), 198–200. For a more general consideration see Janet Harris, "L's Poems on Slavery," *CLQ*, 14 (1978), 85–92.

11 The other is the sonnet written in honor of Fanny Kemble's readings from Shakespeare in *The Seaside and the Fireside.*

12 Michael Zimmerman's "War and Peace: L's The Occultation of Orion," *AL,* 35 (1966–67), 540–46, is the only detailed study of this poem.

13 Harry Hayden Clark, ed., *Major American Poets* (ABC, 1936), p. 853. This magnificent anthology contains valuable material on Longfellow and all the other poets included.

14 H. Z. Kip, "The Origin of L's 'The Arrow and the Song,' " *PQ,* 9 (1930), 76–78, compares the poem, with suggestion of indebtedness, to four verses in Goethe's *"Sprüche in Reimen"* in his *Sprichwörterbuch.*

15 See John William Scholl, "L and Schiller's *'Lied von der Glocke,'* " *MLN,* 28 (1913), 49–50, who also finds traces of Schiller in the Second Interlude of *Christus,* "The Hanging of the Crane," and "Kéramos," and C. R. Lefcourt, *"L'Influence de* 'Das Lied von der Glocke' *sur* 'The Building of the Ship' *de* HWL," *Revue des Langues Vivantes,* 33 (1967), 495–98. Hans-Joachim Lang and Fritz Fleischmann, in " 'All This Beauty, All This Grace': L's 'The Building of the Ship,' " *NEQ,* 54 (1981), 104–18, not only argue Longfellow's use of Mackenzie's articles on "Ship," "Navigation," and "Navy" in the *Encyclopedia Americana,* but document the poet's interest in politics and in Mackenzie's career and offer besides an excellent analysis of the poem and an account of its fame and reputation. Oral Sumner Coad, "The Bride of the Sea," *AL,* 9 (1937–38), 71–73, compares Longfellow's description of the launching of a vessel in terms of sexual union with Whittier's "The Ship-Builders," and suggests a "faint parallel" to Wordsworth's

sonnet, "On the Extinction of the Venetian Republic." See also Robert S. Ward, "L and Melville: The Ship and the Whale," *ESQ,* No. 22 (1961), pp. 57-63, on similarities between the "Ship" and *White-Jacket.*

16 The patriotic and partisan ending of "The Building of the Ship," though primarily responsible for its fame, was an afterthought. The original ending was gloomy and elegiac:

> But where, oh where,
> Shall end this form so rare?
> . . . Wrecked upon some treacherous rock,
> Rotting in some loathsome dock,
> Such the end must be at length
> Of all this loveliness and strength!

The new ending was decided upon after a dinner with Charles Sumner following a Free Soil meeting in Tremont Temple, and the first revised version read:

> We will not doubt, we will not fear,
> But sail right on with hearts of cheer,
> Our hearts, our fortunes go with these. . . .
> Sail on, nor fear to breast the sea!
> Sail on, sail on forever more. . . .
> Our faith and trust, that banish fears,
> Are all with thee—are all with thee!

All this and much more is detailed in Henry Wadsworth Longfellow Dana's study of the manuscript in his " 'Sail On, O Ship of State!': How L Came to Write These Lines One Hundred Years Ago," *CLQ,* Second Series, 1947–50, pp. 209–14, where he also gives an account of the revival the poem experienced during World War II, when President Roosevelt sent its climax to Winston Churchill and it created a sensation in England. The union with Britain that Roosevelt was thinking of, however, was far from Longfellow's thought.

17 Gerald R. Griffin's "L's 'Tegnér's Drapa': A Reappraisal," *American Transcendental Quarterly,* No. 40 (1978), 379–87,

is the only detailed exposition of the meaning of the poem. Griffin's principal concern is an attempt to reconcile the glorification of Balder and the sagas in the first part of the poem with the idea of all this being supplanted by Christ and Christianity in the last part.

V: Evangeline

1 Manning Hawthorne and H. W. L. Dana, "The Origin and Development of L's *Evangeline*," *PBSA,* 41 (1947), 165–203. This important article is the fullest account we have of the sources and writing of the poem.

2 Though the morality of the removal of the Acadians hardly seems debatable, it is not surprising that it should find defenders in a world in which much worse outrages are still being condoned. See Archibald MacMechan, *"Evangeline* and the Real Acadians," *Atlantic Monthly,* 99 (1907), 202–13, and Erving Winslow, "Historical Inaccuracies in L's *Evangeline,"* *Dial,* 60 (1916), 105–107. Both these writers blame the Acadians for their own fate, and MacMechan declares that "Thanks to *Evangeline,* the Expulsion will never be understood." Clifford Millard describes "The Acadians in Virginia," *Virginia Magazine of History and Biography,* 40 (1932), 241–58, and H. L. Sayler's "The Real Evangeline," *Bkm,* 18 (1900), 17–25, is an illustrated article on the Lousiana background. Rose M. Davis, " 'The Tents of Grace' in L's *Evangeline*: Their History and Fate," *Pennsylvania History,* 18 (1951), 269–92, takes its point of departure from the lines,

> Now in the Tents of Grace of the meek Moravian
>   Missions,
> Now in the noisy camps and the battle-fields of the
>   army,
> Now in secluded hamlets, in towns and populous
>   cities,
> Like a phantom she came, and passed away
>   unremembered.

This article describes the Moravian missions and includes some account of Francis Huebner's 1902 novel, *Charles Killbuck,* in which Evangeline is a character.

3 See Manning Hawthorne, "Hawthorne and 'The Man of God,' " *Col, N.S.* Vol. 2, No. 2, Winter 1937, pp. 262–82. Hawthorne's review of *Evangeline* in the *Salem Advertiser* was reprinted, with an introduction, by Hubert H. Hoeltje in *NEQ,* 23 (1950), 232–235.

4 See Edward Thornstenberg, "Is L's *Evangeline* a Product of Swedish Influence?" *P-L,* 19 (1908), 301–17; A. H. Applemann, "The Relation of L's *Evangeline* to Tegnér's *Frithiof's Saga,*" *Publications of the Society for the Advancement of Scandinavian Study,* 2 (1914–16), 165–80, and "L's *Evangeline* and Tegnér's *Frithiof's Saga,*" *Anglia,* 49 (1925), 153–72; Murray Gardner Hill, "Some of L's Sources for the Second Part of *Evangeline,*" *PMLA,* 31 (1916), 161–80. There is also a book-length study by Ernest Martin, *L'Évangéline de L et la suite merveilleuse d'um poème* (Librarie Hachette, 1936). For an account of Banvard and his contemporaries see John Francis McDonnell, *The Lost Panoramas of the Mississippi* (University of Chicago Press, 1951).

5 Edward L. Hirsh, *HWL* (University of Minnesota Press, 1964), p. 35.

6 See, further, on this subjet, R. B. Steele, "The Meter of *Evangeline,*" *MLN,* 9 (1894), 414–18, and T. M. Campbell, "L and the Hexameter," *MLN,* 23 (1908), 96 (cf. correction by Charles Eliot Norton on p. 231).

7 There is only one Homeric simile in *Evangeline,* a somewhat violent one for a poem of this character:

> As when the air is serene in the sultry solstice of
>   summer,
> Suddenly gathers a storm, and the deadly sling of the
>   hailstones
> Beats down the farmer's corn in the field, and shatters
>   his windows,

> Hiding the sun, and strewing the ground with thatch
>   from the house-roofs,
> Bellowing fly the herds, and seek to break their
>   enclosures;
> So on the hearts of the people descended the words of
>   the speaker.

But there are a number of Biblical allusions and references to both European and American Indian folklore.

VI: The Song of Hiawatha

1 Since there has been some discussion about the pronunciation of the hero's name, let it be recorded that Longfellow pronounced it He-ah-wah-thah, with the stress on the third syllable. See his letter to an unidentified correspondent, in Hilen, *Letters,* Vol. III, p. 541.

2 The fullest account of Schoolcraft and his relation to Longfellow is in Chase S. and Stellanova Osborn, *Schoolcraft—L—Hiawatha* (Lancaster, Pa., The Jacques Cattell Press, 1912). On the historical Hiawatha, consult Joseph S. Promechen, "The Making of *Hiawatha,*" *NYFQ,* 28 (1972), 150–60, as well as Albert Keiser, *The Indian In American Literature* (OUP, 1933), who points out that the poem "has not a single fact or fiction relating to the great historic Iroquoian reformer and statesman" but moves him from central New York "to live and move among inveterate Algonquin enemies on the southern shore of Lake Superior." See also James Cleland Hamilton, "The Algonquin Manabozho and *Hiawatha,*" *Journal of American Folklore,* 16 (1903), 229–33; Douglas Leechman, "L's *Hiawatha,*" *Queen's Quarterly,* 51 (1944–45), 307–13; Arthur C. Parker, "Who Was Hiawatha?" *NYFQ,* 10 (1964), 285–88.

3 In a letter to G. W. Greene, February 15, 1875 (Hilen, *Letters,* Vol. VI, p. 23), Longfellow himself points out the resemblance between the legend of Wenonah and the West Wind and that of Flora and Zephirus in Ovid's *Fasti.* David W. Berry, "The Hiawatha Saga: Bayard Taylor's Possible

Contribution,'' *CLQ,* 17 (1981), 256–58, concerns Taylor's "Mon-da-min,'' in *A Book of Romances, Lyrics, and Songs* (1852).

4 See Rena N. Coen's detailed and elaborately illustrated article, "L, Hiawatha and Some Nineteenth Century American Painters,'' in *PPLCC.*

5 See Longfellow's letters to Moncure D. Conway and Charles Sumner, in Hilen, *Letters,* Vol. III, pp. 505–506. But the controversy on this point has been keen. Waino Nyland, *"Kalevala* as a Reputed Source of L's *Song of Hiawatha,''* *AL,* 22 (1950), 1–20, supports Longfellow's denial of indebtedness to the *Kalevala* for anything more than meter and poetic devices. Wilbur L. Schramm, *"Hiawatha* and its Predecessors,'' *PQ,* 11 (1932), 321–43, finds that the American Indian romances in verse that preceded *Hiawatha* had created a tradition of which Longfellow could hardly have been unaware and that he "was advised by a tradition as old as 1790 to write in tetrameters, and he was advised by Schoolcraft to write in trochees.'' See also Douglas Hardy, "Influence of Finnish *Kalevala* in the Composition of L's *Song of Hiawatha,''* *Brigham Young University Studies,* 4 (1962), 140–47. But Ernest J. Moyne, Hiawatha *and* Kalevala: *A Study of the Relationship Between L's "Indian Edda'' and the Finnish Epic* (Helsinki, Academia Scientiarum Fennica, 1965) argued that some incidents for which Longfellow had "only the barest hints in his Indian sources'' were built up on Finnish models and that he "adapted the metre, structural form, and much of the coloring of *Kalevala* to transform the crude Indian legends and myths recounted by Schoolcraft and others into a widely read poem,'' and in his review of Moyne's book in *NEQ,* 38 (1965), 96–99, Andrew Hilen accepted it as having "finally resolved'' the question of Longfellow's dependence upon *Kalevala.*

6 See Henry E. Legler, "L's *Hiawatha:* Bibliographical Notes Concerning its Origin, its Translations, and its Contemporary Parodies,'' *Literary Collector,* 9 (1904), 1–19, and Ernest J. Moyne, "Parodies of L's *Song of Hiawatha,''* *Delaware Notes,* Thirtieth Series, 1957, pp. 93–108.

7 C. Hugh Holman, "The *Hiawatha* Metre in *The Yemassee*," *MLN*, 67 (192), 418–19; Newton Arvin, *L: His Life and Work*, p. 169.

8 At least two scholars have disagreed with Longfellow about this however. Cecelia Tiche, "L's Motives for the Structure of *Hiawatha*," *AL*, 42 (1970–71), 548–53, argues that the ending has been better prepared for than has been recognized. The advent of Christianity is "the civilizing apotheosis" for which the Indians have been gradually prepared throughout the poem. "Longfellow appears . . . to have designed *Hiawatha* as a groundwork of native materials in a land whereon European culture could possibly be grafted." But his own words show that he did not thus *design* it; if she is right, then in this particular he "builded better than he knew." Robert A. Ferguson, "L's Political Fears: Civic Authority and the Role of the Artist in *Hiawatha* and *The Courtship of Miles Standish*," *AL*, 50 (1978–79), 187–215, finds in the poem an expression of Longfellow's convictions about art and the state and the relations between them. Ferguson sees the old Indian culture as in a state of disintegration before Hiawatha's departure. The latter's alliance with Chibiabos and Kwasind indicates the necessary union of wisdom, culture, and power in the service of the state. Iagoo is the artist as buffoon and Pau-Puk-Keewis "the alienated, antisocial artist" whose darker powers are released by death. Upon this basis, Ferguson explains what has seemed to many Hiawatha's exaggerated mourning for Chibiabos.

9 *Midwest Folklore*, 7 (1956–57). 5–25.

10 "The Indian Legend of Hiawatha," *PMLA*, 37 (1922), 128–40. Thompson states that though Longfellow "selected his materials so as to produce a unity that the original will not warrant" and is "not wholly faithful to the Indian spirit," his statement that the legends he relates are real Indian legends is literally true. He never departs from them except as he was misled by Schoolcraft, and though he almost completely humanizes his hero, he weaves around him, "usually with a high degree of accuracy, typical experiences of Indian life."

11 It would be hard to find anything in nineteenth-century literature more likely to enrage late twentieth-century

feminists than Hiawatha's musings at the beginning of Canto 10:

> "As unto the bow the cord is,
> So unto the man is woman,
>
> Though she bends him, she obeys him,
> Though she draws him, yet she follows,
> Useless each without the other."

12 As the text stands, Hiawatha grieves seven times as long for Chibiabos as for Minnehaha, but with all due respect to Robert A. Ferguson's interpretation (see note 8), this is probably due to inadvertence or carelessness on Longfellow's part rather than to deliberate or meaningful design.

13 "Mercerized Folklore," *P-L,* 31 (1920), 538–75.

14 *Genre,* 6 (1973), 315–32.

VII: The Courtship of Miles Standish

1 Charles Francis Adams, Jr., *Three Episodes in Massachusetts History* (HM, 1892) criticizes the changes Longfellow made in his account of Standish's Indian expedition, but this criticism is not entered upon aesthetic grounds.

2 Perry, "The Centenary of L," in his *Park-Street Papers* (HM, 1908). James Russell Lowell's comments on Longfellow's hexameters, and on English hexameters in general, in his review of *The Courtship of Miles Standish,* reprinted in *The Function of the Poet and Other Essays* (HM, 1920), are less enthusiastic but of considerable interest. He praises the poem highly, however, and doubts that we have had "more purely objective narrative" since Chaucer.

3 Robert A. Ferguson, "L's Political Fears," etc. (see notes to Chapter VI), embraces *Miles Standish* as well as *Hiawatha,* but overreaches himself, I believe, when he sees John Alden not only as representing the artist and his place in society but also Longfellow himself. Alden "remains paralyzed for much of the poem, caught by conflicting loyalties and

feelings of irrelevance within a community endangered by war. His dilemma reflects Longfellow's own inability to decide upon a meaningful course of action during the late 1850s.'' Ferguson is more interesting when he sees Standish's admiration for Caesar and Caesar's desire to be first, his blasphemies, and his lack of control as alienating him from Longfellow's readers, who, he believes, thought of Caesar primarily as having subverted Rome's republican institutions.

4 Hirsh, *HWL,* pp. 36–37.

VIII: Tales of a Wayside Inn

1 It is not necessary to agree with Arvin in this judgment, nor yet to accept his extremely high estimate of ''The Saga of King Olaf'' (pp. 227–36), but it is impossible not to acknowledge gratefully that his chapter (XII) on the *Tales,* in his *L: His Life and Work,* is by all means the best comprehensive general critical evaluation of the work that has been made.

2 The first series of tales is told on an evening, the second on the following morning, when it is too rainy to go out, and the last on the evening of the next day. The tale-tellers all depart on the morning after the second evening of tale-telling.

3 Samuel Chamberlain, *Open House in New England* (Hastings House, 1937), pp. 50–51.

4 For details see John van Schaick, Jr., *Characters in Tales of a Wayside Inn* (Universalist Publishing House, 1939), half of which is taken up with letters of Longfellow, Monti, and Parsons. Mrs. C. Van D. Chenoweth, ''The Landlord of the Wayside Inn,'' *New-England Magazine, N.S.* 10 (1894), 265–72, is an interesting, illustrated popular article on the Howes and their inn. For additional material on the Spanish Jew, Isaac Edrehi, see John J. Appel, ''HWL's Presentation of the Spanish Jew,'' *Publication of the American Jewish Historcal Society,* 45 (1955), 20–34. Appel connects

Longfellow's interest in Spanish Jews with his interest in the Spanish language and literature and sees him presenting them symbolically rather than realistically "as transmitters of Oriental culture to the West, and . . . as a link connecting Spanish with American literature."

5 The Musician, the Spanish Jew, and the Sicilian are Europeans. Of the four Americans, all except the Landlord, the only one to tell only two tales, are in some sense intellectuals. Is it because he feels somewhat out of place in the company that he disappears during the second session of story-telling, choosing to spend the rainy day doing his chores in the barn?

6 The American tales are "Paul Revere's Ride," "The Birds of Killingworth," "Lady Wentworth," "Elizabeth," "The Rhyme of Sir Christopher," and in part "The Baron of Saint Castine." All are set in New England except "Elizabeth" (New Jersey). The Italian stories are "The Falcon of Ser Federigo," "King Robert of Sicily," "The Bell of Atri," "The Monk of Casal-Maggiore," and possibly the indefinitely localized "Legend Beautiful."

7 "The Legend of Rabbi Ben Ezra," "Kambalu," "Azrael," and "Scanderberg."

8 "The Legend of Rabbi Ben Ezra," "King Robert of Sicily," "Torquemada," "The Cobbler of Hagenau," "The Legend Beautiful," "Elizabeth," and "The Monk of Casal-Maggiore." It is the underside of religion that predominates, however, in "Torquemada" and, less seriously, in "The Cobbler of Hagenau," while "The Monk of Casal-Maggiore" is religious only in the sense that its leading characters are clerics. On the religious aspects of "The Saga of King Olaf" see my discussion of that tale.

9 "The Legend of Rabbi Ben Levi," "King Robert of Sicily," "The Ballad of Carmilhan," "The Legend Beautiful," "Azrael," "The Mother's Ghost."

10 Arvin, *L: His Life and Work*, pp. 213–15, gives further details.

11 But see Steven Allaback, "L's 'Galgano,' " *AL,* 46 (1974–75), 210–19, for a reprint, with suitable historical and critical comment, of Longfellow's translation of a tale from Fiorentino's *Il Pecorone,* which he had intended for the place now occupied by "The Falcon of Ser Federigo." On August 29, 1863, he wrote Fields that the falcon has "begun his flight, and is ready to tear 'Galgano's' eyes out." "Galgano" is considerably more erotic than "The Falcon," though less so than "Emma and Eginhard."

12 The most elaborate general account, necessarily omitting twentieth-century research, is still Hermann Varnhagen, *L's* Tales of a Wayside Inn *und ihre Quellen nebst Nachweisen und Untersuchungen über die vom Dichter bearbeiten Stoffe* (Berlin, Weichmannsche Buchhandlung, 1884). See also the notes to Volume IV of the Craigie Edition.

13 As preserved in *Massachusetts Historical Society Collections,* First Series, V.

14 See William E. A. Axon, "On L's 'Birds of Killingworth,' " *Papers of the Manchester Literary Club,* 33 (1907), 224–27.

15 Hjalmar Edgren, "Antecedents of L's 'King Robert of Sicily,' " *P-L,* 14 (1903), 127–33, traces the story clear back to India, summarizes the various versions, and describes the differences between them.

16 See Andrew Hilen, *L and Scandinavia,* pp. 90–103, where may also be read the section of "King Olaf" excluded from the final version, "The Revel of Earl Sigvald," in which Christ and St. Michael are toasted by drunken revelers. Cf. Hilen, "L and Scandinavia Revisited," in *PPLCC,* especially pp. 9–10.

17 Roscoe H. Miller, "Baron of Saint-Castine, American Pioneer," *Americana,* 28 (1934), 92–97, gives an account of the actual French nobleman after whom Castine, Maine, was named.

18 See J. Perry Worden, "L's Tales and Their Origin," *Anglia*,
    23 (1901), 316–22, pointed out the source and recorded that
    Longfellow first heard the story in a lecture by the American
    art critic, Charles Perkins.

19 Carl L. Johnson, "Three Notes on L" (see Ch. IV, n. 3) in-
    cludes a detailed investigation of the sources of "Emma and
    Eginhard."

IX: Later Poems

 1 See James Taft Hatfield's fascinating article, "L's 'Lapland
    Song,' " *PMLA*, 45 (1930), 1188–92, in which the manu-
    script of Longfellow's original version of "My Lost Youth" is
    reproduced in facsimile. The song, which was importantly
    connected with the beginnings of interest in folk poetry, was
    first taken down from a native Laplander and printed in Ger-
    many in 1673. A new translation appeared in *The Spectator*
    in 1712, and Herder translated it four times. Longfellow
    misinterpreted or deliberately changed the meaning from
    "the will of boys is the will of the wind" to "a boy's mind is
    full of vague prophecies and longings; he has outreaching
    visions and dreams." Hatfield gives many examples of
    echoes of the song in modern literature and life. See also
    George Arms, "The Revision of 'My Lost Youth,' " *MLN*,
    61 (1946), 389–92.

 2 John J. Appel, "HWL's Presentation of the Spanish Jews"
    (see chapter 8, note 4) points out that "Sandolphon" was
    "based on a legend which Emmanuel Scherb read
    [Longfellow] from Heinrich Corrodi's *Kritische Geschichte
    des Chiliasmus*" and that he also consulted John Peter
    Stehelin's *Traditions of the Jews.*

 3 This is rather startlingly like Jim Burden's studying Virgil
    and thinking of the "hired girls" on the farm in Willa
    Cather's *My Ántonia:* "It came over me, as it had never done
    before, the relation between girls like those and the poetry of
    Virgil. If there were no girls like them in the world, there
    would be no poetry."

4 See "Emma Lazarus," in Edward Wagenknecht, *Daughters of the Covenant* (University of Massachusetts Press, 1983).

5 On "The Jewish Cemetery at Newport" see Ely Stock, "L's 'The Jewish Cemetery at Newport,'" *Rhode Island History,* 20 (1961), 81–87; Hammett W. Smith, "A Note on L's The Jewish Cemetery at Newport,'" *College English,* 18 (1956), 103–104; and Irving Fitzig, "L and 'The Jewish Cemetery at Newport," *American Heritage,* Vol. 13, No. 2, February 1962, pp. 60–63, which is largely devoted to excellent color photographs. G. R. Elliott, "Gentle Shades of L," in *The Cycle of Modern Poetry* (Princeton University Press, 1929), finds the poem superior to Gray's "Elegy Written in a Country Church-Yard" because "while lacking Gray's finest touches, it lacks also his pompous melancholy and sentimental egoism. It catches, through a rich local condition (a characteristically American one), a pathos far wider and more valid than that which Gray read into the lives of his ideal-stolid yokels. And it is beautifully architectured." Elliott also records having sent copies of the first stanza of "In the Churchyard at Cambridge" to "a number of young college persons much interested in current verse, some of them promising poets themselves. 'Who wrote this?' I queried; "I have been it quoted . . . a new poem?'—Quite new to them, their answers showed, but acceptable as supposedly belonging to our age!" He quotes passages from Longfellow which remind him of Sandburg, Frost, Robinson, Amy Lowell, and the imagists.

6 This has been recorded for Deutsche Grammophon by the great German baritone Dietrich Fischer-Dieskau ("Charles Ives: Songs," DG 2530 696).

7 Of which my discussion must be deferred since in this volume all the sonnets are to be considered together.

8 Ferris Greenslet, *The Life of Thomas Bailey Aldrich* (HM, 1908).

9 This factual error does not of course affect the poetic quality of the composition. In Longfellow's time Chaucer was generally believed to have been born in 1328. The generally accepted conjectural date is now 1340, and it has even been argued that he might have been born as late as 1343 or 1344. Longfellow seems to have been much impressed by Chaucer's supposed advanced age; he brings it up again in two fine sonnets, "Chaucer" and "Woodstock."

10 *The Sonnets of HWL,* Arranged with an Introduction by Ferris Greenslet (HM, 1907).

11 Samuel Longfellow says that the suggestion for this sonnet came to his brother from "looking over . . . an illustrated book of Western scenery," where he supposedly saw the picture of which a framed reproduction still hangs in the Longfellows' bedroom. Rena Coen has recently suggested that the poet may have seen Thomas Moran's spectacular painting, "The Mountain of the Holy Cross," when it was exhibited in Boston in 1875 (see *PPLCC,* p. 83). James M. Cox, "Longfellow and his Cross of Snow," *PMLA,* 75 (1960), 97–100, sees resemblances between "The Cross of Snow" and the fourth of the "Divina Commedia" sonnets, from which he proceeds to deductions concerning Longfellow's relationship to both Dante and Mrs. Longfellow. Though I do not doubt that Fanny was Longfellow's Beatrice, I do not find this convincing. I may add that if "Palingenesis" and "The Bridge of Cloud" contain references to Mrs. Longfellow, as Newton Arvin (p. 139) suggested, it can only be in the most general possible way.

12 John D. Rae, "L's 'Nature,' " *MP,* 18 (1920), 48, suggests that Longfellow took the idea for this sonnet from a passage in Robert Southey's *Commonplace Book* which Southey described as a Yorkshire epitaph:

> As careful nurses to the bed do lay
> Their children which too long would wanton play,
> So to prevent all my ensuing crimes
> Nature my nurse laid me to bed betimes.

13 Nancy L. Tenfelde's "L's 'Chaucer,' " *Expl,* 22 (1964), Item 55, is an admirable detailed analysis of this sonnet, demonstrating Longfellow's thorough knowledge of his subject.

14 See further R. E. Amacher, "L's 'Jugurtha,' " *Expl,* 6 (1947), Item 29.

15 Richard F. Benton, "L's 'Helen of Tyre," *ESQ,* No. 10 (1958), 25–28. See also his "Helen of Tyre," *Expl,* 16 (1958), Item 54. These articles constitute the most authoritative commentaries on this poem.

X: Dramatic Works

1 This piece is included in Ray W. Pettingill, ed., *L's Boyhood Poems.*

2 Longfellow considered many more subjects for dramatic treatment than he ever produced; cf. Edward Wagenknecht, *L: A Full Length Portrait,* Appendix A: "Longfellow's Unwritten Works."

3 As Lawrance Thompson points out in "L Sells *The Spanish Student,"* *AL,* 6 (1934–35), 141–50, this work was the author's "most sustained poetical composition" up to the date of its composition. Thompson's article is a detailed account of the arrangements made for its publication and of its relation to the author's other literary interests and endeavors at this time.

4 For more detailed commentary on *The Spanish Student,* see Iris Lilian Whitman, *L and Spain.*

5 Quoted from Poe's article on "The American Drama." In the Stedman-Woodberry Edition of Poe, this piece appears in Volume VI of the Scribner edition.

6 See G. Thomas Tanselle, "L's 'Serenade,' *The Spanish Student,"* *Expl,* 23 (1965), Item 48.

7   See Longfellow's letter to Sara Jewett, March 7, 1881, in
    Hilen, *Letters,* Vol. VI, pp. 694–95. The altered text was
    printed as a pamphlet at the Riverside Press, with Blanche
    Roosevelt's picture on the cover, apparently for sale at the
    theater. There are copies in both the Widener Library and
    the Longfellow House.

8   Newton Arvin, *L: His Life and Work,* pp. 273–74, gives
    some account of the differences between this and the final
    version.

9   When, in the next scene, "A body is thrown from the
    tower," one can hardly avoid remembering the corpse
    "precipitated over the waterfall" in Longfellow's juvenile
    drama, "The Poor Student."

10 The fullest studies of *The Divine Tragedy* are in Alfred G.
    Schmidt, *L's Divine Tragedy* (Lucka S.-A., Druck von
    Reinhold Berger, 1905) and Sr. Mary Charles's 1955 Univer-
    sity of Pennsylvania dissertation, "L's *Christus.*"

11 Though at one point he rather oddly allows the prince to
    remark that his heart "has become a dull lagoon, / Which a
    kind of leprosy drinks and drains."

12 In "L's *Golden Legend* and its Analogues," *P-L,* 4 (1892),
    91–100, P.A.C. calls the poem "a curious blending of the
    'Faust Legend' with the Alkestis myth." This writer gives an
    interesting account of analogues and includes a careful sum-
    mary of *Der Arme Heinrich.* Carl Hammer, Jr., *L's Golden
    Legend and Goethe's* Faust (LSUP, 1952) "seeks to deter-
    mine the extent of Faustian elements in Longfellow's *The
    Golden Legend,* whether patent borrowings or features
    suggesting spiritual kinship with Goethe's *Lebenswerk.*"
    The method primarily employed is that of citation of parallel
    passages. The most fully annotated edition of *The Golden
    Legend* was prepared by S. Arthur Bent for HM and
    published in the Riverside Literature Series in 1887. John T.
    Krumpelmann, "L's *Golden Legend* and the *Armer
    Heinrich* Theme in Modern German Literature," *Journal of*

English and Germanic Philology, 25 (1926), 173–92, is mainly concerned with Gerhart Hauptmann's play and the question of Longfellow's influence.

13 An "illumination" by Edwin Stafford Doolittle, illustrating the soliloquy of Friar Pacificus, was exhibited at the Centennial Exhibition in Philadelphia, and Dudley Buck's cantata on the *Legend* won one thousand dollars at the Cincinnati Music Festival in 1880 for "the best composition for solo voices, chorus, and orchestra."

14 The fullest study of these matters is Edward L. Tucker's "L's Play *John Endicott,*" in *PPLCC.*

15 In view of the suicidal passages in *The Golden Legend,* one of Giles Corey's speeches takes on an added interest.

> But a voice
> Was whispering in my ear continually,
> "Self-murder is no crime. The life of man
> Is his, to keep it or to throw away!"

16 "Literature and Orthodoxy in Boston after the Civil War," *American Quarterly,* 1 (1949), 149–65. As might be inferred from its title, this article is primarily important for its consideration of the religious meaning of *Christus.*

17 Though he was, to be sure, no more a dogmatic Unitarian than he was dogmatic about anything else. There is an interesting 1881 fragment among his "Elegiac Verse":

> How can the Three be One? you ask me; I answer
>   by asking
>   Hail and snow and rain, are they not three, and
>   yet one?

18 "The Sources of L's *Michael Angelo,*" *Romanic Review,* 25 (1934), 314–24.

XI: The Man

1 See Edward Wagenknecht, "Dickens in L's Letters and Journals," in his *Dickens and the Scandalmongers: Essays in Criticism* (Okla, 1965).

2 "L's Income from his Writings, 1840–1852," *PBSA*, 38 (1944), 9–21.

3 *The Spanish Background of American Literature* (YUP, 1955), Vol. I, pp. 119–20, 249; Vol. II, p. 160.

4 Orie W. Long, *Literary Pioneers* (HUP, 1935).

5 *American Poets and Their Theology* (The Griffith and Rowland Press, 1926). A more liberal Protestant point of view is expressed by E. J. Bailey, *Religious Thought in the Greater American Poets* (Pilgrim Press, 1922). For the Catholic point of view see Joseph E. O'Neill, "HWL, Poet of the Feeling Heart," in Harold S. Gardiner, ed., *American Classics Reconsidered* (Scribners, 1958).

6 See the impressive testimonials presented in the last chapter of the present writer's *L: A Full-Length Portrait*.

7 Gamaliel Bradford, *Biography and the Human Heart* (HM, 1932); W. D. Howells, *Literary Friends and Acquaintance* (Harpers, 1900).

Appendix: Translations and Anthologies

1 Hilen, *Letters*, Vol. I, p. 320.

2 White, "L's Interest in Scandinavia During the Years 1838–47," *SSN*, 17 (1942), 70–82. The fullest account of the "little Longfellow war," more Poe-slanted than Longfellow-slanted, is Chapter 5, "Culmination of a Campaign: Poe and L," in Sidney P. Moss, *Poe's Literary Battles* (Duke University Press, 1962); see also the present writer's *Edgar Allan Poe: The Man Behind the Legend* (OUP, 1963), pp. 132–35. In all fairness, however, it must be admitted that questions involved in Longfellow's possible use of

materials by other writers have been raised by critics much more friendly to him than Poe. See especially Andrew Hilen's article, "L's 'A Lay of Courage,' " *PMLA*, 67 (1952), 949–59, and the discussion thereof in the present writer's *HWL: Portrait of an American Humanist*, pp. 227–28, note 21, which contains some material not included in his earlier discussion in *L: A Full-Length Portrait*, pp. 157–58, and compare the references there cited.

3 Two lectures on Dante, prepared for Longfellow's classes and also delivered by him in a course he gave at the Mercantile Library in New York, were printed in the Blue and Gold Edition of his prose and used in part in *The Poets and Poetry of Europe*. In "H. W. L's Interest in Dante," in *PPLCC*. J. Chesley Mathews traces this interest throughout Longfellow's career, describes the writing of his translation, and points out passages reminiscent of Dante in his poems, with which compare his article, "Echoes of Dante in L's Poetry,' *I*, 26 (1949), 242–59.

4 Howells, who was sometimes present, has written interestingly of these meetings; cf. Edward Wagenknecht, "L and Howells," *ESQ*, No. 58 (1970), pp. 52–56.

5 For a careful and sympathetic description and evaluation of Longfellow's translation, see John Fiskle, "L's Dante," in *The Unseen World and Other Essays* (HM, 1876).

6 Daniel Kilham Dodge, "L's Scandinavian Translations," *SSN*, 6 (1920–21), 187–97; John Leighly, "Inaccuracies in L's Translation of Tegnér's 'Nattvardsbarnen,' " *SSN*, 21 (1949–50), 171–80; Walter Silz, "L's Translation of Goethe's 'Ueber allen Gipfeln,' " *PMLA*, 71 (1956), 344–45; Carl Hammer, Jr., "L's Lyrics 'From the German,' " in Waldo F. McNeir, ed., *Studies in Comparative Literature* (LSUP, 1962).

7 W. P. Trent, *L and Other Essays* (Crowell, 1910).

8 See R. Baird Shuman, "L, Poe and *The Waif*," *PMLA*, 76 (1961), 155–56.

Suggestions for Further Reading

An elaborate Longfellow bibliography is included in my *L: A Full-Length Portrait,* pp. 328–42, which is abridged and reprinted with alterations in my *HWL: Portrait of an American Humanist,* pp. 237–41. The fullest list of uncollected articles is probably still H. W. L. Dana's in *The Cambridge History of American Literature* (Putnam, 1917), Vol. II, pp. 425–36.

The most desirable editions of Longfellow's works are the Riverside Edition, eleven volumes (1886), the Standard Library Edition, fourteen volumes (1891), which adds Samuel Longfellow's biography, and the more attractive, illustrated Craigie Edition, also issued as a limited, large paper Edition de Luxe (1904). The best one-volume edition of the poems is the oft-reprinted Cambridge Edition. All these editions are published by HM. The ten-volume edition published by the Davos Press, New York, in 1909, includes some prose not reprinted in the HM editions.

Early poems, not elsewhere collected, will be found in Richard Herne Shepherd, ed., *The Early Poems of HWL* (London, Pickering and Co., 1878) and Ray W. Pettingill, ed., *L's Boyhood Poems* (Saratoga Springs, The Author, 1925). The best volumes of selections are Odell Shepard, ed., *HWL: Representative Selections* (ABC, 1934); Louis Untermeyer, ed., *The Poems of HWL* (The Limited Editions Club and The Heritage Club, 1943); *Favorite Poems of HWL,* with an Introduction by Henry Seidel Canby (Doubleday, 1947); and Howard Nemerov, ed., *L* (Dell Publishing Company, 1959). It is not possible to list

here the multitudinous illustrated editions, but see the Frederic
Remington edition of *The Song of Hiawatha* (1891), the editions
of *Evangeline* illustrated by F. O. C. Darley (1892) and by Violet
Oakley and Jessie Willcox Smith (1897), and the Pilgrim Ter-
centary Edition of *The Courtship of Miles Standish*, with
reproductions of gorgeous paintings by N. C. Wyeth, all
published by HM. Violet Oakley's pictures in the 1897
Evangeline are outstanding; both she and Jessie Willcox Smith
were pupils of Howard Pyle, who contributed a note to this
edition. See also Edward A. Wilson's pictures in the Doubleday
edition noted above and Boyd Hanna's in the LEC-Heritage
edition.

There is no comprehensive modern biography of Longfellow.
The authorized biography was his brother Samuel's, first
published as *Life of HWL, with Extracts from his Journals and
Correspondence,* two volumes (Ticknor, 1886) and *Final
Memorials of HWL* (1887). These works were integrated and
republished as *Life of HWL,* three volumes (Houghton Mifflin,
1891). The only other early books now likely to attract the
general reader are George Rice Carpenter, *HWL* (Small,
Maynard, 1901) and Thomas Wentworth Higginson, *HWL,* in
the American Men of Letters series (HM, 1903), which makes use
of some material not used by Samuel Longfellow. Herbert S.
Gorman's *A Victorian American, HWL* (George H. Doran,
1923) is of no value and has no interest except to illustrate the
"debunking" tendencies of one school of biographers of the
1920s at their worst. Lawrance Thompson's *Young L
(1807–1843)* (M, 1983), though unsympathetic, is thoroughly
researched for the period indicated. Edward Wagenknecht's *L: A
Full-Length Portrait* (LG, 1955) and its revision, *HWL: Portrait
of an American Humanist* OUP, 1966) are researched works
covering the whole life, but these books are "portraits" or
psychographs rather than, in the narrower sense of the term,
biographies. Newton Arvin's *L: His Life and Work* (Atlantic-
Little, Brown, 1963) is excellent for criticism but adds nothing to
biography. Cecil B. Williams, *HWL,* in Twayne's United States
Authors Series (1964) is the latest good, allover survey at this
date of writing.

At present the closest approach to a modern biography,

written in the light of all that is presently known about Longfellow, will be found in the biographical introductions to the
various sections of our most important monument of Longfellow
scholarship, Andrew Hilen's six-volume collection of *The Letters
of HWL* (The Belknap Press of HUP, 1966–82). Longfellow's
journals are reported being readied for publication by J. Chesley
Mathews.

There are a number of scholarly book-length studies of special
subjects: James Taft Hatfield, *New Light on L, with Special
Reference to his Relations with Germany* (HM, 1933); Carl L.
Johnson, *Professor L of Harvard* (University of Oregon, 1944); R.
P. Hickey, *Catholic Influence on L* (Kirkwood, Missouri:
Maryhurst Normal Press, 1928), which is valuable particularly for
its consideration of foreign and Catholic works not noted
elsewhere; Andrew Hilen, *L and Scandinavia* (YUP, 1947); Paul
Morin, *Les Sources de l'Oeuvre de HWL* (Paris, Emile Larose,
1913); Iris Lilian Whitman, *L and Spain* (Institudo de la Españas
en los Estados Unidos, 1927). Mention may also be made of a
number of unpublished doctoral dissertations: Theodore Bar-
dacke, "A Critical Study of L's Poetry," Syracuse, 1950; Thomas
E. Bellavance, "The Periodical Prose of L," Michigan State,
1970; Robert R. Crosby, "L as a Dramatist," Indiana, 1958; Carl
L. Johnson, "L and France," Harvard, 1933; Sr. Mary Charles,
"L's *Christus,*" Pennsylvania, 1955; Joseph Eugene O'Neill,
"L's Imagery," California, 1955; Linda J. Robinson, "L's
Hiawatha: An American Epic, Tulane, 1968; J. C. A.
Schumacher, "The Sources of L's Poetry," Yale, 1894; Robert
Stafford Ward, "L's *Lehrjahre,*" Boston University, 1951.

Many references to articles about Longfellow and books
devoted in part to other subjects will be found in the preceding
notes.

Index of Names

Index of Titles